STALIN'S WAR
THROUGH THE EYES
OF HIS COMMANDERS

STALIN'S WAR
THROUGH THE EYES
OF HIS COMMANDERS

ALBERT AXELL

ARMS AND
ARMOUR

Arms and Armour Press
An Imprint of the Cassell Group
Wellington House, 125 Strand, London WC2R 0BB

Distributed in the USA by Sterling Publishing Co. Inc.,
387 Park Avenue South, New York, NY 10016-8810.

British Library Cataloguing-in-Publication Data:
a catalogue record for this book is available from
the British Library

ISBN 1-85409-402-5

Designed and edited by DAG Publications Ltd.
Designed by David Gibbons; edited by Michael Boxall;
Printed and Bound in Great Britain by
Creative Print and Design Wales, Ebbw Vale.

CONTENTS

INTRODUCTION

Western images of Stalin changed radically after World War II. In wartime, the highest American, British and other Western leaders hailed Stalin as a brilliant Commander-in-Chief and defender of Western civilisation. Later, the image of Stalin as a hero in the war against Hitler was dashed when the West, enveloped in the Cold War, dug up old and new records of Stalin's crimes. These included the pre-war purges, the mass migrations in Russia, and the gulags. Stalin, once hailed by politicians in Washington and London as a loyal ally, came to be widely regarded as the devil incarnate. A recent well-documented book says that after the war the CIA at one time considered – and rejected – the possibility of assassinating Joseph Stalin. (See Peter Grose, *Gentleman Spy: The Life of Allen Dulles*, London 1994.)

After the war a plethora of Stalin books appeared, many critical of the dictator as wartime Supreme Commander of Russia's armed forces. Some writers showed ill-concealed bias, although few could match the pre-war outpouring of abuse from Stalin's arch-rival Trotsky, who was murdered in Mexico in 1940, apparently on orders from the Kremlin. The noted Stalin and Trotsky biographer General Dmitri Volkogonov, once said that 'Nobody wrote as many caustic, malicious, offensive, vile, and degrading remarks about Stalin as Trotsky.'

Post-war writers and historians began to equate the crimes of Hitler and Stalin. Oxford historian Alan Bullock, himself the author of a hefty volume in which he compares the two dictators, makes the point that the Hitler–Stalin comparison has been used by polemicists to promote the view that the crimes against humanity committed in Stalin's Russia mitigated the offence of those committed in Hitler's Germany.

My book is, I believe, the first since the war to record interviews with Stalin's surviving combat generals. Most of the interviews were tape-recorded when I was Moscow correspondent for a Wall Street newspaper. The victor generals praise their Supreme Commander but they are not a servile claque; they do not refrain from criticism.

I have included some of history's most decisive battles which were fought on the Eastern Front. In each Stalin was closely involved. When America's General Dwight Eisenhower visited Russia at the end of the war, he told Stalin that his victories at Moscow, Stalingrad and Berlin would in the future be studied by cadets at the US Military Academy at West Point just as avidly as once they had studied the ancient Battle of Cannae.

Some of the items in this book appear in print for the first time.

Note: In an attempt to make this book as accurate and impartial as possible, I asked an international group of experts and scholars to read all or part of the manuscript. American, British, Russian and Finnish experts were kind enough to offer their suggestions and encouragement.

HITLER AND STALIN

★★★ NAPOLEON'S GAMBLE – AND HITLER'S ★★★

The ghost of Napoleon Bonaparte haunted the wartime German High Command. Napoleon was also often in Stalin's thoughts, especially his 1812 campaign in Russia that became one of the great tragedies of history. In his *Outline of History,* H. G. Wells says that the *Grande Armée* of 600,000 men which entered Russia under the supreme command of the new emperor, quitted the country frost-bitten, lean and ragged – and less than 5,000 strong.

Shortly after Hitler attacked Russia some Nazi commanders, like Günther von Kluge, began to read memoirs of the ill-fated Napoleonic invasion. Eventually an order banned the circulation of these memoirs. German General Kurt von Tippelskirch says that during Christmas 1941, six months after the invasion, Nazi troops lived under the shadow of Napoleon's retreat from the burned-out city of Moscow. Shortly after Christmas, a ghoulish cartoon appeared in *Krokodil* magazine published in Moscow. A skeleton in the uniform of one of Napoleon's soldiers stands by the side of a road, a wicked grin on its chalky face. The skeleton is beating a drum as columns of bedraggled German soldiers trudge past corpses of their comrades. The cartoon is entitled: 'On the Old Smolensk Road, 1812–1942'.

Meanwhile, a Swedish journalist, Arvid Fredborg reported from Berlin at the end of 1941: 'The pessimists remembered Napoleon's war with Russia, and all the literature about the *Grande Armée* suddenly had a marked revival. The fortune-tellers busied themselves with Napoleon's fate and there was a boom in astrology.'

Hitler, who cleverly spiced some of his speeches with the word 'peace', also evoked the memory of Napoleon during the war.

Said Hitler:

'I, perhaps better than anyone else, can well imagine the torments suffered by Napoleon, longing, as he was, for the triumph of peace and yet compelled to continue waging war, without ceasing and without seeing any prospect of ceasing – and still persisting in the hope eternal of at last achieving peace.'

Stalin invoked both the images of Hitler and Napoleon in his Revolution Day address in November 1941:

'We are assured that Hitler acts like Napoleon, and is like Napoleon in everything. I can tell you that Hitler no more resembles Napoleon than a kitten resembles a lion. Secondly, Napoleon based himself on the forces of reaction, whereas Hitler bases himself on reaction itself.'

While thanking Roosevelt and Churchill for their laudatory messages concerning the staunchness of the Red Army, he sought to remind them that Hitler's army was nothing like Napoleon's. In 1942 Stalin referred to the

Grande Armée when he called for the opening of a Second Front in Europe: 'The German invasion of our country is often compared to Napoleon's invasion of Russia. But this comparison will not bear criticism. Of the 600,000 troops which started out on the march against Russia, Napoleon brought to Borodino barely 130,000 or 140,000. That was all he had at his disposal at Moscow. Well, we now have facing the Red Army more than 3,000,000 troops, and troops armed with all the implements of modern warfare. What comparison can there be here?"

Two years later, highly impressed with Operation 'Overlord', the Allied cross-channel invasion of France, Stalin told US Ambassador Averell Harriman: 'The history of war has never witnessed such a grandiose operation. Napoleon himself never attempted it.'

Before Hitler invaded Russia, Stalin awarded the prize bearing his name – the highest state award – to a well-known historian, Professor Evgeny Tarle, for his book on Napoleon (*Napoleon's Invasion of Russia: 1812*). In it Tarle says: 'Napoleon burst upon Russia as a conqueror, a beast of prey, a ruthless destroyer.' And: 'For the Russian peasants, the defence of Russia from the invading army was a defence of their lives, their families, their property.'

It was, in truth, a scenario for 1941 when the population of Russia, as in 1812, rallied to drive out the invader, meeting the attempt at foreign conquest with a popular war of self-defence.

Russian peasants in 1812 saw Napoleon's invasion in much the same way as the Russians saw Hitler's in 1941. Although Napoleon, before crowning himself Emperor, had apparently supported the French Revolution with its banner of 'Liberty, Equality and Fraternity', he had in 1812 no interest in setting free Russia's serfs, an act which he believed would cause chaos. In the opening weeks of his Russian campaign, Napoleon demonstrated to the people that his invasion would be for the worse, that the Russian nobles, peasants and serfs would gain nothing from a French conquest.

Tarle shows how groundless were the fears in St. Petersburg court circles that Napoleon might arouse the masses against the Tsarist regime. The Russian people saw the ruthlessness with which French troops suppressed the uprising, for example, of Lithuanian peasants against their harsh noble masters. Russian peasants, regarding the French as a hated enemy, burned their harvests and farmhouses – a measure duplicated by their descendants more than a century later, which became known as Stalin's 'scorched earth' policy.

Tarle explains: 'At first glance we are confronted by a paradox: the peasants who loathed their servitude, who protested by murders of landowners recorded in annual statistics and by revolts which had, only 37 years before, imperilled the entire feudal order in the Pugachev insurrection – the same peasants met Napoleon as a fierce enemy, fighting with all their strength as no other peasants had fought him except those of Spain.' In self-defence, the peasants rose against the invaders. (Note: Yemelyan Pugachev, a Don Cossack, raised an army of 30,000 discontented peasants and Cossacks in the Volga area and the Urals in a popular uprising in 1773–5. He promised the people 'freedom in perpetuity' and liberation of the serfs. His was the largest peasant revolt in Europe at that time and was suppressed with great difficulty and severity. Pugachev was finally captured, brought to Moscow and quartered.)

Hitler, of course, had a different objective. In addition to suppressing the Russian *Untermensch* ('lower races') – he wanted most of the Slavic population 'kept in pigsties' – the Führer was intent on the destruction of the communist regime.

Both Napoleon's and Hitler's armies had a mix of nationalities. Napoleon's had included hundreds of thousands of Germans, Italians, Dutch, Poles and Dalmatians, plus Spanish volunteers. Hitler brought with him Italian, Hungarian, Rumanian, Finnish and Spanish troops.

Another similarity between 1812 and 1941 is the stratagem used by the Russian commanders of shifting suddenly from defence to offence. In 1812 the Russian Commander-in-Chief, Field Marshal Prince Mikhail Kutuzov, pointed out the importance of keeping the army intact. Only that way promised the hope of eventually turning the tide. Kutuzov reasoned that a Russian Army which could retreat intact could afford to 'sell' territory at high cost to the enemy, until the invader's lines were drawn out and gripped by winter when they would be easy prey for a counter-attack. In the end Napoleon found himself in precisely this position. When Kutuzov's army counter-attacked, aided by swarms of Cossacks and guerrilla fighters, it was brilliantly successful.

During Napoleon's last years, when he was a sick man aware of approaching death, he prepared his memoirs which were designed to put himself in an attractive light and minimise his worst blunders. He made many observations on the Russian war, which he thought should have been the most popular of any in modern times. He said: 'I had no wish to obtain any new acquisition; and I reserved for myself only the glory of doing good, and the blessings of posterity. Yet this undertaking failed, and proved my ruin, though I never acted more disinterestedly, and never better merited success.' He also uttered these pathetic words: 'There is a day in every conqueror's life when the military lines have grown so long and so thin that everything that has been won by blood has to be lost by still more blood.' The extraordinary length of his lines in Russia had sealed his doom.

The basic story of the calamity of Napoleon's *Grand Armée* on the great Russian land mass was known to every Red Army soldier. Details of the battles were studied in Stalin's military schools. During the war Professor Tarle delivered lectures on Napoleon to Red Army soldiers. V. V. Kovanov, a Russian surgeon during World War II, records that Tarle gave lectures to wounded soldiers in front-line hospitals. In discussing action on the Nazi–Soviet fronts, Tarle would draw comparisons with the war against Napoleon, 'painting a colourful picture of the retreat of Napoleon's armies from Moscow, and would then, with the insight of a strategist, analyse the rout of Hitler's armies near Moscow'.

Nazi leaders knew the smallest details of the Napoleonic fiasco in Russia, but closed their eyes to the possibility that their hitherto undefeated armies might suffer a similar fate.

A diary entry of Dr. Joseph Goebbels on 9 July 1941, a few weeks after the invasion, is unequivocal: We are colossally superior to the enemy. Space is the only difficulty for us. But there can be no repetition of Napoleon's case, although by irony of fate we attacked Bolshevism on the same night that Napoleon crossed the Russian frontier, that is, on the night of 21 June. We went into action not only with marching infantry, but with tanks. It will be incomparably easier for us to negotiate the vast expanses in the East.'

The precise dates of Napoleon's conquests were known to at least some of Hitler's generals. As Nazi troops swept into Lithuania, Franz Halder, the Army Chief of Staff, wrote in his diary on 24 June 1941: 'Interesting historical coincidence that Napoleon also took Vilna on 24 June.'

Colonel-General Erich Hoepner, Commander of 4th Panzer Group, which attacked historic Borodino in October 1941, was struck by another coincidence: 'Just as they had 129 years ago, the Russians put up extremely stiff resistance in an effort to block the way to the sacred city of Moscow,' he wrote, adding: 'An engagement ensued which was even fiercer and longer than the previous one; it was fought with all the modern means of warfare.'

In their euphoria at the beginning of the *Blitzkrieg*, Nazi leaders ignored a prophetic remark by General Wilhelm Groener, who had headed the German occupation of the Ukraine back in 1918:

'Anyone who wants to grasp the strategic nature of the Eastern War Theatre must not overlook historical recollections. Beside the gate of the vast lowland between the Vistula and the Urals, which is the home of one state and one people, stands the warning figure of Napoleon, whose fate should implant in anyone who attacks Russia a sense of horror and foreboding.'

It may be calculated that it took Napoleon's army 83 days to enter Moscow, on 14 September 1812. By contrast, Hitler's Field Marshal Fedor von Bock's motorised and armoured divisions needed 167 days to arrive at the approaches to Moscow, but they never entered the capital.

The factors that helped defeat Napoleon were now working against Hitler. His soldiers, like Napoleon's, fought bloody but indecisive battles as they approached Moscow. Both armies plodded great distances along terrible roads and both were punished by the Russian winter. Hitler's soldiers also came up against something unexpected – the tenacity of the Russian people. But Napoleon's army had been similarly stunned.

An item in the *Petersburg Gazette* of 2 October 1812 under the headline 'For Information by Special Command' could have provided a lesson for the future:

'Whatever may be the progress of the enemy we would rather drain the last drop of the cup of misery, than by a scandalous peace, to subject Russia to a foreign yoke.'

★★★ STALIN'S WAR CREDENTIALS ★★★

When Hitler invaded Russia on 22 June 1941, Stalin was the more experienced war leader of the two. Hitler a corporal during World War I, was a novice in operational and strategic matters. He was unable to provide effective military guidance in World War II. Stalin, although not a trained soldier, had absorbed military knowledge in the Russian Civil War (1918–21) where he moved from one chaotic front to another. His role in civil war strategy is documented in war records and memoirs. In one operation he mounted an unorthodox seaborne assault which military professionals opposed, calling it too risky. When it proved successful, Stalin told Lenin that he had lost faith in 'experts'. He was deeply involved in a series of important military operations and dutifully telegraphed the results to Lenin.

Adolf Hitler had reportedly spent four years in the trenches during World War I and was decorated with the Iron Cross. But shortly before he was murdered, General Kurt von Schleicher, a high official of the Weimar Republic (this republic existed in Germany from 1919 until Hitler's dictatorship), had been curious as to how a mere corporal had received the Iron Cross, 1st Class, a top military award in the Kaiser's Germany.

As Schleicher discovered, Hitler's name was missing from the official honours list of the regiment in which he had served. The record showed that Hitler as the orderly of a company commander had carried out a messenger's duties. So there could be no question of an Iron Cross decoration. Further investigation revealed that Hitler had apparently received his award fraudulently several years after the war.

The German historian Werner Maser, a biographer of Hitler, writes that the Führer's account of his own war experiences is 'not altogether free of falsification and hyperbole'. In his opus on the German–Soviet war, British historian Alan Clark calls Hitler a 'brave man' who had studied military affairs all his life and who won the Iron Cross in the field. Clark's work was published six years Maser's, and he may not have been aware of the discrepancy over Hitler's decoration.

Military memoirists have pointed to Stalin's ability to plan strategy and organise troops on a big scale. According to Marshal Georgi Zhukov, Stalin was not only conversant with the basic principles of planning the operations of fronts but was also familiar with major strategic concepts.

Zhukov and other marshals such as K. K. Rokossovsky, Ivan Konev, A. M. Vasilevsky, Kiril Meretskov and Ivan Bagramyan, speak positively of Stalin as Supreme Commander. By contrast, esteem for Hitler was not high among a number of Nazi generals. Nazi Panzer General Heinz Guderian, for example, speaks of the 'muddled' assessment of Hitler's strategic abilities by his advisers.

A look at Stalin's bookshelves shows that before World War II he had paid close attention to military theory. Annotated volumes on war history, ancient and modern, as well as biographies of eminent soldiers, filled his library. Conspicuous among them were many volumes on Napoleon's military campaigns. A Russian researcher who examined Stalin's library after his death mentions the copious notes in the margins of these books written in the dictator's hand.

The official Soviet biographies of Stalin that were written in wartime decorate him with a halo of genius for his part in the war against Hitler and, earlier, in the Civil War. But despite the embellishments in the wartime biographies, there is evidence that Stalin made a significant contribution to the defeat of the White Guards. Perhaps the biggest triumph of this former rebellious divinity student in Georgia was his 1918 defence of the southern city of Tsaritsyn on the Volga (sometimes referred to as the 'Red Verdun'), later renamed Stalingrad in his honour.

The records say that in June of that year Stalin set out for Tsaritsyn with a detachment of soldiers and two armoured cars. The people of Moscow and Petrograd were running short of food but bands of counter-revolutionary Cossacks and others stymied efforts to collect grain in the south. British-led troops were meanwhile approaching the oil port of Baku. In the Urals an army of restless Czech troops was becoming increasingly hostile to the Bolsheviks.

As civil war simmered, telegrams shot back and forth between Lenin and Stalin. If Tsaritsyn were lost, the whole of the rich grain-producing region of the North Caucasus might also go. Reporting on the situation in Tsaritsyn, Stalin told Lenin that there was a 'bacchanalia of profiteering and speculation' in that city. On 7 July 1918, before going to the front, which was to the south of Tsaritsyn, Stalin telegraphed Lenin:

> 'I am driving and bullying all who require it. Hope soon to restore the position! You can rest assured that we shall spare nobody, ourselves or others, and the grain will be obtained. If only our military "specialists" – cobblers! – would not sleep and idle, the line would not have been broken; and if we restore the line, it will not be thanks to the officers, but in spite of them. STALIN'

The tone of Stalin's telegrams apparently irritated Leon Trotsky who called them "provocative braggadocio."

A few days later he telegraphed Lenin again:

> 'Everything is complicated by the fact that the Headquarters Staff of the North-Caucasus Command has proved to be absolutely incapable of fighting against the counter-revolution. It is not only that our "specialists" are psychologically incapable of striking a decisive blow against the counter-revolution, but also that they, as "Staff" workers, are capable only of "drafting plans" and elaborating schemes of reorganisation, but are entirely indifferent to military operations – and generally speaking behave as though they were outsiders, or guests. STALIN'

In Moscow, Stalin's competence in military affairs being recognised, he was placed in charge of all Red forces on the Tsaritsyn Front and was immediately instructed to 'restore order, amalgamate detachments into regular army units, appoint proper authorities, and drive out all the undisciplined'.

As the Civil War continued, the Red Army saw a rapid expansion. In May 1918 it numbered 300,000 troops, but, according to the records, by the end of 1919 its strength had risen to three million, and it continued to rise.

A year after Stalin had helped organise the defence of Tsaritsyn, he was in Petrograd, the present St. Petersburg. Lenin sent him this telegram:

> 'TO J. V. STALIN
>
> 'Knowing Petrograd's constant tendency towards independent activity, I think you should help the Revolutionary Military Council of the front to unite all the armies. The other Western armies besides the 7th should be taken care of, too. (3 June 1919) LENIN'

Two weeks later, several regiments and the entire garrison of Fort Krasnaya Gorka revolted. Morale was at a low ebb in the 7th Army which was loyal to Lenin. Again Lenin fired off a telegram.

> 'TO J. V. STALIN
>
> 'According to information from the sailors who captured the fort of Krasnaya Gorka, an English naval force of twenty-three vessels from Libau is expected to reach Kronstadt today, the 16th. I trust you have taken all measures. Send me a map of the front. (16 June 1919) LENIN'

The mutiny of the forts of Krasnaya Gorka and Seraya Loshad occurred in the rear of the Red Army. The Whites broke through to the gates of Petrograd but were repulsed by Red Army forces led by Stalin whose units then captured the mutinous forts by a combined blow from land and sea.

It is noteworthy that three weeks after Stalin's arrival, it was reported that laxity among loyalist troops had been eliminated. As stated in an official report, 'the enemies and traitors were mercilessly destroyed'. Stalin, then 40 years old, already had two decades of revolutionary activity behind him. He sent this telegram to Lenin:

> 'Following the capture of Fort Krasnaya Gorka, Fort Seraya Loshad has also been captured. Their guns are in perfect order; the rapid rebuilding of all forts and strongholds is under way. The naval experts assert that the capture of Krasnaya Gorka from the sea runs counter to all naval science. I can only deplore this so-called science.'

He goes on to explain how he managed the victory:

> 'The swift capture of Gorka was due to the grossest interference in the operations by me and by civilians generally, even to the point of countermanding orders on land and sea and imposing my own. I consider it my duty to declare that I shall continue to act in this way in future, despite all my reverence for science. STALIN'

Six days later he telegraphed this battle report to Lenin:

'Our offensive began yesterday. Although promised reserves have not yet come up, to have remained on this line any further was out of the question – we were too near Petrograd. So far the offensive is developing successfully. The Whites are on the run. STALIN'

He concluded his message by asking for the urgent dispatch of two million rounds of cartridges.

Early in 1920 when Stalin was back in southern Russia, Lenin informed him by telegram of ominous developments in that sector:

'To Comrade Stalin, Member of the Revolutionary Military Council of the South-Western Front

'The situation on the Caucasian Front is assuming a more serious character. In the situation obtaining today we may possibly lose Rostov and Novocherkassk and the enemy may attempt to develop his successes further to the north and threaten the Donets area. Adopt exceptional measures to hasten the transfer of the 42nd and the Latvian divisions and strengthen their fighting potential. I expect that you will appreciate the general situation and bend all your efforts to achieve important results. (20 February 1920) LENIN'

During the Civil War a new medal was struck – the Order of the Red Banner – in recognition of combat excellence in the Red Army and Navy. On Lenin's recommendation, Stalin was awarded this medal in November 1919 for his performance during the Civil War.

Some historians point out that Leon Trotsky, who had been appointed War Commissar – an 'inspired appointment' according to a number of observers – was the architect of the Bolshevik victory over the Whites. In any case the West believed at the time that Trotsky was the sole warlord of the Red Army and didn't know that there was a rivalry between Trotsky and Stalin which sometimes gave rise to conflict. This happened at Tsaritsyn when Trotsky, as War Commissar, sent Stalin a cable ordering him to reinstate some Red officers he had abruptly dismissed. When Stalin read the cable, he scrawled on it 'Pay no attention.' The cable is preserved in the archives.

In October 1919 the White Guards under General Yudenich launched an attack against Petrograd that was strong enough to make Lenin consider abandoning that city. It was the second such attack, the first having been repulsed some months earlier under Stalin's leadership. This time Trotsky rallied the defenders, and Yudenich, making no headway, had to retreat. When there was a revolt on the Island of Kronstadt in March 1921, Trotsky acted quickly, brutally crushing the insurgents in ten days of fighting in blinding snow-storms.

In a 1919 speech to the Eighth Party Congress, Stalin said that it was important to establish a powerful military force. 'Either we create a real worker and peasant – primarily peasant – strictly disciplined army and defend the republic, or we perish.' This was five years before Lenin's death.

Stalin later wrote an essay on strategy and tactics: 'The principal task of strategy is to determine the main direction in which troops are to advance and along which it is most advantageous to deliver the main blow at the enemy in order to achieve the desired aims.' The future Generalissimo added: 'A strategic plan is a plan for the organisation of the decisive blow in the direction in which it is most likely to produce the maximum results. In other words,' he said, 'to define the direction of the main blow means to predetermine the character of the operations throughout the duration of the war, and, consequently, to predetermine, to the extent of nine-tenths, the fate of the war itself. That is the aim of strategy.'

Stalin's essay was written in relatively simple terms. Defining the relation of tactics to strategy, he said tactics was part of strategy, subordinated to and serving the latter. 'Tactics deals not with a war as a whole, but with individual episodes in the war, with engagements, with battles. Whereas the aim of strategy is to win the war, or to carry to conclusion the struggle, let us say, against Tsarism. The aim of tactics is rather to win individual engagements, individual battles, to carry out successfully individual campaigns, individual actions, corresponding more or less to the concrete circumstances of the struggle at any given moment. The principal task of tactics is to determine the ways and means, the forms and methods of struggle that are most suited to the concrete circumstances at the given moment and are most certain to prepare a strategic success. That is why tactical actions and their results should be appraised not by themselves, not from the viewpoint of their immediate effect, but from the viewpoint of the aims and possibilities of strategy.'

It should be borne in mind that many Bolsheviks, including Stalin, had what may be called a siege mentality. Having experienced the Civil War and the intervention at that time of foreign armies (including British, American and Japanese forces), they expected Red Russia once again to be under foreign attack. So it is not surprising that Stalin delved into the art of the counter-offensive. Before the war, he had written:

'I believe that a well-organised counter-offensive is a very interesting manoeuvre. The old Parthians knew of such a counter-offensive when they drew the Roman General Crassus and his troops deep into their country and then dealt a counter-offensive and destroyed them. Our brilliant General Kutuzov also knew about this very well; he destroyed Napoleon and his army with the aid of a well-prepared counter-offensive.'

Counter-offensive strategy figured prominently in Stalin's World War II orders. As his armies gained strength and combat experience they used this strategy often and to good advantage against Hitler's soldiers.

★★★ INTERVIEW: THE GENERALS SPEAK ★★★
GENERAL OF THE ARMY IVAN SHAVROV

(I met General Shavrov on 17 April 1991, when he was a member of the Defence Ministry's Institute of Military History. From 1943 to 1945 he was Chief of Staff of a tank corps on a number of fronts. A decorated veteran of the war, Shavrov was wounded in the Battle of Stalingrad.)

Author: General, did Stalin do everything to prepare for the Nazi invasion?

Shavrov: Yes and no. He made everything possible and even did the impossible to prepare the country as a whole for defence. If the industrialisation hadn't been achieved, and if there had been no base for the defence industry, we couldn't have managed during the war. That's a plus. But Stalin hadn't done everything possible. On the eve of the war, knowing that Hitler was preparing the invasion, informed about the heavy concentration of troops, he did not take specific steps to mobilise the border military regions.

But, then, there is one concealed reason for this. Stalin really believed in the pact signed by German Foreign Minister Ribbentrop on 23 August 1939. That's one thing. Second, he didn't want to give Hitler a pretext for invading our country. If Stalin started mobilising the troops and began taking various measures in the border military districts, Hitler could claim that Stalin was getting ready for war. But the last thing Stalin wanted was to provoke a war. That's why in one of his speeches in 1941 Stalin said that when Hitler invaded he 'announced' himself as the aggressor and the whole world saw it. [Stalin stated this in a radio address on 3 July 1941.] In any case, the eve of invasion was a very complicated moment. Stalin stood for delaying mobilisation in the border regions but finally had to listen to the military and issue orders to prepare the troops. Of course, Hitler would have succeeded at the very beginning in any case because our army divisions were weak and not at full strength compared to the Germans. But our casualties could have been considerably less. Yes, Stalin did not do everything necessary.

Author: General, is it certain that casualties would have been fewer if Stalin had placed the bulk of his armies on the border?

Shavrov: If we had concentrated many more troops in the border areas – as Hitler wanted us to do – they could all have been destroyed then and there. We were short of tanks, anti-tank weapons and aircraft and, in this sense, you are right, we could have had more casualties at the border.

Author: Do you think the Red Army commanders at the border should have done more at the start of the war?

Shavrov: Yes, of course the commanders at the borders could have done something additionally, to improve the situation, to be more prepared – maybe just by bringing the divisions up to a higher battle standard. For example, if you take Admiral Nikolai Kuznetsov, just on the eve of the German attack he took all his warships out of their home bases and they were actually at their battle stations and firing at the enemy, without Stalin's orders. And he saved the fleet and meted out casualties to the German side.

Author: General, what puzzles me is why would Stalin undercut himself, I mean weaken the army with the pre-war purges? [Note: German historian Georg von

Rauch says that of six thousand of Stalin's highest-ranking officers who were arrested on charges of treason, 1,500 were executed.]

Shavrov: I can tell you this fact. I'm a member of the staff of the journal *Tekhnika I Vooruzhenie* (Arms and Technologies). Not long ago we conducted research on the development of the wartime T-34 tank project. The T-34 was delivered to the Army in 1939 by the officials of the plant that produced the tank. And government inspectors looked at everything, including the tank's weak points.

And it was found that although the diesel engine of the tank was designed by a very talented engineer who spent two years training at diesel plants in the United States, the working life of the engine was too short. So the tank was immediately sent back to the factory. In general the tank was accepted with only a few desired modifications, and mass production was to have started in 1940. But in two months' time, after the tank was sent back to the factory, the whole research team on the T-34 was arrested and only those who were left behind were able to continue working on the tank. And at our journal we are at a loss. What were the reasons for arresting all these engineers and technicians? Who gave the order? We don't think it was Stalin. Nobody knows for certain who was responsible. Was it treason? Of course Hitler was interested in this. He was getting ready to invade our country and said that within a few months' time he would be in Moscow – and even further east, to the Urals! That was Germany's plan. You see, this is only one example but there are a lot of others.

Author: But these mistakes were very damaging to the military.

Shavrov: That's what I want to say. I know another case. I was in the Far East, at the Lake Khasan battle against the Japanese Army in 1938. I was a platoon commander of PT-5 tanks. When the Japanese struck we were about 200 miles away from the fighting. To defeat the Japanese we had to concentrate troops. Nobody at the time knew how the battle would develop. That night, and for a few more days, our regimental commanders, divisional commanders, and senior commanders were arrested. At the very moment of the Japanese attack! I knew the commander of one brigade, Vasiliev. I forget his first name. He was arrested. Did Stalin do it? Who did it? This question is still unanswered.

So this is my evaluation of Stalin. As the leader of the state and the Party he was responsible for everything. He was obliged to look into problems and sort them out. And he is not to be excused. His is a very controversial personality.

Author: I read that the Red Army didn't have anti-tank weapons at the start of the war. Is that true?

Shavrov: You probably don't know this because history books don't tell you about it, but at the beginning of the war we didn't have anti-tank weapons and were compelled to make use of dogs in destroying Hitler's tanks. Few people know this. Ordinary dogs were trained to eat only under tanks that had their engines running. On the backs of these dogs we attached anti-tank mines. A soldier in our trench held the dog and, when the German panzers attacked, were about 200 yards away, the dog was eager to race to the approaching tank and eat beneath it. And our soldiers would release the dogs and the bottoms of the Nazi T-3 and T-4 tanks were weak enough so that the mines carried by the dogs would explode and destroy the tanks.

I was attached to the 238th Tank Division at that time and I assisted in feeding the dogs. By the way, the Germans protested to the International Red Cross about our use of dogs in the war. And their protests were made at the time that Nazi Germany was burning human beings, including our men, women and children, in their death camps.

Author: In your opinion what greater efforts could have been made to defend your country in 1941?

Shavrov: Now, more than half a century after the war, we can criticise from contemporary positions. Now the situation is like this: Many historians and writers of these events sometimes distort, exaggerate, make mistakes in describing the situation in those years, twisting the facts. Of course there are people who say we could have avoided a lot of mistakes – especially in repulsing Hitler's armies. But this fails to take into account the political decisions that were involved. But, to repeat, it's hard to say now after many years what else could have been done beforehand for the actual struggle with the Germans.

Author: Was Hitler's army stronger than the Red Army?

Shavrov: I will say this: The German Army was a very strong army and fully mobilised. Its divisions were at full strength, both in personnel and all necessary equipment. They were, you might say, perfect in the military sense. Besides, this army for a few years had smashed through many European countries and gained experience with their victories; for instance, the occupation of France, Czechoslovakia, Belgium and other European countries. And however the ease of these victories, it still was war. So there are two major factors that favoured Hitler's armies: first, a full supply of arms and, second, combat experience in operations against other European countries. When we were attacked, the Nazi strike force had almost 200 divisions in addition to 160 brigades. Separate brigades. It had about 4,000 tanks and 5,000 aircraft. The Nazi aircraft were superior to ours. They were the best in the world at that time. I want to add that most of these divisions (about 180) were German divisions. They were supplied with trucks and arms captured from France and Czechoslovakia. Therefore the Germans were well mechanised and well armed. And of course they had their own industry working full-time for the army.

[General Pavel Kurochkin, who distinguished himself at the 1941 Battle of Smolensk and in other engagements, told a post-war conference of historians that in training, experience, equipment and degree of mobilisation, the Wehrmacht was "overwhelmingly superior" to the Red Army at the time of Hitler's invasion.]

Author: A question on Soviet generalship: Does Zhukov rank with Suvorov and Kutuzov, who are the greatest heroes in Russia's history? Does the adjective "great" belong in front of Zhukov's name?

Shavrov: (Answers with a resounding *da*) Yes! If we try and compare the Great Patriotic War with those battles fought by Suvorov and Kutuzov, we cannot. Against the Nazis we fielded a great mechanised army spread over 4,000 kilometres. The history of humanity never had such a war. Towards the end of the war there were 10 big Red Army operations – we called them the "ten Stalin strikes" – being fought on a 4,000 kilometre front. This was very great strategic planning, during the end of 1944 and the beginning of 1945. As a final word on this point, paying due respect to the military leadership of Suvorov and Kutuzov in their time, I personally, knowing

Zhukov, studying him, consider that he is on just as high a plane, if not higher, than those who came before him.

Author: General, how did you react when you heard of the opening of the 'Second Front' in Normandy by the Allies?

Shavrov: I've read a lot about the operations of the US Army after the landing in France in June 1944. At that time our army had already waged many offensive operations, but when the US Army together with the British Army landed in Normandy, we took a deep breath and we were very pleased. We had been fighting alone in Europe for three years and had hoped for this day for a long time and, when it happened, our troops were jubilant. And when we heard about the landing of the Allies, we celebrated it and made it known to all the troops. The Normandy landing helped improve the morale of our troops. That's the mood we were in. We used this event to raise the fighting spirit of our soldiers and officers.

(General Shavrov omits mention of the Anglo-American landings in Sicily and Italy in the summer of 1943. While the Russians viewed this as a relatively small operation, Stalin congratulated Roosevelt and Churchill inAugust on the "outstanding success" of the Sicily operation; and, on 10 September, sent them a "personal and secret message" saying: "There can be no doubt that the landing in the Naples area and Italy's break with Germany will be yet another blow to Hitler's Germany and considerably facilitate the Soviet armies' operations on the Soviet-German front.")

★★★ BUILDING TWO RUSSIAS ★★★

"The Bolsheviks are trying to accomplish in five years what under optimum conditions would require 50 years." — The Times *of London, 1929*

Seeing a palpable foreign danger to Russia, Stalin sounded a tocsin for the Russian people in 1931. 'We are 50 to 100 years behind the advanced countries,' Stalin said in February of that year, addressing a group of industrial managers. 'We must cover this distance in ten years. Either we do this or they will crush us.'

British scholar Joseph McCabe has an interesting observation about political leaders in the early and mid-1930s. He says in his wartime biography of Winston Churchill that the 'supreme test' of any statesman in those years was his foresight or the clearness and urgency of the warning he gave about the approach of a new world war.

In Britain some politicians like Churchill and Anthony Eden spoke occasionally of the war peril. But until 1937 Churchill continued to downplay the danger of war, recommending that Herr Hitler be disarmed by concessions.

Stalin, whose country was almost universally despised and therefore in the greatest danger, issued frequent warnings. By the 'advanced countries' Stalin meant mainly the capitalist West. Hitler's takeover of Germany was then (1931) a few years off. Stalin, a student of Marx and Lenin, cited the 'jungle law' of capitalism: 'You are backward, you are weak, so you are wrong, hence you can be beaten and enslaved. You are mighty, so you are right, hence, we must be wary of you.' 'That is why', said Stalin, 'we must no longer be backward.'

In a desperate attempt to propel Russia out of backwardness, Stalin promulgated the brutal Five-Year Plan with its ambitious targets. According to the blueprints, after completion of several five-year plans, Russia would attain the production levels of the advanced European states. Meanwhile, the creation of powerful armed forces and a modern war industry would – it was believed – be able to halt any aggression against Russia. Nobody then could imagine that the coming upheavals in industry and agriculture would be so costly in life and property.

Here it is important to say a word about Russia's status in Europe in the first decades of the 20th century. Even three decades into the century, Russia was estimated to be fifty or more years behind Germany in terms of industry and literacy, and probably fifteen or twenty years in terms of military equipment. In the aftermath of the World War I Russia was held in low esteem by many Europeans who regarded her population as lazy and degraded, even barbarous. In a book entitled *Russian Characteristics* published in London before the Russian Revolution, its author, Emile J. Dillon, described the average Russian as 'untruthful', 'dishonest', 'shifty', 'drunken' and 'weak'. Paul Milyukov, a Russian historian and politician, agreed with this unfavourable evaluation when he later wrote his own book on the people and culture of Russia.

The possibility of bridging the gap between a poor, stagnant and demoralised Russia and the advanced European countries in just a few years was seen by most Western experts as wildly unrealistic. The implementation of such plans could be achieved only by Herculean energy and utter ruthlessness.

The first of the Five-Year Plans actually dated from 1928. At least some of the people involved were dreamy-eyed idealists. Given their orders, an army of workers fanned out to the Ural Mountains. They included exiled *kulaks*, party activists, nomads from Central Asia and a few hundred American, British, French and German engineers, agronomists, horticulturists, teachers and other experts.

The targets set by the planners seemed impossible: to double oil and coal production, triple the output of tools and machines and raw materials, double the output of consumer goods, quadruple the country's electric power, and expand Russia's railways. Simultaneously there was a drive to train doctors and nurses to combat the diseases common to a poor country, and teachers to wipe out illiteracy.

Some foreigners who flocked to Russia with a belief in the 'communist utopia' shouldered heavy work loads because of the scarcity of Russian specialists. Other foreigners went for the adventure or the guarantee of a job. One of the former was Bill Shatoff of Chicago who became chief of police of what is now St. Petersburg; at the same time he took over as the construction boss of the 'Turk-Sib' railway (while on temporary leave from his police job); and became simultaneously a civilian administrator at an army unit.

The empty plains of Russia began to change. When completed, the new building complexes and new cities in Siberia and Soviet Central Asia were said to be equal to the creation of a 'second Russia', the new one being tucked away behind the Urals, far from a potential invading army. In size, this broad hinterland with its hundreds of newly built factories, farms, oil fields, coal fields and mines was as large as Western Europe.

When war came to Russia, another giant task had to be tackled. In five months, from June to November 1941, more than 10 million people and $1\frac{1}{2}$ million railway wagons filled with machines and spare parts were evacuated from the western areas of the country. Looking back at that period, former US Ambassador to Moscow Averell Harriman told me: 'Stalin did a remarkable job of rebuilding the war industries. You know, when the government withdrew from Moscow, when there was danger it might be overrun in the latter part of 1941, they put the machine tools from factories into railway boxcars and they put the operators in the same cars. And they moved together to the location, wherever it was. And they restarted production rapidly. And Stalin was involved in that, I know, because we discussed the details of that. He had a great deal of detailed knowledge of supply questions. And not only in 1941 but throughout the war.'

When war came, the peasant country of Russia was gone – eliminated by the Five–Year Plan and the collective farm.

One of the construction projects of the First Five-Year Plan that captured the attention of the West was built on the doorstep of the Urals on thirty square miles of land. Nearby a new city of half a million people arose. In a few years the city, called Magnitogorsk ('Magnet Mountain'), boasted the largest iron foundry and steel mill in the world.

In January 1933 Stalin made a startling announcement. The former peasant country of Russia, he said, had become the world's second industrial power. The First Five-Year Plan had been completed in little more than four years, from October 1928 to December 1932. The number of industrial workers had doubled, from 11 million to 22 million. Stalin spoke of Russia's development:

'Formerly we did not have an iron and steel industry. Now we have such an industry.

'We did not have a tractor industry. Now we have one.

'We did not have an automobile industry. Now we have one.

'We did not have an engineering industry. Now we have one.'

Stalin also mentioned an aviation industry, chemical industry and others, adding: 'We have achieved these on a scale that makes the scale of European industry pale.' This was, be it noted, the time of the 'great depression' in the West.

Only in an oblique detail did Stalin touch on the inevitable tragedies that affected whole populations, of harvests disorganised, of famine, of arrests and exile and executions. 'We could not', he said, 'refrain from whipping up a country that was a hundred years behind and which, owing to its backwardness, was faced with mortal danger.'

The growth figures were impressive. At the end of three pre-war five-year plans, 9,000 new industrial plants and complexes had mushroomed, many equipped with American machinery. Stalin and his functionaries made sure that the plans concentrated on heavy industry so that if war broke out production could quickly turn to howitzers, projectiles and tanks. Most experts say that the new industries that were built deep in the interior, in Siberia and Central Asia, no doubt saved Russia from defeat in the war.

In the dizzy drive for greater productivity, Russian agriculture suddenly found itself hobbled. British author and scholar H. G. Wells, who visited Russia and met Stalin, called the collective farms 'unnecessarily brutal'. He said 'all successful peasants were labelled *kulaks*' and 'thousands were deported to Siberia'. Fifty per cent of Russia's entire livestock was slaughtered. (But playwright George Bernard Shaw, who had written a 500-page book on economics, saw things differently. In a letter to Wells, he saw the battle as between the collective farm and the *moujik*, or Russian peasant. Shaw wrote that collective farming was not only a success under Stalin but was 'the only chance for our own agriculture; but we stick helplessly to the *moujik* and the *kulak*.')

In the rural areas of Russia poor peasants in newly collectivised farms were pitted against their richer neighbours, the *kulaks*, often with tragic results. The late General Dmitri Volkogonov, a historian and former chief of the Soviet military's psychological warfare department, said in an interview published in *The New York Times* on 1 August 1995, that the 'tragedy of the *kulaks*' began under Lenin. He had discovered in the archives an order by Lenin that as a warning to others several hundred *kulaks* should be hanged in a public place and not cut down.

In his memoirs Churchill says that after Stalin told him of the modernisation of agriculture (some Russian sources say that upwards of a million peasants died; other sources put casualties at 'many millions'), the British Prime Minister quoted to his host Burke's dictum: 'If I cannot have reform without injustice, I will not have reform.'

Stalin may or may not have retorted with this quotation from Cardinal Richelieu: 'I find it easier to tolerate injustice than disorder.' (British diplomat and Russian expert Bruce Lockhart quotes this probable Churchill–Stalin exchange in his 1952 book of reminiscences, *My Europe*. He adds: 'The fact remains that in the Soviet Union there is no disorder.')

In the Russian countryside millions of peasants, perhaps the most ferocious of individualists, refused to join the new socialised-collective farms. Rather than give up their animals to the collectives, they slaughtered them. On 31 August 1930 *Pravda*, the official Party newspaper, admitted that during this rural upheaval almost half the country's pigs, one-third of its sheep and a quarter of its cattle were slaughtered, causing a nation-wide meat shortage.

An eye-witness to this initial crippling of Russian agriculture was American engineer John D. Littlepage, who wrote in October 1938: 'The liquidation of the *kulaks* was pretty hard on the people of Russia in that they went short of food for years because of the removal of so many competent farmers from the land. It also caused many *kulaks* to destroy their domestic animals so that now, after almost ten years, there is still a shortage of meat and dairy produce in Russia.' (In an attempt to halt the meat shortage, planners in 1934 tried to persuade Russians to eat rabbit meat, and breeding farms for rabbits appeared. But rabbits never became popular. Some Russians referred to them as 'Stalin's cows'.)

A few brave souls protested. One of them was Mikhail Sholokhov, later to receive the Nobel Prize for his novel of the revolution, *And Quiet Flows the Don*. In the summer of 1929 this writer of Cossack origin, seeing with his own eyes the sins of collectivisation in his home region in Russia's south, wrote a stinging letter to a friend denouncing the outrages. The friend sent the letter on to Stalin. Sholokhov said that six years earlier he had himself been a 'tough, over-zealous commissar' in the drive for collectivisation in Cossack territory. It is a remarkable letter. Here is an excerpt:

> 'You should see the goings-on in our and neighbouring areas. The kulak is being pressed but the average peasant has already been squashed. The poor peasants are starving and the property – down to samovars and children's blankets – of the truest middle peasants, who are quite often very weak economically, is being sold off. The people are running berserk, their mood is depressed, and the areas sown for the next year will shrink disastrously. And the fact (a horrible fact) of the emergence of political gangs in the neighbouring area comes as the result of the heavy pressure on the kulak.'

Sholokhov, unwilling to hide his feelings, ended his letter by saying that everyone in the Kremlin 'should be given a good whipping'. This meant, he said, 'everyone who shrieks hypocritically, like a Pharisee about the alliance [of the worker] with the average peasant and, at the same time, is strangling the very same peasant.'

The Sholokhov letter came to light only recently. A year before the letter was written, Stalin had referred to Sholokhov as 'a well-known writer of our time'. Almost certainly Stalin read the letter – but not the sentence about whipping. The friend who sent the letter to Stalin protected the novelist by rewriting the letter and removing the offending words.

Sholokhov went on to gain favour with Stalin, and his next novel was apparently printed only after Stalin interceded on the author's behalf. During the 1933 famine Sholokhov is said to have saved thousands of lives by persuading Stalin to send grain to the Upper Don region. The author sent Stalin several letters during that famine, and Stalin never failed to answer them; he acknowledged one letter with these words: 'You ought to have telegraphed, not written.'

Writing to a friend, the Cossack author depicted the tragedy of that era. 'The good news: a starving collective farmer getting 400 grams of bread full of chaff and fulfilling his daily quota. The bad news: a hamlet of 65 farmsteads, where 150 people have died since 1 February. [Three months.] In fact, the entire hamlet has died.'

In his well-known 'Dizzy With Success' speech delivered some months after the first Sholokhov letter reached him, Stalin denounced 'stupid bungling' by communists in rural areas. He also cautioned against 'pushing ahead too fast'.

Peasants refusing to join collective farms weren't the only disaffected group in Russia. Industrial workers with grievances against the system took revenge in the factories and became known as 'wreckers'. Even if their number was grossly exaggerated by the Kremlin, some no doubt existed. A few foreign engineers like Littlepage personally witnessed sabotage of the Five-Year Plans.

He said: 'I know from my own experiences that a good deal of industrial sabotage was going on all the time in Soviet mines, and that some of it could hardly have occurred without the complicity of highly placed communist managers.'

Another American engineer was approached by a secret police investigator at his factory, shown some metal parts, and asked if he could identify them. 'Certainly,' he said. 'They are parts of a heavy machine-gun.' The investigator then surprised him with the news that such weapons were being made in his own shop on the night shift.

Some Western observers have concluded that the opposition to the National Plan, and the resulting reprisals and reign of terror, caused more deaths than the notorious deportations to the far-flung camps of the 'archipelago'.

Meanwhile, reports of a regenerated Russia propelled by Stalin's five-year plans began to attract world-wide attention. An editorial in one New York newspaper in 1931 stated that 'a vast majority of Russians is being made to sit up and do completely new tricks by the whiplash of the State'. In 1932 America's *Fortune* magazine devoted its entire March issue to the 'panorama' of the Five-Year Plan. Four years later a German military expert recorded his impressions: 'The new industrial centres are situated so far inside Russian territory that even the loss of a zone 500 miles deep will not constitute a serious danger to the industries producing motors, tractors, tanks, or aircraft.'

But some Germans began to be anxious about a 'creeping danger' to their nation from Stalin's Russia. Prior to the outbreak of war, the German Ambassador in London, Herbert von Dirksen, said that a German politician told him: 'As for Russia, a certain fear psychosis at the success of the Five-Year Plan is to be observed in Germany, and there are people who conclude from this that a change of attitude towards the Soviet Republic and new alignments are necessary.'

When Hitler's armies invaded Russia, many of Stalin's new factories changed overnight to war production. For instance, the Magnitogorsk Steel Mill – 900 miles east of Moscow – began to manufacture steel plate for tanks. Within a few months Hitler's troops seized almost 50 per cent of Russia's arable area and actually looted some of the country's rich topsoil. In his booklet, *Renewal of Land Resources* (Moscow, 1985), Dr. Zia Nuriev says: 'The Nazis robbed our people of everything they could, carting off to Germany machine tools, cattle, ore, coal and railway tracks. They even shipped to Germany trainloads of the famous Ukrainian black soil to fertilise German fields.'

Even apple trees became a casualty when Hitler's armies retreated across the Ukraine in 1943. The Russian writer Ilya Ehrenburg wrote in his book, *The War, 1941–1945*: 'There was an hour when my heart turned to water. I saw the orchards of Glukhov and the posthumous fruit of the apple trees cut down by the foe. The leaves trembled; all was empty.'

Despite the devastation caused by Hitler's occupiers, by the end of the first year of war the cultivated areas in the newly developed Central Asian regions had increased by 10 million acres. At the factories in the interior workers expanded defence production. The State Planning Committee announced that the fall in industrial production had ceased from December 1941.

★★★ AN ARMY FOR WINNING ★★★

The Red Army literally sang Stalin's praises. I found there were in the archives an estimated 2,000 chants and hymns celebrating all phases of Stalin's rule, including his contribution to the building up of military might. One musical piece, entitled *The Stalin Cantata*, was composed by A. V. Alexandrov, founder of the well-known Red Army Chorus. There is also the famous *Stalin Song* with music by Aram Khachaturian.

That Stalin gave absolute priority to defence problems is shown by the new aircraft factories, yearly military exercises, enormous mass parachute descents and annual aerial reviews. In the mid-thirties, when the country's first assembly lines were beginning to turn out bad trucks, Russia was exhibiting what was billed as the world's largest aircraft, the 'Maksim Gorky'. (It later crashed.)

Stalin's build-up of the armed forces came at a time when militarism and naked aggression were becoming evident in Europe and Asia. The same year (1931) that Stalin delivered his 'advance-or-die' speech, a Japanese army invaded Manchuria, and an early warning about German militarism was sounded by the British military attaché in Berlin. The world paid scant attention to events in Asia. (Few nations protested Japan's action, the League of Nations merely asking both parties to settle their conflict amicably.) More attention was paid to developments in Germany. Reporting from Berlin, the British attaché, Colonel J. H. Marshall-Cornwall, wrote: 'The danger [from Germany] is not imminent, but it is throwing its shadow ahead.' His warning was made public forty years later, but is worth quoting further because it shows that some observers saw the writing on the wall two years *before* Hitler attained power.

> 'The past twelve months have been marked by a gradual but quite distinct stiffening of the military spirit in Germany. New weapons are being tested and their manufacture organised. Reserve stocks of ammunition are being accumulated and new methods of transport and communication developed. So far it has proved impossible to do much in the way of training illegal reserves of manpower, but the patriotic associations have successfully upheld the military tradition and fostered the fighting spirit.'

Five years later (1936), General Erich Ludendorff's book *Total War* showed the extent to which militarism had entered the thinking of some top German officers. 'War and politics help the people to survive, but war is the supreme expression of the people's will and life. For this reason politics must serve the waging of war.'

Stalin's military experts, meanwhile, held that a future war would have three characteristics: First, great mobility at the start of the war, based on air power in conjunction with highly mechanised ground forces. Second, a *Blitz* attack. Third, an emphasis on 'permanent factors'. If a first assault did not quickly achieve victory, the conflict would pass into a static war of position; and the outcome of that would be decided by such factors as economic power, war reserves and morale.

Pinpointing Germany and Japan as potential enemies, the Kremlin undertook vigorous counter-measures.

In 1932, writing in the journal of the Japanese Admiralty, the Japanese military attaché in Moscow said: 'The mechanisation of the Red Army astonishes all the foreign attachés who are present at its parades.'

In 1934 Moscow was ready to show off its armed forces. It published a 100-page photographic review of Russia's new army and navy. On the book jacket (an English text was provided for foreigners), was a quotation from Stalin: 'We do not covet one inch of foreign soil, we will not yield an iota of our own.'

Interestingly, in addition to the glossy photographs, the text contained quotations from Mikhail Tukhachevsky and Jan Gamarnik, two of Stalin's marshals later purged; the former shot, the latter a suicide.

Stalin's army showed steady growth:

1934	900,000 men
1935	1,300,000 men
1938	2,000,000 men
1939	3,000,000 men
1940	4,000,000 men

(The 1940 complement was actually 5,000,000 if security police and militia are counted.)

Hitler's army was also expanding rapidly. It had 31 divisions in 1936, but this number rose to 52 in late 1938 and 103 towards the autumn of 1939. The total numerical strength of the German Army grew within the seven pre-war years (1932–9) from 104,218 to 3,754,104 officers and men – an increase of more than 35 times. But by the start of the Russo–German war, Hitler had doubled the strength of his army and reinforced it with the armies of Italy, Hungary, Rumania and Finland plus pro-Nazi contingents from occupied European countries.

Perhaps the single most important fact about Germany between the two world wars was that German disarmament, as planned by the Allies in the 1919 Treaty of Versailles, was turned into the most rapid rearmament the world had ever seen. The British Minister of Information, Brendan Bracken, in a wartime speech said: 'No country ever entered a war more thoroughly prepared than Germany in 1939. Her civilians were almost as carefully groomed for total warfare as her soldiers.' The West, he said, was paying a heavy price for the 'folly' of ignoring the huge military build-up in pre-war Germany.

That Stalin was closely monitoring events in Europe, particularly German rearmament, was borne out by Russia's own increasing military build-up. On a visit to Moscow in 1934, French Air Minister Pierre Cot said that he was impressed with Stalin's air force. He called it the best in Europe. Some observers said that Russia had already achieved the level of western Europe in armaments.

In that same year, reports said there was a large increase in the number of Red Army tanks. Naval tonnage was also up sharply. 'Frontier defence' was the reason given for the expansion of the Red Army. In 1934 Russia had a fleet of airships modelled after Germany's *Graf Zeppelin* which had flown into Moscow a few years earlier, dazzling Stalin and his military chiefs. It was announced that more than 5,000 Soviet paratroops had completed training. From a strategic point of view, the airships and paratroops could be used for a surprise landing of large forces in an enemy's rear.

The exact number of Red Army aircraft and tanks had always been classified, the West's knowledge of them being mainly guesswork. But a French air mission visiting Russia in 1936 estimated that the Russians had 5,000 military aircraft operational, and were producing 5,000 annually. This figure was confirmed by Swedish and German experts and by the fact that in the May Day parades of 1934 and 1935 at least 3,000 military aircraft took part in fly-pasts over six cities. (But when Hitler attacked in 1941, much of Stalin's air force consisted of inferior or even obsolete aircraft.)

In 1935, German General Heinz Guderian, later to become one of Hitler's best panzer commanders on the Eastern Front, estimated the number of tanks in the Red Army at more than 10,000. He also placed the Red Army at the head of all armies in motor transport. Guderian's colleagues scoffed at his 'tall estimate'.

But Guderian was on the mark. Stalin had at least that number when war began although, like his aircraft, many were obsolete. After nine weeks of war, the world was shocked when Moscow admitted its losses included 5,000 tanks and 7,500 guns. An army that could still wage war after such heavy losses must have had the largest or second largest arsenal in the world.

In 1939 German General Gebhard von Schroeder had written that Russia's aircraft industry had a capacity exceeding Germany's. He calculated that Russia had 18,000 tanks, 8,000 military aircraft, 142,000 military motor vehicles, and a total army mobilisation strength of twenty-six million men.

It is ironic that the country that fielded this huge military force had but a decade earlier been the world's leading proponent of disarmament. Just one proposal out of others made by Maxim Litvinov, Stalin's Foreign Minister, to a 1927 Disarmament Conference was so comprehensive it could aptly be called 'the mother of disarmament proposals'. Its list of items to be destroyed included all munitions factories, flame-throwers, chemical materials, high-powered rifles and all other means of annihilation. It envisaged disbandment of armed forces, the abolition of war ministries, dissolution of general staffs, and a ban on all military training. But the other powers ignored Litvinov's proposal and began preparing for war.

Before war broke out in Europe, the Russian Defence Ministry had announced a few changes in the Red Army. One embodied a new oath for recruits that was aimed at expressing loyalty not, as of old, towards the 'international proletariat' but towards the Russian motherland. Political screening also became an important element in recruiting soldiers. In August 1938 the Red Army began subjecting new recruits to the most careful political testing so that 'new enemies would not be admitted'.

The long arm of Stalin's purges had already reached deep into the ranks of the Army and Navy, according to the official announcement, to 'weed out those guilty of disloyalty'.

'Those who try to attack our country will receive a stinging rebuff to teach them not to poke their pigs' snouts into our Soviet garden.' (Stalin, circa 1935.)

'One arrives at the conclusion that there is a gap in the fence of [Stalin's] lovely garden, because as late as in 1938 the entire "pig" was there, and is almost certainly there still – in 1940.'

(Colonel Victor Kaledin, in *The Moscow-Berlin Secret Service*, London, 1940)

★★★ ESPIONAGE IN STALIN'S RUSSIA ★★★

Stalin promoted the idea that Russia was a Mecca for German and Japanese spies during the pre-war era. He maintained that the Great Purge Trials of civilians and military officers in the middle and late 1930s were needed to wipe out espionage and sabotage. Saying that the 'bourgeois states' were out to stuff Russia with enemy agents, he once gave this rationale for his actions:

'France and England are now swarming with German spies and diversionists and, on the other hand, Anglo–French spies and diversionists are active in turn in Germany. America is swarming with Japanese spies and diversionists, and Japan with Americans. Such is the law of the mutual relations between bourgeois states.

'The question arises: Why should bourgeois states be milder and more neighbourly towards the Soviet Socialist State than toward bourgeois states of their own type? Why should they send to the rear of the Soviet Union fewer spies, wreckers, diversionists and murderers than they send to the rear of the bourgeois state akin to them?'

In conclusion, he charged the Western states and Japan with trying to send into Russia three times as many 'wreckers, spies and murderers' as they had done in the past. Except for the verdicts of the purge trials, which have long been open to question, evidence of a 'swarm of foreign spies' in Russia bent on subverting the Red Army is difficult to obtain, but some Russian historians have given details about enemy agents in the Soviet Union prior to the German invasion.

Mikhail Semiryaga in *Barbarossa Plan*, Moscow, 1986, says that from October 1939 to December 1940, Russian counter-intelligence apprehended nearly 5,000 German agents and 'put out of action' a number of armed saboteur groups. He adds that during the first half of 1941 the number of German agents who infiltrated into Soviet territory 'considerably increased'.

Semiryaga goes on to say that to co-ordinate and direct all forms of Nazi espionage and sabotage activity inside Russia, a special staff code-named 'Walli' was set up near Warsaw. It was in charge of special teams attached to the *Wehrmacht*. Particular attention was given to the training of officers for operations in the Soviet rear and, a year before the invasion, the German High Command set up a sabotage unit code-named 'Brandenburg' that consisted of ethnic Germans residing outside Germany.

General of the Army Ivan Shavrov, a former member of the Defence Ministry's Institute of Military History, is explicit: 'We had a Fifth Column in our country. I don't know if this extended to the Ministry [of Defence] but it was definitely there at the border, and Hitler therefore knew the position of our Army thanks to this Fifth Column, and the state of our industry, and he was in a hurry because time was very short for the Germans in their time-table for attacking our country.'

Shavrov asserts that pro-Hitler agents survived in Russia even after the 'show trials' of the 1930s.

On 11 June 1937, the world was shocked by the announcement in Moscow that a group of high-ranking generals had been arrested and charged with treason, espionage and plotting to overthrow the government. Stalin spoke of a 'military-Fascist conspiracy' against his regime and included among its leaders not only Trotsky but prominent marshals of the Red Army. A plot to assassinate the leaders of the Kremlin including Stalin was alleged. Stalin demanded the uprooting of 'enemies of the people' who he said were hiding in the army. In Stalin's language these men were puppets in the hands of the *Reichswehr*. German generals wished to throttle the Red Army so that it could not defend the country. They wanted to make of Russia a 'second Spain'.

The newspapers claimed that the arrested generals, and other defendants at the trials, had received German and Japanese gold. These and other ranking officers were shot.

(The Japanese and Germans were mentioned so often at the Moscow trials that they felt compelled to speak out. In January 1937 the Japanese Foreign Office called the trials 'fantastic' and said the confessions elicited at the trials were 'farcical'. Similar comments came from Berlin. In a riposte, the Party newspaper *Pravda* said that Japan and Germany 'are already wailing over the loss of their valuable agents'. *Pravda* urged citizens 'who love their country to go on smoking out of their holes spies, traitors and wreckers' against the Red Army.)

The military trials followed a mass of open 'show trials' affecting Party leaders, administrators, diplomats and others. But the purge of the military was the most harmful to the security of the country.

Among those arrested was Marshal Mikhail Tukhachevsky, one of the senior officers of the Red Army and a pioneer in its reorganisation. Tukhachevsky had served in World War I as a Tsarist officer but in 1918 he had joined the Bolshevik Party and volunteered for the Red Army. Also court-martialled at the same time were seven other top officers, all accused of treason. German documents, apparently forgeries, were uncovered that implicated Tukhachevsky in a proposed coup. The German secret service was said to be behind the forgeries.

Most writers and historians hold that Tukhachevsky was entirely innocent of any crime. Although the military trials were held behind closed doors, it was believed that one of the charges against Tukhachevsky was that he was 'too close' to German officers. Only a small minority questions whether Tukhachevsky's loyalty to Stalin might have oscillated. Curiously, at the time of the military trials it was alleged by some diplomats that Tukhachevsky was guilty of 'indiscretions' with attractive Western, including British, ladies.

More serious was Tukhachevsky's apparent defeatist attitude towards the German Army. A respected French journalist, Geneviève Tabouis, mentions in her book, *They Called Me Cassandra*, of a meeting with Tukhachevsky and being astonished by his opinion of Hitler's war machine. 'They [the Nazis] are already invincible', she quotes him as telling her 'over and over again'.

Another marshal charged with treason, Jan Gamarnik, a high Defence Ministry official, was found dead, apparently by his own hand. (Military historian Volkogonov told me in 1989 that Gamarnik was asked to be a member of the court to judge Tukhachevsky, but he couldn't because he was Tukhachevsky's friend. But he knew that if he refused to join the 'jurors' he would be shot. 'So Gamarnik chose the only possible way of protesting: he shot himself.' Volkogonov added: 'There were quite a number of cases like that – officers who committed suicide as their way of expressing disagreement with Stalin.')

One bizarre case involved Lieutenant-General A. Y. Lapin, Commander of the Far Eastern Air Force, who was reported to have killed himself in prison after being arrested in the Stalin purge. According to *The Times* of London, Lapin had written a letter 'in blood' that was, apparently, smuggled out of prison. The letter said: 'I falsely testified to matters of which I knew nothing and under the constant menace of new tortures I affirmed everything imputed to me. I am not a counter-revolutionary and have no connection with such elements whatsoever.'

Before Hitler assumed power there had been exceptionally close military ties between Germany and Russia, originating after World War I when the two countries signed the Rapallo Treaty of Friendship in 1922. Germany was allowed to manufacture in Russian plants certain types of armaments barred to her by the Treaty of Versailles. German soldiers trained with these weapons on Russian soil, and some German officers even gave lectures on strategy and tactics at selected Soviet military schools.

The Moscow–Berlin link was an anomaly, but it is said to have produced a pro-Russian bloc of German generals which included Hans von Seeckt and, later, Werner von Fritsch. But after Hitler's assumption of power in 1933, and his regime's outspoken anti-Bolshevism, all Russo–German military ties, at least on the official level, were cut off.

Given Berlin's attitudes, it's not surprising that Berlin wished to create as much disorder in Red Russia as possible, it being the strongest, most feared and despised country on Hitler's 'black list'. There is a curious reference to Nazi trouble-making in Russia in an American edition of Hitler's *Mein Kampf* published in 1939. A footnote by a team of American editors seems to support Stalin's accusations. It says: 'Since 1933, the Nazis have certainly done everything in their power to foment trouble in Russia. There may be more real fact behind the Stalin "purge" than has as yet leaked out.'

In 1937–8 the Red Army had an estimated 80,000 regular plus about the same number of reserve officers. The purges eliminated three-fourths of the Supreme War Council, at least 60 out of 85 corps commanders, 110 out of 195 divisional commanders and 220 out of 406 brigade commanders.

At least 60 per cent of all colonels and generals were reported to have been arrested – as many as 20,000 officers. Some were reprieved; others were sent to labour camps, and some were later released and re-entered military service. (General Gorbatov, in his book, *Years Off My Life,* records his own arrest and pathetic existence in a Siberian gulag before being summoned back for front-line duty against Hitler's forces.)

One high-ranking security officer who escaped to Japan said the military purges had affected more than 10,000 high military and political officers as well as more than 1,000,000 civilians and soldiers of the Red Army.

In 1990, General Igor Sergeyev, who was Deputy Commander-in-Chief of Russia's Strategic Rocket Forces, disclosed that 35,000 'commanders' were expelled from the Party and arrested in 1937–8. Between 1932 and 1939, the army's numerical strength actually decreased. He said that experienced officers were replaced with 'hastily-trained men'.

It was apparent that no army could sustain such blows and not lose credibility as a fighting force.

In July, 1938, in the midst of the Moscow trials, one of Stalin's generals defected to Japan, which caused a new sensation. Major-General Genrick Samoirovich Lyushkov, Stalin's general who was head of military counter-intelligence in the Far East, told the Japanese that he had been in charge of a sweeping purge of the Soviet Far Eastern Army but decided to defect because he feared he himself would soon be among the victims. Reports had previously reached Moscow of the shooting in the Far East of 61 'leaders and members of a Trotskyist–Japanese–German terroristic spy, diversionist organisation working on the Far Eastern railways and systematically supplying espionage information to a certain foreign intelligence service'.

Lyushkov spoke of widespread discontent in the Red Army because of the purges. He told his hosts that there was the possibility (he called it a 'danger') that the army would collapse if the Japanese struck against Russia. He also said that he had received an official reprimand three months earlier from Marshal Vasily Blyukher, the commander of the Far Eastern Army, who was himself a later victim of the purges. He did not clarify the reasons for the reprimand, but historian Roy A. Medvedev has written that although Lyushkov 'exposed' Stalin's crimes when he defected to Japan, he had himself been an active participant in those crimes.

At least a part of what the world believes about the Moscow purge trials was laid out by Lyushkov in lengthy statements made in Tokyo in 1938. In one he said: 'With full responsibility for what I say before world opinion, I declare that these alleged conspiracies have no ground in reality but were entirely concocted by the Kremlin leaders.' He added that the proceedings of the Moscow purge trials against alleged 'enemies of the people' were deliberate fabrications by Stalin who systematically planned to 'liquidate his rivals'.

How reliable was Lyushkov as a source of information? After publishing his disclosures, *The Times* of London made a candid assessment on 9 August 1938: 'Some parts [of Lyushkov's testimony] bear the stamp of truth and others that of familiarity with the Japanese official thesis.'

In Moscow, meanwhile, more trials, more executions followed. The president of the White Russian Republic was charged with treason and reportedly killed himself.

The Czech President Eduard Beneš, in his post-war memoirs, said that he learned in 1937 of the existence of an 'anti-Stalin clique' in the Red Army which had close contacts with Nazi officers. Other authors say that Beneš gave a dossier on the 'Tukhachevsky affair' to the Russian Ambassador to be forwarded to Stalin. But no trace of this dossier has yet been found in Russian archives.

Czech officials are said to have been shocked to learn that their country's military secrets, hitherto known only to the Russians through their mutual aid alliance, were also known to the German High Command. The secrets, they claimed, were given to Berlin by Tukhachevsky. Some corroboration came from G. E. R. Gedye, Prague correspondent of *The New York Times*, who cabled on 18 June that 'two of the highest officials in Prague' say that they have 'definite knowledge that secret connections between the German General Staff and certain high Russian generals have existed since Rapallo'.

At one of the Moscow show trials evidence was given that Stalin twice narrowly escaped assassination – in 1933 and 1935. Were Stalin's – or Hitler's – secret services behind these real or fictitious assassination plots? According to the impartial British *Annual Register*, a chief of the local OGPU (the secret police) in Georgia and two border guards had fired at Stalin's cutter when he was cruising off the Black Sea coast in the summer of 1933. The attempt failed because of the cutter's speed and distance from the Georgian shore. A second attempt with a German automatic rifle in 1935 was frustrated by the late arrival of the 'conspirators' at the place where Stalin was spending his holiday. The instructions for the planned assassinations had, it was claimed, come from Yuri Piatakov, the Deputy Commissar for Heavy Industry, who was alleged to have close ties with Leon Trotsky. Piatakov later was accused of treason and executed.

Stalin's biographer, General Volkogonov, told me that he is certain the assassination plots were fabricated. 'I'm absolutely sure that there were no plots, no attempts on Stalin's life during this time.' He added: 'There was not a single person who would make an attempt on his life. If it was in the United States, Stalin would be definitely assassinated because Americans wouldn't tolerate a tyrant like Stalin. But it was easy for Stalin to govern the Russian people; they were treating him as a god while at the same time he was annihilating millions of people.'

But Volkogonov's remarks may be too categorical. The tremendous upheavals of the 1930s were guaranteed to create dissidents or disaffected elements, or saboteurs, in Russia. (See comments by the US engineer John Littlepage and others above.) In addition, Stalin had very real enemies abroad. Volkogonov himself said that Stalin's rival Trotsky – who was living in Mexico before his murder in 1940 – retained one 'maniacal passion' to the end of his life: hatred of Stalin. There was, moreover, the ominous build–up of war potential in a Germany which hated Bolshevism and regarded Stalin's Russia as its No. 1 prey.

The military trials were sandwiched between other sensational 'trials of spies and saboteurs', for example, the 'Trial of the Seventeen', in which the defendants confessed to plotting to wreck Stalin's second Five-Year Plan and maintaining 'treasonable links' with Trotsky, in exile in Mexico. All were sentenced to death except Karl Radek who promised to reveal important new facts if his life were spared.

Radek allegedly furnished material about 'treason in the High Command of the Army' that helped implicate Tukhachevsky. The German-speaking Radek apparently had close contacts in Germany, including Count Ernst zu Reventlow, a prominent Nazi, who is said to have once conferred with Radek about forming a Russo–German alliance.

Prior to his arrest, Karl Radek, an ex-newspaper commentator and rector of Sun Yat-sen University in Moscow, made an extraordinary statement about enemies of the Stalin regime: 'There are in this country semi-Trotskyists, quarter-Trotskyists, one-eighth Trotskyists. To these people we say that whoever has the slightest rift with the Party, let him realise that tomorrow he may be a diversionist, tomorrow he may be a traitor, if he does not thoroughly heal the rift by complete and utter frankness to the Party.'

British writer Sir John Maynard says that this statement is of particular interest because in it Radek perhaps 'unconsciously furnished a clue to the riddle of the confessions'. (On the mass confessions at the trials and the allegations that drugs were used to elicit them, see comments by Sir Bruce Lockhart and Sidney and Beatrice Webb in the Notes.)

Many disclosures at the Moscow purge trials still seem incredible. For instance, on 20 December 1938, two military doctors were sentenced to death by a court-martial, being accused of plotting the mass infection of Russian troops in wartime. One was described as a Russian-born German, the other as a 'Trotskyist–Bukharinist spy.'

German historian Georg von Rauch, appraising the Moscow trials and the Tukhachevsky affair, says: 'Even if Tukhachevsky did not prepare an uprising, it is not unlikely that he would have been ready to take such an action if he felt that Stalin's measures endangered the revolutionary achievements. This possibility was enough for Stalin to rid himself of a potential rival. The sacrifice of the one man of necessity led to that of the others.'

To Nazi leaders with their slogan of *Drang nach Osten* (march to the east), the massacre of Russia's officer corps was of maximum interest, not to mention gratification. At the Nuremberg War Crimes Trials (1945–6), Field Marshal Wilhelm Keitel said that when German generals warned Hitler about attacking such a strong opponent as Russia, Hitler rejected their warnings, saying: 'The best high-ranking officers were wiped out by Stalin in 1937.' In January, five months before the onslaught, Hitler told his generals who were planning the invasion of Russia: 'They do not have good commanders.'

But not all German generals felt that Stalin's purges had blunted the effectiveness of the Red Army. For example, SS General Hermann Behrens said that the execution of many ranking officers such as Marshal Tukhachevsky and other generals sapped the Red Army's strength only 'for a short while'.

When, in the summer of 1939, two years after the purge trials, Stalin showed interest in a common front with Britain and France against Hitler, the British Prime Minister (Chamberlain) did not believe that the Russians had enough military power to be of much use to the Western allies. Historian William L. Shirer says that the British military and air attachés in Moscow were filing dispatches to London saying that while the defensive capabilities of the Red Army and Air Force were formidable, they really could not mount a serious offensive. (On the other hand, it was believed in at least some Western diplomatic circles that the performance of Russian aircraft and tanks in the Spanish Civil War had had a 'chilling effect' on the German and Japanese high commands.)

The Russian historian Andrei Mertsalov says that the Red Army was able to compensate for the purge losses in the ranks of its commanders, and that the best test of its real strength was the outcome of the German–Soviet war.

According to German historian von Rauch, after the huge losses to the military purges, the Soviet High Command was forced to enroll 10,000 officer candidates as junior lieutenants, six months before completion of their training, and in the meantime, a rehabilitation commission investigated, cleared and reinstated about 3,000 officers who included K. K. Rokossovsky and F. I. Tolbukhin, both of whom became outstanding marshals during World War II.

Russian military historian General Pavel Zhilin has written that 800,000 officers were trained in 1941–2 alone. From 1941 until the end of the war, Russia's military academies graduated 90,000 officers. From military schools of all levels, 1,300,000 officers were graduated. A further 320,000 officers underwent advanced training. In addition, the best soldiers were given officers' insignia. More than a quarter of a million enlisted men were commissioned during the war.

The Moscow trials aroused militant anti-communism around the world. The influence of foreign communist parties declined. At least one influential newspaper in Paris, saying the trials were obvious frame-ups, demanded that the Soviet–French Treaty of Mutual Assistance be denounced. In general the European and American press saw the trials as striking cases of hysteria and self-slander.

In 1996 a biographer of Zhukov and of other Russian marshals, General Mikhail Ipatovich Belov (he lost one brother to the Stalinist purges and three in the war), could still be sceptical about the military trials. 'Even now not everything is known,' Belov told me. 'We still can't say conclusively whether or not there was some truth in the charges [of espionage and treason] against some of the accused officers.'

Virtually all the victims of the Moscow trials, both military and civilian, have been 'rehabilitated' posthumously. In many cases the process has taken almost half a century.

★★★ WHAT HITLER EDITED OUT OF *MEIN KAMPF* ★★★

As ominous war clouds drifted over Europe, some prominent British politicians discovered that they had been duped about Hitler's true intentions. This was revealed, for example, during a private meeting between Russian Ambassador Ivan Maisky and British elder statesman and ex-Prime Minister David Lloyd-George who had visited Germany the previous year and held lengthy talks with Adolf Hitler. Maisky and Lloyd-George knew each other and there was mutual respect between them. Their meeting took place near London in July 1937.

Maisky: One of Hitler's objectives mentioned in *Mein Kampf* is the gaining of *Lebensraum* [living space] in the East – Poland, the Baltic lands.

Lloyd-George: There is nothing of the kind in the book. I've read *Mein Kampf.*

Maisky: You must have read it in the English translation.

Lloyd-George: I did.

Maisky: But it is all there in the original. The most offensive parts have been left out in the English and the French translations so as not to frighten readers.

Lloyd-George: The deuce!

It was true. Politicians who read *Mein Kampf* in English or French translation were unaware that Hitler had censored parts of his book to placate British and French sentiments. (Hitler's cunning also extended to the Middle East. For the text distributed in that region he eliminated certain racist passages to make the book palatable to Arabs.)

Winston Churchill, it appears, was also deceived if only temporarily. He had written a book, *Great Contemporaries,* in 1935 (republished without change in 1937) which plainly showed that he was familiar only with the expurgated version of Hitler's work. In his book Churchill calls Hitler 'a genius born of the miseries of Germany' and speculates: 'We may yet live to see Hitler a gentler figure in a happier age.' That was Churchill's message to the British people in 1935.

The British scholar Joseph McCabe said that two years later he himself translated the 'aggressive parts' that had been removed from Hitler's book, which was on sale in Britain, and offered them to several London newspapers so as to give the British reading public the full version of *Mein Kampf.* But the papers rejected his offer.

McCabe said that Hitler's plan to annex the Ukraine, seize the French region of Alsace–Lorraine, and unite all parts of German-speaking Europe, was laid out ten years earlier, in 1925, in Hitler's book. Hitler apparently disallowed publication of the book outside Germany without the 'sanitary' cuts. In the early 1930s Hitler's lawyers filed suit against a French publisher who attempted to put out an unabridged translation of the book.

Politicians and the public were duped, said McCabe, because only a 'corrupt' and 'abridged' edition of Hitler's major work was available in the West, including the United States.

Making an about-face from his earlier optimism, Churchill now sought ways to contain the Führer's cravings. He invited Ambassador Maisky to a private lunch. Churchill was still a few years away from taking up the Prime Minister's residence at No. 10 Downing Street, but many, including Maisky, believed his time would come.

Churchill was quite blunt in his remarks to the Russian diplomat:

'Remember my words. Disaster will fall in a year or two. Germany cannot come to a halt so simply, for the Berlin maniac is obsessed with the idea of taking over the whole world. The only thing that can curb him is the bloc of peaceable but resolute nations. Today all other political problems must be subordinated to the struggle against Hitler.'

Maisky was all ears. He knew that some British leaders were still attempting to come to terms with the Führer. In November 1937 Lord Halifax had travelled to Germany as a special envoy of the British Cabinet and flattered Hitler, saying that fate had ordained the Nazi leader to be the West's 'bastion against Bolshevism'. A few days earlier, unknown to Halifax, the Nazis at a secret meeting approved plans to seize more living space, the first victims to be Austria and Czechoslovakia.

In the autumn of that year, Alexander Troyanovsky, Stalin's first ambassador to the United States, met privately in Washington with William Dodd, the American Ambassador to Germany who was on home leave. Dodd belonged to a small group of liberal politicians who believed that Hitler and Nazism endangered the existence of the Western democracies.

Hitler, said Dodd, could wage war at any time. 'I think Hitler will listen to reason only if all democratic forces join efforts against him. With a solid Nazi front being built up from Rome to Tokyo, it would be a great thing for the United States, England, and France to unite with Russia and simply say to Hitler: "Enough!"' Troyanovsky not only agreed but suggested the drawing up of collective security pacts for Europe and Asia.

But political as well as clerical bias hindered improved relations with Stalin's Russia; and in any event few politicians in the Western democracies showed interest in a security pact with Moscow. Stalin's overture to America in June 1937 to sign a Pacific Pact as a safeguard against Japanese belligerency is now almost forgotten. Roosevelt rejected a pact with Moscow, telling Stalin's ambassador that the 'best shield' against a bellicose Japan was a powerful navy. This was four years before Japan knocked out the US fleet (except for aircraft carriers) in Hawaii. When, a few days after the loss of America's battleships on 7 December 1941, Japan sank a new British battleship and a heavy cruiser in the South China Sea, it meant that Japan reigned supreme from the Indian Ocean to California.

In July 1938 the French Foreign Minister Georges Bonnet held a formal meeting in Paris with Moscow's envoy, Yakov Surits, in which they discussed the problem of the Sudetenland, a part of the Czech state populated by Germans. Bonnet told Surits that a semi-drunk Hermann Göring had recently confided to a French woman at a cocktail party: 'It's a pity we shall apparently have to fight each other over the Sudetenland. We Germans were such fools not to have grabbed it earlier with Austria. Nobody would then have raised a finger!'

Surits complained to Bonnet that France seemed never to take Russia into account, though the French were 'perfectly aware' that the future of the world was being decided in Czechoslovakia and that, when Hitler seized that country, Germany would dominate Europe. Surits said that there was an absence of co-ordination, although – and he stressed this point – both nations and Czecho-slovakia were joined by a system of mutual aid pacts. That evening Surits sent an 'urgent' telegram to Moscow:

> 'In France I see mounting fear, mixed with awe, of Nazi Germany's might. Day after day I witness endless circumspection, concessions and a gradual erosion of an independent stance in foreign policy. Finally, I see pro-Nazism rearing its head with every passing day and becoming increasingly insolent.'

From London, meanwhile, Maisky sent a 'highly urgent' telegram to Foreign Minister Maxim Litvinov in Moscow:

> 'I have told Lord Halifax (in accordance with your instructions) that the USSR is becoming increasingly disillusioned with the policy of Britain and France, that it considered such a policy ineffectual, short-sighted and only capable of encouraging the aggressor to further leaps, and that the Western countries would be responsible for the approach and onset of a new world war.'

A month later, Britain's Lord Runciman visited Prague as a mediator in the Czech–German crisis and told Czech leaders in blunt language that if they refused Hitler's terms, Britain and France would leave that country to its own devices.

As Europe edged closer to war, all attempts to draw up a pact of mutual assistance between Britain, France and Russia were in vain. Some months before he was replaced by Neville Chamberlain in 1937, the British Prime Minister, Stanley Baldwin, discussing with colleagues Hitler's desire for living space, said: 'And if he should move east, I should not break my heart.' Chamberlain doubted whether Russia could give aid to anyone who needed it in the event of war. He made no secret of his loathing for Stalin and said that any agreement with Russia would become a yoke around Britain's neck.

Meanwhile, the desire to improve relations with Adolf Hitler was at that time strong among some British diplomats. It is recorded by the German Ambassador Herbert von Dirksen that Lord Halifax told him it would be 'the finest moment in my life' to see the Führer drive along the Mall in front of Bucking-ham Palace together with the British royal family.

On 21 July 1939 Britain was rocked by a scandal: newspapers reported that at a 'private talk' in London, Helmuth Wohlthat, a close friend of Her-mann Göring, and Robert Hudson, the British Parliamentary Secretary for Overseas Trade, had discussed granting an international loan to Germany, up to one billion pounds sterling. The two men also spoke of an Anglo–German concord on global 'spheres of influence'. The report appeared at a time when British, French and Soviet officials were meeting to discuss a pact of mutual security.

★★★ THE HITLER–STALIN LETTERS ★★★

Anti-Bolshevism had long been a fixation of Adolf Hitler's. Stalin often attacked fascism and, after Hitler came to power, Nazi aggressiveness. So it is not surprising that Hitler and Stalin never came within sight of each other and hardly ever corresponded.

But Hitler's posture abruptly changed in the summer of 1939. Seeking a concordat with Stalin, he hastened to open a dialogue with the Kremlin. The Führer wrote an agitated letter to Stalin in which he hinted broadly that war with Poland (he used the word 'crisis') might erupt in the near future, and proffered a half-hearted invitation to Stalin to visit Berlin.

Stalin had no intention of visiting Nazi Germany. But the idea of a 'non-aggression' pact with his bellicose opponent had great appeal. Seeing himself in a good bargaining position, the Kremlin dictator asked for a number of conditions to which Berlin readily agreed. One was a request that Germany use her influence on Japan to persuade that country to mend its relations with Moscow. Hitler agreed; which turned out to be a coup for Moscow.

When Hitler's Foreign Minister Ribbentrop later visited Moscow, Stalin mentioned Japan, saying: 'There are limits to our patience with regard to Japanese provocations.' Japanese army units had been making incursions into Soviet territory in the Far East and also into Mongolia, which was closely allied to Russia. Stalin said: 'If Japan desires war, it can have it.' Russia, he said, was not afraid of Japan and was prepared for war. But 'If Japan desires peace – so much the better!' He said that German help in this direction would be useful, but he added that he did not want Tokyo to get the impression that the initiative had come from Moscow.

Hitler had a built-in dilemma *vis-à-vis* Stalin's Russia: how to transmute years of hate into instant friendship? Over the years the Führer had frequently used street language in referring to the Bolsheviks. In *Mein Kampf* he forswore any deal with Russian communism. 'How', Hitler wrote, 'can one explain to the German worker that Bolshevism is an execrable crime if one allies oneself with this hell-born monster?' Another passage should have alerted Stalin: 'Any treaty links between Germany and present-day Bolshevist Russia would be without any value whatsoever.'

To promote this 'new face' of Nazi Germany towards Russia was the task of Foreign Minister Ribbentrop. His well-crafted message to Stalin on 14 August 1939 began:

'The ideological contradictions between National Socialist Germany and the Soviet Union were in past years the sole reason why Germany and the USSR stood opposed to each other in two separate and hostile camps. The developments of the recent period seem to show that differing world outlooks do not prohibit a reasonable relationship between the two states, and the restoration of co-operation of a new and friendly type. The period of opposition in foreign policy can be brought to an end once and for all and the way lies open for a new sort of future for both countries.'

This message, paving the way for a new relationship between the sworn enemies of the past, continued:

'There exist no real conflicts of interest between Germany and the USSR. The living-spaces of Germany and the USSR touch each other, but in their natural requirements they do not conflict. Thus there is lacking all cause for an aggressive attitude on the part of one country against the other. Germany has no aggressive intentions against the USSR. The Reich Government is of the opinion that there is no question between the Baltic and the Black Seas which cannot be settled to the complete satisfaction of both countries.'

Meanwhile, as a starting-point in the new relationship, Russian and German officials put their signatures to a new commercial treaty that offered trade advantages to both sides.

As soon as the urgent Ribbentrop message had been sent, Russia was asked to receive a visit from the Foreign Minister as soon as possible in order to work out the details of a non-aggression treaty. The German Ambassador in Moscow, Count Friedrich von der Schulenburg, took the opportunity to tell his home government that only a few months earlier Moscow had asked England to send its Foreign Minister to Russia to speed up negotiations on a trilateral security pact (England–France–Russia). But Lord Halifax refused to visit Moscow, and the makeup of the delegation actually sent was of such inferior rank as to be thought offensive by some observers.

On 20 August 1939, three days before the signing of the German-Soviet pact, Hitler sent Stalin a 'Very Urgent' letter which reached the Kremlin the following day:

'Herr Stalin, Moscow.

(1) I sincerely welcome the signing of the new German-Soviet Commercial Agreement as the first stop in the re-ordering of German–Soviet relations.

(2) The conclusion of a non-aggression pact with the Soviet Union means to me the establishment of a long-range German policy. Germany thereby resumes a political course that was beneficial to both states during bygone centuries. The Government of the Reich is therefore resolved in such case to act entirely consistent with such a far-reaching change.

(3) I accept the draft of the non-aggression pact that your Foreign Minister, Herr Molotov, delivered, but consider it urgently necessary to clarify the questions connected with it as soon as possible.

(4) The supplementary protocol desired by the Government of the Soviet Union can, I am convinced, be substantially clarified in

the shortest possible time if a responsible German statesman can come to Moscow himself to negotiate. Otherwise the Government of the Reich is not clear as to how the supplementary protocol could be cleared up and settled in a short time.

(5) The tension between Germany and Poland has become intolerable. Polish demeanour toward a great power is such that a crisis may arise any day. Germany is determined, at any rate, in the face of this presumption, from now on to look after the interests of the Reich with all the means at its disposal.

(6) In my opinion, it is desirable, in view of the intentions of the two states to enter into a new relation to each other, not to lose any time. I therefore again propose that you receive my Foreign Minister on Tuesday, 22 August, but at the latest on Wednesday, 23 August. The Reich Foreign Minister has full powers to draw up and sign the non-aggression pact as well as the protocol. A longer stay by the Reich Foreign Minister in Moscow than one to two days at most is impossible in view of the international situation. I should be glad to receive your early answer. ADOLF HITLER'

Stalin sent off a reply the same day. (The German Ambassador in Moscow, Schulenburg, who first received it, said Stalin's letter was 'couched in very conciliatory form in reply to the Führer's message.')

'21 August 1939. To the Chancellor of the German Reich, A. Hitler.

'I thank you for the letter. I hope that the German–Soviet non-aggression pact will mark a decided turn for the better in the political relations between our countries.

'The people of our countries need peaceful relations with each other. The assent of the German Government to the conclusion of a non-aggression pact provides the foundation for eliminating the political tension and for the establishment of peace and cooperation between our countries.

'The Soviet Government has authorised me to inform you that it agrees to Herr von Ribbentrop's arriving in Moscow on 23 August. J. STALIN'

Stalin took part in the negotiations. To Ribbentrop's suggestion to inject a few words about Russo–German friendship into a preamble to the final document, Stalin replied:

'The Soviet Government cannot suddenly present to the nation assurances of friendship when the National Socialist Government has been slinging mud at it for six years.'

But the talks proceeded rapidly and the Pact was signed on 23 August.

Shock gripped the Western world. In the East the Japanese government was stunned, then collapsed. One French diplomat aptly called it a *coup de théâtre*. When journalists reported that Stalin had toasted Hitler's health ('I know how much the German people loves its Führer; I should therefore like to drink to his health'), it added to the shock and dismay of many people in the West.

Several months later Hitler told an audience in Munich: 'I regard it as a triumph for common sense that we have reached an agreement with Russia.'

Stalin's birthday was on 21 December, and Hitler sent greetings: 'I beg you to accept my sincere wishes on your 60th birthday. I unite herewith my best wishes for your personal well-being and a happy future for the nations of the friendly Soviet Union.'

Stalin's reply was diplomatic: 'The friendship of the peoples of Germany and the Soviet Union, cemented in blood, has every reason to be lasting and firm.'

Although a number of quarrels arose between the new friends, the Germans once more discussed among themselves the sending of an invitation to Stalin to visit Germany, or perhaps to attend a meeting with Hitler at a border town where they could discuss mutual problems. But no such meeting ever took place, and Stalin never invited Hitler to Moscow.

★★★ MASTER STROKE – OR BLUNDER? ★★★

Controversy lingers: Did Stalin betray the West by signing a non-aggression pact with Hitler? And was the pact much more advantageous for Stalin than Hitler?

Before the signing of the pact, the Russians were disenchanted with their future British and French allies. In July 1939, two months before World War II erupted, when Anglo–French–Russian talks were stalemated, Stalin's Foreign Minister, V. M. Molotov, spoke coarsely about the British and French negotiators. They were, he said, 'crooks and cheats'. 'Our partners are resorting to all kinds of trickery and disgraceful subterfuge, was Molotov's coded message to Russian ambassadors in London and Paris.

Earlier, Stalin's envoys had received this message from Moscow: 'The fact that France and England would like to prod Germany to take action against the East is quite understandable and is well known. It is also true that they would like to direct the aggression exclusively against us, so that Poland should not be affected ...'

The talks between Britain, France and Russia were held in the grim aftermath of Munich. Virtually all Western historians are now agreed that at Munich in 1938 the British and French reached the limits of cynicism in agreeing to Hitler's demands on Czechoslovakia. German historian Josef Henke says that after Munich 'the occupation under any circumstances of Warsaw became Hitler's immediate goal'. Another German historian, Christian Zentner, says that Hitler's invasion of Austria followed by the Munich Agreement 'geographically and strategically' were determined by the interests of the coming war against Stalin's Russia.

Historian Charles Bloch of France concluded in his 1986 book *Le III Reich et le Monde* that Munich made World War II inevitable. 'This was the last opportunity to stop Hitler and prevent a world catastrophe, and that opportunity was missed.' A contemporary Russian academician, Dr. Andrei Mertsalov, is blunt: Munich is 'perhaps the most shameful diplomatic deal ever known to the civilised world'. (See Appendix for additional comment on the Munich Conference.)

At the time of Munich, Vladimir Potemkin, the deputy head of the Soviet Foreign Office, warned French Ambassador Robert Coulondre that the decisions taken in that German city would lead to the 'partition' of Poland. The Ambassador understood the significance of Potemkin's warning: Hitler had in effect received from Paris and London a permit to wage war against Poland, and Russia would not stand by idly.

Meeting President Roosevelt at the February 1945 Yalta conference in the Crimea, Stalin informed him that he had agreed to the Non-aggression Pact with Hitler for one reason only – Munich.

What happened at the Anglo–French–Soviet talks of 1939 makes for unpleasant reading. Averell Harriman, who met Stalin on four evenings in September–October 1941 (and many times thereafter), gave me the following account of Stalin and Munich. 'Stalin told me that he'd been ready at the time of Munich to join with the Western Allies against Hitler and, to use his own words, he said about the tripartite talks in 1939: "We expected one of your statesmen to come, one of your principal political figures to come [to Moscow]." And then Anthony Eden [a prominent British politician; Foreign Secretary Lord Halifax had declined to come] offered to come, but Chamberlain rejected his offer and Stalin said they sent a clerk in the person of William Strang who was a Foreign Service officer. Not quite a clerk, but not an actual political personality. And Stalin looked on this as an indication that the British were not interested in the talks and he always maintained that Chamberlain was attempting to direct German aggression towards him; that that was Chamberlain's objective.'

Harriman added, 'So that was Stalin's point of view when there was an argument about his pact with Berlin.'

Right off, the Russians were disillusioned about prospects for a military convention against Hitler. What he calls the 'thick-headedness' of the British and French was evident when on 3 August 1939, Stalin's Ambassador to Britain, Ivan Maisky, hosted a luncheon for the Anglo-French military mission to Russia which was to depart for Moscow next day. The ranking guest was Sir Reginald Drax, a British Admiral, who would head the Allied mission. Moscow had voiced a preference for Lord Gort, the Chief of the British General Staff, but he was reported to be 'too busy' to go. At this time World War II was one month away. During the luncheon the following exchange took place:

Maisky: Tell me, Admiral, when are you leaving for Moscow?
Drax: It has not yet been decided, but I think in the next few days.

45

Maisky: You're flying, of course? Time is running short, for the European situation is very tense.

Drax: No, it's not convenient. There are almost 40 people in the two delegations, including the ancillary personnel, and we have lots of baggage.

Maisky: If an aeroplane won't do, then perhaps you'll be going on one of your fast cruisers. That would be very stylish and impressive: military delegations on board a warship. Besides, it would take little time to get from London to Leningrad.

Drax: No, a cruiser would not suit either. If we go by cruiser, we'll have to evict some two dozen officers from their cabins and use their berths. Why cause such inconvenience? No, no, we won't go by cruiser.

The British and French delegations left for Moscow two days later in the ageing 13-knot cargo-passenger steamer *The City of Exeter*. The steamer took five days to get to Leningrad, arriving on 10 August. Venting his frustration, Maisky called it a 'phenomenal delay' amidst a 'spirit of sabotage'.

Aboard the steamship, the British and French delegates enjoyed table-tennis and ate exotic Indian dishes while they studied their official instructions. One British delegate said: 'The British government is unwilling to enter into any detailed commitments that are likely to tie our hands in all circumstances. Endeavours should therefore be made to confine the Military Agreement to the most general terms. Something on the lines of an agreed statement of policy may meet the case.'

In only two more weeks, Hitler's Foreign Minister Ribbentrop would fly to Moscow in the Führer's personal aircraft and discuss, amend and sign the Pact with Stalin in less than 24 hours and then return to Berlin.

In Moscow the Anglo-French delegation attended a dinner given by Marshal Klementi Voroshilov who would lead the talks on the Russian side. Stalin put in a brief appearance and said a few words to Drax and his French counterpart.

Stalin (to French General J. E. A. Doumenc): How many divisions will France muster against Germany in case of mobilisation?

Doumenc: About a hundred.

Stalin: (to Admiral Drax): And how many will Britain send?

Drax: Two, and another two later.

Stalin: Ah, two, and two more later.

Obviously not believing his ears, Stalin gave the British admiral a long, piercing look, one that, as the officer later recorded, made him think that he 'should never have sailed from London in that damned steamer'. It is doubtful if other international talks of such importance ever got off to such a poor start.

From the outset Voroshilov raised two key points: first, Moscow wanted reciprocity with Britain and France on military commitments. This meant, for example, joint military action if Hitler invaded Russia through the Baltic states. Second, Russia sought Poland's permission to allow the Red Army to enter its territory as there was no other way to help Poland if it were attacked by Germany.

Later, when the talks had been aborted, Voroshilov commented: 'We wanted to fight the common enemy, but had to ask for permission to do so. When the question of transit for Soviet troops through some regions of Poland arose, the negotiations stalled.'

Adding to the Kremlin's vexations, the Russians noted that Admiral Drax had no plenipotentiary powers, which meant that he had no authority to sign a treaty document.

The adversarial nature of the tripartite talks was shown by the adoption of secret hand signals among the French and British. If, for example, a question were raised making it important for the British and French positions to be brought 'into line,' or if any of the British and French delegates should 'let their tongues run away with them', it was agreed that someone should start scratching the end of his nose in as natural a way as possible, so as not to arouse the suspicion of the Russians.

Russian Professor of History Fyodor Volkov, a contemporary specialist on Britain, is unequivocal: 'Such a "signalling system" was in no way compatible with the basic ethics of vital interstate negotiations on the issues of war and peace.'

On 17 August Drax asked for a recess so that the British and French could consult their home governments. A few days later, Germany and Russia announced the signing of a trade agreement under which Moscow received a two-year credit for the purchase of German goods.

Hitler, anxious to obtain a non-aggression pact with Moscow prior to his attack on Poland, sent an urgent message to Stalin, asking him to receive his Foreign Minister, Ribbentrop. Meanwhile the British and French were unable to comply with Voroshilov's request for clear answers to the two key questions. (Voroshilov would later refer to the talks as 'frivolous make-believe negotiations'.)

Hitler, impatient, send another telegram to Stalin, this time containing a 'sweetener': Berlin was ready to stop all anti-Soviet activities and recognise the inviolability of Russia's frontiers. When Hitler again pressed Stalin to receive his Foreign Minister, Stalin agreed and began putting his own finishing touches to a draft treaty of non-aggression. Ribbentrop flew to Moscow to iron out the final kinks in the treaty. (When Ribbentrop arrived, the band played the *Horst Wessel Lied*, a part of the Nazi anthem, but in the newsreel footage shown in Russia's cinemas the editors wisely omitted the soundtrack.)

The Hitler–Stalin treaty evoked unbridled fury in the West. Stalin was accused of betrayal. Less than 10 days after the Pact was signed, Hitler invaded Poland. A few weeks later, under a secret protocol to the treaty, Stalin ordered the Red Army to cross the Polish border and occupy a part of Poland's eastern territory. Moscow declared that the territory, prior to World War I, had been part of Tsarist Russia.

Stalin claimed that Russia derived valuable benefits from the treaty, mainly time to prepare the country for war. Also, Russia was able to get equipment and technology from Berlin unavailable to it on French, British or American markets. (Between the two world wars there was a virtual quarantine in the West against Red Russia. During the mid-1930s, Stalin asked America to build a battleship for Russia. In his diaries, US Ambassador to Moscow Joseph E. Davies tells of Stalin's personal appeal for the warship, to be paid for in cash. Stalin said that building the warship would give jobs to American workers. But Washington said no, citing 'security interests'.) The official volume, *The German Reich and the Second World War*, published in Germany in 1983, says 'deliveries of German equipment [under the Nazi–Soviet Pact] contributed to the intensive development of the Soviet war industry'.

An offshoot of the pact with Hitler was the conclusion of a similar pact with Japan, signed in April 1941. Tokyo's subsequent decision to send its armies south and not strike at Russia, enabled Stalin during the war to detach some of his divisions stationed in the Far East for use against Hitler.

Another plus was the bolstering of Russia's forward defences. In late 1939 Russia secured bases near the Baltic ports of Liepaja and Ventspils, artillery positions in the Gulf of Riga, and airfields in Lithuania and Estonia. Situated on the Gulf of Finland, almost touching Finland, the city of Leningrad (now St. Petersburg) was extremely vulnerable in time of war and these acquisitions helped to protect the city. After Stalin's brief but costly war with Finland, the Russians acquired additional buffer territory around Leningrad.

As a by-product of the pact, Stalin obtained some late-model German aircraft, the result apparently of a German blunder. In the late summer of 1939 a group of Russian aviation specialists were invited to Berlin, including aircraft designer Alexander Yakovlev, and General Ivan Petrov, an experienced pilot and himself an expert in aircraft design. In Germany, Petrov was given *carte blanche* to visit aircraft and related factories. In the space of several weeks he says he was able to visit 200 factories.

Shown the latest German fighters and bombers, the Russians drew up a shopping-list, asking the Germans for one of each aircraft to take back to Moscow. Their hosts agreed, but the Russians had to meet certain conditions: payment in cash and permission for a German delegation to visit at least one aircraft factory in Moscow. When he heard about the sales, Hitler was said to be so furious that he ordered an immediate investigation and harsh punishment for those involved. The Luftwaffe general who approved the Russian requests is reported to have committed suicide.

Before the Russians left for Berlin, Stalin had told them: 'It is extremely important that we know the daily output of their aircraft!' Petrov discovered it to be – 84 per day. Petrov recalls: 'We couldn't believe that figure because our own production barely amounted to 20 aircraft a day. But no matter how much I checked and rechecked the figure came out the same.' This and other information gathered by the Russian mission proved valuable to Russia's defence.

For Hitler, the pact with Stalin not only removed the danger of a two-front war, but it provided Germany with a steady supply of Russian petroleum, platinum, cotton, scrap and pig iron, timber, feed grains and vegetables.

These supplies to Hitler aroused anger among the Western democracies who accused Russia of helping Hitler's war effort. But, to be fair, Russia was a junior partner compared to Nazi Germany's brisk commerce with the West. American companies, for instance, had nearly 60 branches in Germany and heavy investments in that country. (In 1943 American Senator Harley Kilgore, a member of the War Investigations Committee, said these investments were actually impeding the US war effort. A Senate report stated that US investment in Germany totalled 1,000 million dollars.)

Britain also aided Hitler. In 1940 the Junkers Ju 87B was the Luftwaffe's most important tactical attack aircraft, delivering aerial artillery right into the front line. Ironically, in view of its use against the West (and later against the Russians), it was initially powered by a British Rolls-Royce engine. In 1935 the first prototype Messerschmitt Bf 109, which became the standard fighter of the German air force, was also equipped with a Rolls-Royce engine, although these were later replaced by German ones.

After 1935 the British firm Vickers began advertising its tanks in German arms trade periodicals. That year the London *Stock Exchange Gazette* breezily divulged the truth: 'Who finances Germany? Without this country as a clearing-house for payments and the opportunity to draw on credits under the [economic] standstill, Germany could not have pursued her plans. We have been so ready to sell to Germany that the question of payment has never been allowed to interfere with the commercial side.'

Some Western financial and industrial magnates initially supported Hitler. In gratitude, the Führer gave Nazi decorations to some of these prominent business leaders. A few, like Thomas J. Watson, the head of IBM, alarmed by Hitler's aggressive acts, returned the medals. At the end of the war Hjalmar Schacht, who had been Hitler's Minister of Finance, told the Nuremberg War Crimes Tribunal: 'If you want to bring to trial the industrialists who helped the re-armament of Germany, you will have to try your own industrialists.'

Did the Hitler–Stalin Pact actually trigger World War II? Many Western historians say yes. A minority, including the German historian Dr. Ingebord Fleischhauer, demurs.

'Most books now available on the Pact and the preceding events', she says, 'were written during the Cold War when attempts were being made to shift the responsibility for the outbreak of World War II on to Moscow. Here ideology blatantly overshadows historical objectivity. As I read those books, I saw that most concepts were based on sheer allegations. A serious historian cannot put up with it. So I studied facts, and facts alone, and got a picture quite different from what most Western historians painted.'

On 3 April 1939, months before the pact with Moscow was signed, Hitler had decided to attack Poland (*Plan Weiss*), and envisaged the war spreading into the Baltic states, says Fleischhauer. If this had happened, the *Wehrmacht* would have held positions much closer to Stalin's borders.

The British historian Sir Bernard Pares, who had served as a diplomat in Moscow, says that with the Pact, Stalin could watch the 'novelties' of the war unfolding in Western Europe, including dive-bomber formations and panzer tactics. Also, Russian generals could study Hitler's *Blitzkrieg* tactics. During the eighteen months that the pact was in force, Stalin stockpiled some weapons, partly reorganised his army, and began to implement a system of defence in depth. In addition, seeking buffer zones, he annexed the Baltic states and then launched the 'Winter War' with Finland.

★★★ INTERVIEW: THE GENERALS SPEAK ★★★
'CLEVER ON THE STAIRCASE' – MARSHAL SERGEI RUDENKO
(This interview with Marshal Sergei Ignatyevich Rudenko took place in Moscow on 2 February 1985 at the Institute of Military History. In 1923 at the age of 19 he joined the Red Army. In World War II he was chief of the 16th Air Army which fought in many battles including Stalingrad, Kursk and Berlin. For heroism Rudenko received a gold star medal, the highest combat award.)

Author: Do you agree with Marshal Georgi Zhukov and General S. M. Shtemenko, as recorded in their memoirs, that practically everything was done to prepare for the Nazi attack?

Rudenko: Of course. Everything was done to prepare for the attack – and also to avoid it.

Author: So does that mean that if I criticise your country for not being ready, if I criticise Stalin on this point, I am misinformed?

Rudenko: Yes. About the situation prevailing at the time: there are people who are 'clever on the staircase', our expression for knowing something after the fact. Some of them make judgements long after the event. Say, forty or fifty years later, they criticise what happened in the 1930s or 1940s, and this is regrettable. Of course we had some serious shortcomings. But war is war. It is not a simple thing. Remember, this was the most critical hour in the history of our Army and the most critical for our leadership – in trying to regain control in those first few days. It was a tremendous challenge to try to regain the initiative.

And both the government and the nation managed to be masters of the situation – to recapture the initiative. And the result is that the Germans came up to Leningrad and were stopped; and in the Moscow direction also they were stopped. For two months the Battle of Smolensk raged. And behind the River Dnieper also the enemy forces were stopped in their tracks.

Author: How do you account, then, for the fall of Kharkov?

Rudenko: Such was the combat situation – I cannot explain it.

Author: In the documentary film 'Zhukov', Marshal Zhukov says that Stalin was not a dictator; that he, Zhukov, could argue with Stalin, that he was able to stand up to Stalin and say '*Nyet*, Comrade Stalin, *nyet*.' Is this true in your opinion?

Rudenko: Yes. A dictator in the formal sense is someone who never agrees with anyone else's opinion, only his own. But you could argue with Stalin. Zhukov did, Rokossovsky did, Meretskov did. When these marshals stuck to their guns and proved they were correct, Stalin changed his mind.

But you must also remember that we were at war and were military men and Stalin was the Supreme Commander-in-Chief; we were subordinate to him and had to comply with his orders. In this way, all armies are the same.

Author: Did you ever meet Stalin?

Rudenko: Yes. I remember being summoned to Stalin's office after I had made some mistakes. So I was prepared to take the consequences. I have to admit that when I was on my way – and I knew I had made some real blunders – I thought I would be severely punished. As the Japanese put it, I was in a '*hara-kiri* situation'. And in the presence of our chief commanders, Stalin was kind enough to listen to my report and, instead of *hara-kiri*, of punishing me, I actually got a promotion and was assigned to another post. That is, everything said by Zhukov – about Stalin giving you a chance to explain your side of the question – is true. I should stress that Zhukov always treated Stalin as his boss. Zhukov was Deputy Supreme Commander, Stalin the Supreme Commander. I was fighting under Zhukov. Well, as long as we are on this question, in the Battle of Moscow I commanded an air division and Zhukov was the Front Commander. Later, in January 1942, I was assigned as Commander of the Air Forces of the Kalinin Front. The Front Commander then was Marshal Ivan Konev.

Author: Did you meet with any Nazi generals – as prisoners?

Rudenko: Yes. Many times I talked to German generals who were POWs. My impression and the conclusion I drew is that they all thought the same way that Field Marshal Paulus did. You remember his saying after his surrender at Stalingrad, 'I am a soldier and I complied with my orders'? This is not, I want to say, a 'creative' type of thinking. Those German commanders were blindly obedient to the tasks given them. By the way, at the Nuremberg Trials Field Marshal Paulus was asked by the lawyer representing one of the Nazi defendants if he had given 'lectures' to the Russians on strategy while he was our POW. He replied that our strategy proved so much superior to theirs 'that the Russians could hardly need my services for lecturing even in a non-commissioned officers' school. The best proof of this is the outcome of the Battle on the Volga [Stalingrad]. As a result, I found myself a prisoner of war. This also led to all these Herren landing in the dock.'

Author: What were your feelings at the beginning of the war?

Rudenko: I was actively involved from the very first days of the war. So I witnessed all of its hardships. I will dwell on a few of my impressions. The most negative was in July 1941. The roads were stuffed with our people. Women, old people, kids. This is one of my worst memories: Women and children moving along the road and Hitler's planes diving and shooting at them. And I was a witness to all this, to many people being killed and injured. I looked at the terrified eyes of young children. And, of course, my whole being was against this inhuman act, and this stream of refugees. And my depression was doubled because on the road I was wearing the wings of an aviation pilot, and everyone looked at me and asked, with their eyes, 'Why do you allow them to commit such a mockery against us?'

And when we were moving in an easterly direction along the roads where the enemy was not bombing us, in the eyes of those people who saw us retreating we saw a reproach. A reproach such as: why are you leaving us in such a state? This was 1941, 1942. I admit I had an inferiority complex and it stayed with me because we were being reproached by the people, especially us pilots, for allowing such a terrible thing to happen. That is the deepest impression that has remained with me.

But I recall another impression, later, when we made some progress and started throwing the Nazis back. No matter what city you were in, be it Stalingrad or the surrounding cities – all were partly or completely destroyed. The villages were burnt down and the people were in rags because they had lost everything. And there were plenty of hungry people among them, too. We didn't feel differently just because we were now winning, we were the liberators. It was still very depressing to see those people in rags, to see those ruins, the villages burnt down. And when we moved into Poland, the picture was the same, but to a lesser extent; not because the Germans were more sympathetic to the Poles but because in some areas there had been no military action. But, mainly, the picture there was very much the same as in Russia, in those areas where combat had taken place. And all of this was a burden and, you might say, a silent reproach on our souls – and yet we had to struggle to be above feelings of vengeance when we entered Germany.

Author: Nobody in your command thought of taking revenge?

Rudenko: I remember driving to a new command post close to the Polish boundary. At the command post was a sign in the shape of a finger pointing west saying, 'This is the way to Berlin'. And, looking at it, I had the feeling that Germany was the source of all our nation's hardships. These were not only my feelings but of all our officers and men. And it seemed natural that after coming to Germany many of our men would wish to take revenge. But our Supreme Command was very strict on this point: that if the army started looting, started taking revenge on the population, that army ceased to be a combat army. It would not be able to fulfil its mission.

Author: Some books have made claims of widespread rape and looting –

Rudenko: Such claims are untrue! If such cases were brought to the attention of our officers the perpetrators received maximum punishment. But our political advisers and party organisations made strenuous efforts to prevent our soldiers from avenging themselves against Germans. For example, our soldiers were instructed not to act according to the principle that 'because my village was burnt down in Russia, I will burn down your village in Germany'. It would have been a crime to do this. That's why a huge propaganda work was done. Of course you understand how difficult such a job is; it involves tremendous work to teach this to the troops. After all, some of the families of our soldiers had been burned to death or shot by Nazi soldiers.

Author: Still, I have read that many Germans were terrified of the Russian soldiers –

Rudenko: I recall a conversation at one of the airfields in Germany. Many German civilians were nearby. I was wearing a plain military coat without insignia, but judging by our soldiers' attention towards me the Germans understood that I was the Commanding Officer. I went up to an old man, an old German, and he said, 'You are the winners, and you can take everything. Our women are your women, our possessions are your possessions. In short, we are under you.'

I asked him: 'Have you got a woman?' He said, 'Yes, I have one.' And I said, 'Did anybody take her away from you?'

'No, nobody.'

'What about your possessions? Did anybody take them from you?' The reply was no.

We knew that the Nazi propagandists had taught Germans to hate our army and to fear 'drunken Russian soldiers'.

But, anyway, I asked him: 'Why do you consider that we, the victors, want to hurt you by taking your women and your possessions?' It was only logical to raise these questions myself. I said: 'Nobody will loot from you and nobody will rape your women.' He answered by saying that although it had not happened up to now, he was afraid it would occur in the future.

At that point, I reminded him of Germany's responsibility for causing great hardships against the Russians.

Author: Were you in Germany at the war's end?

Rudenko: Yes. I was in Berlin during the Victory Day salute. That was the greatest joy for me — and the fireworks. And I took part in the surrender ceremonies.

Author: Marshal, how did you assess the capabilities of Hitler's commanders?

Rudenko: First of all, I want to say that nobody tries to under-estimate the abilities of the German commanders, as military leaders. No doubt there were quite able ones. But aside from this, it is important to credit the German successes at the start of the war to the fact that the enemy was more ready for war, it had much experience in combat, was very well equipped and well organised, and had a numerical superiority in manpower.

But these were temporary factors that helped the Nazi High Command in the first stage of the war. As for us, it is an 'open secret' how well the major strategic offensive operations of our army were prepared and developed in the air, on land and at sea.

★★★ A RUSSIAN COLONEL IN PARIS ★★★

Semyon Krivoshein was one of Stalin's brightest tank commanders. He was rugged, cool, intelligent, patriotic and — of no small importance — had had military training in France (as part of an exchange programme) and combat experience in Spain.

Krivoshein's kaleidoscopic army career spanned five wars. The son of a poor Russian-Jewish tailor, he fought in the Russian Civil War against White Guard troops. During the Spanish Civil War he had commanded a tank brigade. Later, in the Far East, his armoured unit helped repulse a Japanese military incursion near Vladivostok. In 1939 he participated in the short but fierce 'Winter War' with Finland. Finally, during World War II, he commanded a tank corps in the titanic confrontation with Field Marshal Erich von Manstein's panzers at the Battle of Kursk and, on the eve of victory, stormed into Berlin where his men captured Hitler's headquarters.

After the war, Krivoshein added a literary dimension to his career with two books about cavalry armies in the Russian Civil War, one on the Civil War in Spain (as seen through the eyes of a tank commander), and one on the war with Hitler. According to a colleague, this colourful general was outstanding in another activity: he had won prizes for his skill in Russian and Cossack dances.

Krivoshein's life took a decisive turn in the early 'thirties when Stalin approved plans to train thousands of young officers in tank warfare. Like many cavalrymen he swapped his scarlet and blue trousers and long sabre for the less ostentatious uniform of a tankman. Arriving in France in 1935 for a training period, the young officer had a grandstand view of the rascally conduct of some major powers.

This was the period when Hitler, throwing off the military restraints of the Treaty of Versailles, was raising a new German conscript army of roughly half a million men – almost double the size of the French home army; Mussolini's soldiers were landing in Africa to savage the barefoot Ethiopians; and Japan was consolidating its grip on Manchuria before invading China.

Then, a thunderbolt from London. In June 1935, shortly after Britain had protested Hitler's violation of the Versailles Treaty, she negotiated a naval pact with Nazi Germany which too violated that treaty and virtually gave Hitler the right to build all the warships he desired for at least ten years.

Like many of his Army colleagues, Krivoshein had a premonition that a Nazified Germany would sooner or later engulf Europe in war.

In France during those days of unrest, Krivoshein found a mood of defeatism among French officers. 'I believed even then, before the war, that the French government had already practically surrendered to the Germans. I spoke to many French officers and they were already panic-stricken, afraid of the German armed forces. So, psychologically the French already had surrendered to Hitler. Already they were saying that Hitler would occupy all of Europe. Of course they meant Russia, too. But when I told them that the Germans would never defeat us, they looked at me as if I were crazy.'

Coincidentally, the Russian president, Mikhail Kalinin, gave a warning in that same year (1935) about the coming war and the cancer of defeatism: 'In the next war we must be victorious. Our Army, our fliers, officers and men must regard the very thought of possible defeat as harmful in the highest degree, for even such a thought alone is capable of annihilating the work of decades.'

Recalling the war year 1944, the tank general said that he had personal acquaintance with French patriots during Operation 'Bagration', in Belorussia, when French pilots won acclaim on the Eastern Front as part of a Russian air army. 'Far from all French were defeatist,' said Krivoshein.

After Stalin's army entered Poland in September 1939, following Hitler's attack against that country, Krivoshein found himself part of the occupation force. There he met some of Hitler's best panzer generals, including Heinz Guderian and Erich von Manstein. He would later lock horns with these commanders, one of the biggest battles taking place at the 'Kursk Bulge' in the summer of 1943.

The German war historian Paul Carell *(Scorched Earth: The Russian–German War, 1943–1944)* relates an amusing anecdote involving Krivoshein in Poland prior to the Russo-German war. A dinner party was in progress for top officers of both armies, and Krivoshein, offering a toast to mutual friendship, fumbled his words. Raising a glass of vodka, he used the word *Feindschaft* (fiendship) instead of *Freundschaft* (friendship). There were peals of German laughter.

But mirth was absent a few days later when a dispute flared over the demarcation line separating the two armies. Not wishing German tanks to pass farther east, Krivoshein had placed his own tanks astride the main railway tracks, thereby blocking the trains carrying Guderian's tanks. 'Out of fuel,' quipped Krivoshein.

A photograph taken at that time shows the two feuding commanders standing in a semi-circle of German and Russian tanks. Guderian is grim-faced. Krivoshein, arms folded, looks determined. Eventually Krivoshein removed his tanks when the two generals came to terms about the demarcation line.

On the eve of the historic battle at Kursk in July 1943, Krivoshein's tank corps was bivouacked at the edge of a pine forest, the tanks well camouflaged. Carell says that Krivoshein's corps was 'magnificently equipped', and a reserve tank army had moved up from the rear and was ready for action. Hours before the battle, Krivoshein had discussed with his staff the probable tactics of his opponent, Field Marshal von Manstein, one of the German officers with whom Krivoshein had shaken hands in Poland four years earlier.

On 12 July the greatest tank battle in history began near the village of Prokhorovka, south of Kursk, where von Manstein hoped to smash his way north towards that city. About 1,200 Russian and German tanks and self-propelled guns clashed in a torrent of fire that spelled defeat for the *Wehrmacht* in a graveyard of burning hulks.

Like many Russian generals, Krivoshein respected Stalin as Commander-in-Chief, calling him a 'worthy commander'. He said that he agreed with British Field Marshal Alanbrooke's estimate of Stalin as a man with a 'military brain of the finest order'. But Krivoshein added a proviso. 'Stalin', he said, 'had very good assistants in the armed forces and they managed to tell him which way was the right way. But Stalin was able to use his formidable strength to manage military affairs and achieve victory – which was no small achievement.'

★★★ THE RUSSO–FINNISH WAR ★★★

Peter the Great (1672–1725) never dreamed of long-range guns and aircraft when he built his new capital St. Petersburg, only 20 miles from the Finnish border. But in an age of tanks, aircraft and long-range artillery, the city of Leningrad (as St. Petersburg was called) would have little chance of survival if Finland came under the thumb of Germany. From the Karelian Isthmus enemy aircraft could fly over Leningrad in less than five minutes. And there was always a potential threat of enemy warships in the Gulf of Finland.

For Hitler, Finland offered a northern gateway into Russia. His generals hoped to use Finnish territory to sever the strategic railway running from Murmansk to Moscow. This vital line later carried thousands of tons of 'Lend-Lease' supplies delivered by Anglo–American ship convoys that ran the gauntlet of German aircraft, ships and U-boats.

In 1939 Leningrad had a populace of 3,500,000 – almost equal to the entire population of Finland. Leningrad was Russia's second largest city, and the output from its shipbuilding, chemical, electric power and machine-building plants amounted to almost 25 per cent of the entire industrial output of the USSR.

Early in 1939 Stalin, with security in mind, asked the Finns to meet him for discussions about frontier adjustments, offering to exchange territory. In addition, he wanted the lease of a port on the Gulf of Finland, and asked the Finns to give up other strategic parcels of territory totalling 1,066 square miles in return for nearly twice as much – but less valuable – Russian territory in the far north. No agreement was reached. After the signing of the German–Soviet non-aggression pact and Hitler's invasion of Poland, Stalin again sought territory adjustments with Finland. At a meeting with that country's negotiator, J. K. Paasikivi, he said significantly that although Russia had good relations with Hitler's Germany, 'Everything in this world can change.'

A month earlier he had said virtually the same thing to the Latvian Foreign Minister, Vilhelms Munters: 'Now there is an unexpected turn in the tide [The German–Soviet pact]. That sort of thing may happen in history. But you can not depend on it. You have to get ready for any eventuality in good time.'

By now Russia had practically absorbed the Baltic states. Before approaching Finland, Stalin had obtained 'buffer territories' by bullying Estonia and Latvia into granting rights of occupation to Russian armies. In the south-west, he seized Bessarabia and Bukovina. The war historian, B. H. Liddell Hart, says that after the partition of Poland, Stalin desired to protect his Baltic flank against a threat from his 'temporary colleague' Hitler.

Weeks before the Russo–Finnish War broke out, the Leningrad journal *Krasny Flot* (Red Fleet) spelled out the reasons why it was necessary to agree on mutual Russo–Finnish assistance in time of war. The journal, obviously reflecting official opinion at a very high level, cited the geographical position of Finland, the insecurity of her communications on the Baltic Sea, her economic weakness and 'the absence of any menace to her frontiers from the east' – meaning from Russia. All this, it said, pointed to the necessity of Finland's 'rallying' to the side of Russia. 'Only by way of mutual assistance with the USSR can a country like Finland withstand hostile aviation which could deal untold damage to her national economy.'

On 12 November 1939, commenting on Finnish naval capabilities in the event of a 'third nation' entering the picture, the journal said that the Finnish fleet was extremely weak and capable of undertaking only very limited defensive measures. Moreover, the Finnish armed coastal vessels were very lightly armed and slow, and in conditions where manoeuvring was difficult, especially close to rocks, they would be easy targets for a strong enemy.

But the Finns, proud, mistrustful of the Russians, and convinced of their own strength, clung to the belief that they could remain neutral in a European conflict. They rejected the Russian proposals and mobilised their small but well-trained and well-equipped army. In November 1939 Russia commenced hostilities. Some reports say that they deployed one million men against 175,000 Finns.

For Stalin the 105-day 'Winter War' was an embarrassment. The Communist Parties of the world were stunned; their influence declined. Even staunch friends of Russia were indignant. Britain, France and the USA offered Finland military equipment and food. Greatly outnumbered, the Finns astonished the world, scoring early successes, outwitting and out-manoeuvring the Russians.

Finnish ski troops, fighting on their own territory, had an advantage against the Red Army in a winter campaign. But some reports attributed the early poor showing of the Russians to Stalin's political commissars who allegedly hindered front-line commanders. (See Appendix: The Commissars.) Other reports said that the invasion was not properly planned and that Soviet soldiers, many from the warmer southern parts of Russia, were unprepared for sub-zero temperatures.

A Soviet explanation for the early setbacks was given by the Headquarters of the Leningrad Military District on 23 December 1939:

'The territory of Finland presents most serious difficulties for the movement of troops. The lack of roads and the rugged terrain, impassable forests, innumerable lakes – divided by innumerable isthmuses spanned by several lines of defences consisting of concrete gun and machine-gun emplacements with concrete refuges for troops – these are the conditions hindering the rapid advance of the troops on Finland's territory. Finland was building these fortifications for four years with the aid of three foreign States which fought among themselves for influence in Finland as the base for an attack on Leningrad and later on Moscow.'

Referring to Finland in a broadcast on 20 January 1940, Winston Churchill said that the war 'had exposed, for the world to see, the military incapacity of the Red Army'. Hitler and at least some of his generals apparently reached the same conclusion about Russia.

With the 'Winter War' under way, Britain and France on 5 February 1940 raised the possibility of sending an Expeditionary Force to aid Finland, but it never materialised. This is how the British historian A. J. P. Taylor described the Anglo–French policy of that time: 'The motives for the projected expedition to Finland defy rational analysis. For Great Britain and France to provoke war with Soviet Russia when already at war with Germany seems the product of a madhouse, and it is tempting to suggest a more sinister plan: switching the war on to an anti-Bolshevik course, so that the war against Germany could be forgotten or even ended.'

The three-month 'Winter War' cost the Russians 200,000 dead and many more wounded. Finland's losses were 24,000 dead or missing, 43,500 wounded. Stalin's generals had learned some lessons about winter fighting. As the historian Mark Arnold-Foster says, even before the Finnish war had ended Stalin's soldiers were being taught to fight 'the Finnish way'.

Liddell Hart says that after a negotiated peace was signed in March 1940, Stalin 'showed statesmanship' by offering the Finns 'remarkably moderate terms'.

George Bernard Shaw, in a comment on the Winter War, said that the 'only novelty' about it was that Stalin took only what he needed instead of taking back the whole country as any other Power would have done. (This was an allusion to the fact that before the Russian Revolution, Finland had been a part of the Tsarist Empire.)

Hitler's entry on the 'Finnish stage' was not long in coming. Troops and guns arrived at Finnish ports in September 1940, six months after the war had ended. The Kremlin, learning that a new Finnish–German agreement had been signed allowing the transport of troops through Finland, asked Berlin about the 'secret portions' of the agreement. Foreign Minister Molotov said that the Germans were helping the Finns to build new airports and pointedly asked what Berlin's intentions were in regard to Finland.

Germany's reply, says the American historian, William L. Shirer, was a 'fatuous and at the same time arrogant epistle, abounding in nonsense and lies and subterfuge'.

Max Jakobson, a Finnish authority on the 'Winter War', says that when Hitler invaded Russia, the Finns joined in what they called the 'continuation war' for the purpose of regaining their lost territory. But Marshal Baron Gustaf Mannerheim – he had once served as an officer in the Tsar's army – turned down German appeals to help capture Leningrad and cut the Murmansk–Moscow railway line. After Finland regained the territory lost to Stalin in the Winter War, the Finnish Army moved into South Karelia to establish a defensive line connecting Lake Onega with Lake Ladoga. 'But there they stopped,' Jakobson says, opposing a German request to advance farther into Russia.

In 1944, when Stalin's armies were forcing Hitler's troops back towards Germany, Finland began talks with Moscow about an armistice which resulted in the Finns pulling out of the war. But they then had the task of driving 200,000 formerly fraternal German troops out of their country. (Prior to their departure, the German troops laid waste the Finnish province of Lapland. This, Jakobson says, was 'Hitler's revenge for Finland's treachery, as he called it, in making peace before Germany's final doom'.)

Russian revisionist historians condemn out of hand Stalin's war with Finland, picturing Russia as a bully striking out at a small neighbour. The Moscow historian, Natan Eidelman, calls the Russo–Finnish War a 'dark page' in Soviet history.

But the German leaders understood that Stalin's war with Finland was conducted out of considerations of strategy against Nazi Germany. A memorandum written by Foreign Minister Ribbentrop said that the 1939–40 war with Finland was one of the measures 'extending Moscow's military power wherever the possibility offered itself in the area between the Arctic Ocean and the Black Sea'. Ribbentrop alleged that Stalin's war with Finland was one of the causes of the German invasion of Russia.

Hitler used every means in the endeavour to destroy Leningrad, on some days sending as many as 2,000 bombers at a time. The German troops never got in to the city, but the 900-day siege resulted in more than 500,000 civilian deaths. The Germans plundered the nearby cities, looting historical treasures and destroying the 18th-century grand palace at Pavlovsk, outside Leningrad, that had been built by Empress Catherine II. They also set fire to the summer residence of Peter the Great at Petrodvorets.

Smashed were its 114 gold-trimmed fountains.

★★★ THE SECRET SPEECH ★★★

Stalin's secret speech to his officers on 5 May 1941 was a concise lesson in politics and soldiering, covering war and peace, history and politics, victory and defeat. Stalin suggested a reason for Napoleon's success and failure. He explained why Germany was winning in the second year of World War II and the reason for the collapse of the French Army. He spoke of attitudes in Britain toward the military. He called Hitler's Germany a 'predatory nation'. Hitler's invasion of Russia was only a few weeks off.

By 1941 Stalin was a cult figure to the nation. Millions of Red Army officers and men had read in their history and political textbooks that Stalin was, after Lenin, *the* authentic hero of the Russian Civil War; that he was responsible for the country's economic transformation and was behind the rapid build-up of the Red Army, Navy and Air Force.

Any Stalin speech was a special event. Since officers expected their country to be involved in war with Germany, every one was eager to hear Stalin's views on the world situation. His speech was secret and 'off the record'. Officers were told not to take notes. But somebody did, because a nine-page, virtually verbatim record of the speech is preserved in the archives of the Russian Ministry of Defence.

The secret speech had a history of its own.

Very early on, misinformers in Moscow and Berlin presented doctored versions of the speech. In Moscow, German journalists were told that the main purpose of Stalin's speech was to prepare his military officers for a 'compromise' with Germany. Alexander Werth, a British journalist in Moscow, apparently didn't know that he was reporting a bogus version of the speech, one which predicted a German invasion of Russia in 1942. Another version had it that Stalin had told his generals about Kremlin efforts to delay the start of the war by three or four months.

There were other dubious accounts of the Stalin speech. Gustav Hilger, who had been a wartime counsellor at the German Embassy in Moscow, said that after the war he had interrogated three Russian officer prisoners who said they had heard Stalin's speech and were positive that it included these words: 'The Red Army must finally get used to the idea that we have entered an era when the Socialist Front has to be expanded by force. Those who refuse to see the necessity of an offensive attitude are petty bourgeois idiots.'

After the war was under way, Joseph Goebbels' Propaganda Ministry used a fake version of the speech to blame Stalin for starting the war. In 1942 the Ministry said that the German Army had taken prisoner Russian officers who had been present at the 5 May speech and who 'testified' that Stalin planned a pre-emptive strike against Germany in order to 'expand the socialist front'.

A year later Foreign Minister Ribbentrop, speaking to a Bulgarian official, claimed that Stalin had declared unambiguously in the May speech that Russia would commence hostilities by invading Germany in August 1941.

The Stalin speech was, therefore, used by Berlin as another pretext for making war on Russia. Before starting military action, Hitler invariably sought pretexts. Prior to his invasion of Poland in September 1939 he had told his generals: 'I will give you a propaganda pretext to start the war. I do not care whether that pretext will be convincing. Nobody asks the winner if he has told the truth.' (The pretext was an imaginary 'Polish' military attack on a German border post and radio station at Gleiwitz. German guards staged the attack, forcing hapless prisoners to wear Polish military uniforms in a suicide mission.)

At the time of Stalin's speech, a powerful German invasion force was gathered along Russia's border awaiting the coded signal to attack.

This is the text of the 'secret' speech:

'Comrades!

Soon you will return to your units from Moscow. Red Army men and commanders will start asking you questions about what is happening now. You have studied in the academies. You were quite close to the high commanders. Tell us what is happening in the world? Is the German army really invincible? A commander must be able to do more than just give orders and commands. A commander must know how to talk to the fighting men. A commander must be able to explain things to them, to talk to them in a friendly manner. Our great military leaders were always close to soldiers. We must act as Suvorov did.' [A famous maxim of the Russian Field Marshal Alexander Suvorov says: 'Save your comrade even if you die.' During World War II, Stalin personally approved the award of the Order of Suvorov to a number of Allied generals including Dwight Eisenhower, George Marshall and Omar Bradley. It is the highest Russian decoration for generals commanding large armies.]

'They will ask you – what are the reasons, why is Europe in turmoil, why is France defeated, why is Germany winning? Why does Germany have a superior army? It is a fact that Germany has a better army, technically and organisationally. How are you going to explain this? Lenin once said that defeated armies learned lessons better. This idea of Lenin's fully applies to nations. Defeated nations learn lessons better. The German Army, defeated in 1918, has done its homework well.

'The Germans have critically re-examined the reasons of their defeat and found ways optimally to organise their army, to train and arm it. The military thought has been making a rapid progress in Germany. Latest armaments were adopted by the German Army. The army was also trained in new warfare techniques. Generally speaking, there are two aspects of this problem. It is not enough to have good hardware and good organisation. One must also have more allies. It was exactly because defeated armies learn lessons better that Germany has learned from the experience of the past. In 1870, the Germans beat the French. Why? Because they fought a one-front war.

'The Germans were defeated in 1916–17. Why? because they fought on two fronts at once. Why didn't the French learn anything from the experience of 1914–18. Lenin teaches us: Parties and states perish if they turn a blind eye to their errors, if they get intoxicated with their successes, if they rest on their laurels then their successes make them giddy. The French got giddy with their successes, with their arrogance. The French missed the right time and lost their allies. The Germans got their allies. The French were resting on their laurels.

'Military thought made no progress in France. It remained on the 1918 level. There was no concern for or moral support of the Army in France. New morality appeared that corrupted the Army. The military were looked down on. Commanders started to be viewed as good-for-nothings who had to join the Army because they did not have factories, plants, banks or shops in which to devote their energy. Girls even refused to marry soldiers. It is only in the atmosphere of such contempt that the army apparat could go under the control of the Gamelins and Ironsides who did not know a thing about the military profession. [Maurice Gamelin was Commander-in-Chief of Allied troops in France; William Edmund Ironside was British Commander of Home Defence Forces in 1940].

'A similar attitude to the military was cultivated in Britain too. The Army must enjoy exclusive concern and love of the people and the government – this is the source of the Army's great morale and moral strength. The Army must be cherished. When the aforesaid morality disappears, the Army will never be strong and effective in combat. This is exactly what happened in France. To prepare well for a war does not mean only to have a modern army. To prepare for a war also means to prepare for it politically. What does political preparation for a war mean? To prepare for a war politically means to have enough reliable allies and neutral countries. When it started this war Germany coped with the task successfully. Britain and France did not.

'These are political and military reasons for the French defeat and the German victories.

'Is the German Army really invincible?

'No, it is not. There has never been an invincible army in the world. There are best armies, good armies and weak armies. Germany started the war under the slogan of liberation from the yoke of the Versailles Treaty. This slogan was popular, It was supported and sympathised with by all nations insulted by the Versailles Treaty. Now the situation has changed. Now the German army is fighting under different slogans. It has changed the slogan of liberation from the Versailles yoke for the slogan of a predatory war. The German Army will not be successful fighting under the slogan of a predatory war. This slogan is a dangerous one.

'Napoleon was supported and sympathised with when he fought under the slogan of liberation from serfdom. He had allies, he had success. When Napoleon started predatory wars, he met with a lot of enemies and eventually was defeated. Since the German Army is fighting under the slogan of enslaving other peoples and bringing other peoples under German dominance, this change of slogans will not bring it success.

'From the military point of view, the German Army is nothing special; it does not have any special tanks, or combat aircraft, or guns. A significant part of the German Army is losing its initial enthusiasm. Besides, the German Army has developed arrogance, conceit, complacency. The military thought is not developing. Combat hardware is inferior not only to Soviet combat hardware; even America is starting to produce better aircraft than Germany.

'How could it happen that Germany is winning?

'1. Germany is winning because its defeated army had done its homework, re-organised and re-examined the old values.

'2. Germany is winning because having won in World War I, Britain and France stopped seeking new ways, stopped learning. The French Army was dominant on the continent.

'That is why until recently Germany has been successful in this war. Today, however, Germany is fighting under expansionist slogans. Where the old slogan against Versailles consolidated all those insulted by Versailles, the new German slogan disunites. The German Army has lost the taste for further perfection of its combat hardware. The Germans are sure that their Army is ideal, the best, invincible. This is not so.

'The Army must be tirelessly perfected every day.

'Any politician, any statesman who succumbs to arrogance may confront unpleasant surprises, like France confronted a catastrophe.

'Let me congratulate you once again and wish you all success.'

At 5.30 a.m. on 22 June 1941, Foreign Minister Molotov received Berlin's diplomatic note. Hitler's invasion was almost two hours old. The note slyly accused Russia of 'breaking' and 'violating' its treaties and agreements with Germany.

★★★ THE HESS MANOEUVRE ★★★

Less than a week after Stalin's secret speech, a high official of the Nazi regime floated down over Scotland in a parachute. This was the beginning of the 'Hess affair' that stunned the world. Even now not everything concerning the event has been declassified.

In June 1991 the Russians released documents which claimed that double-agent Kim Philby had supplied Stalin with reports on the 'secret flight' to Britain of Hitler's deputy, Rudolf Hess. In May 1941 Hess had flown to Britain and parachuted near his intended destination in Scotland, the residence of the Duke of Hamilton. The invasion of Russia was just weeks off.

Understandably concerned about the pro-Hitler clique in Britain and possibility of an Anglo-German deal, the mood in the Kremlin was sepulchral. A few months before the Hess flight, Stalin had confided to General (later Marshal) Vasily Chuikov: 'Even now, in this difficult time for the British people, appeasers of the aggressor are rushing back and forth between Berlin and London. They are prepared to make new concessions at any time, provided the aggressor turns his arms against us.'

According to the Russian documents, British intelligence knew in advance about the Hess mission. Philby informed the Russians that the British had intercepted a letter sent by Hitler's Deputy to the Duke of Hamilton some weeks before his solo flight. The Russians didn't say so but presumably the Philby message to Moscow mentioned Hess's offer of peace terms to London.

The British interrogators of Hess said that he brought with him 'a cudgel of an olive branch'. Convinced by Nazi notions of an Aryan Britain, Hess sought before the invasion of Russia, an anti-Slav armistice: Britain would keep her Empire while Germany would rule the Continent. Small wonder, one London newspaper said in 1996, that after the war Hess 'should drink out the chalice of punishment to the last drop'. But at the time of Hess's flight, British leaders understood that if Stalin's armies were defeated, Britain would be subject to Hitler's whims. Naturally, the Hess proposal was unacceptable.

It was doubly distasteful to Churchill because Hess also demanded his removal from office as the price for an armistice. But although the Hess proposal was unacceptable to the British Government, some ministers kept an enigmatic silence, seemingly because they did not want Berlin to know London's real attitude towards the Hess caper.

When the Hess flight was first announced in Britain, a Member of Parliament said: 'This is the most sensational thing that has happened for many hundreds of years.' But scant news of the bizarre flight reached the world. The British lid on the 'Hess affair' so irritated Kremlin leaders that the Party organ, Pravda, asked mischievously: 'What is Hess at the present time – a criminal who must be tried and punished or the plenipotentiary representative in Britain of Hitler's Government enjoying inviolability?'

Some Russian historians say that given the delicate balance of power in the world at that time, and the extent to which Britain had an interest in a war between Germany and Russia, the reason for the silence emanating from London was to let Hitler think that, when he attacked Russia, he would not have to fight a war on two fronts.

A British newspaper commented in 1941: 'Why Churchill and the authorities deliberately chose to maintain a mysterious silence over Hess, when in fact his proposals had been turned down, remains officially unexplained. Was this silence, with its suggestion of some possible complicity, a trap to lure Hitler forward on his desperate enterprise with the hope of some possible eventual support, only to turn on him with the most positive counter-thrust as soon as he had embarked on it? Had some bright wit of British diplomacy devised the scheme to use Hess as a boomerang and to catch Hitler with his own anti-Soviet bait with which he had so often in the past gulled the British Tory class?'

When asked in the House whether Hess had brought with him any proposals for solving Europe's problems, Churchill replied: 'I have no statement to make about this person at the present time; but His Majesty's Government has, of course, kept the United States Government informed on the subject of his flight to this country.'

Twelve days after the Hess flight, Sir Archibald Sinclair, the Secretary of State for Air, said that the Duke of Hamilton 'did not recognise the prisoner Hess, having never met the Deputy Führer'. He added that contrary to reports that had appeared in some newspapers, the Duke had never corresponded with Hess. But according to the British historian, Alan Bullock, Hess and the Duke had met each other during the 1936 Berlin Olympics.

R. R. Stokes, the MP for Ipswich, noted a strange circumstance: during the interrogation the Duke of Hamilton had been left alone with Hess for one and a half hours. Also, Stokes recalled that the Minister of Information, Alfred Duff Cooper, had earlier mentioned that a letter from Hess had indeed been received by the Duke.

On 19 June, three days before Hitler's attack on Russia, Major Vyvyan Adams gave vent to his views on the 'Hess affair' in the House of Commons:

'I believe that Hess came to this country under the fond delusion that he could debauch our aristocracy by saying to them, "Join us, or we join Russia". It seems that he came having in his pocket proposals which might attract the mentality which now wants peace at any cost. There is such a mentality and it is mainly to be found here and there in corners among the well-born and well-to-do, those who have more money than sense, those who whisper the dangerous fallacy, "Better defeat with our possessions, than victory with Bolshevism", which is exactly what Hitler wants them to say.'

Was Hitler unaware of his deputy's intentions? Some books mention a 'baffled', 'furious' and 'shocked' Hitler. (As one British wit put it: 'There is this to be said in favour of that theory: that every apparent inconsistency fits it and every improbability makes the whole thing much more probable.') After the Hess flight, Goebbels' Propaganda Ministry alleged that Hess had been in a 'state of hallucination' when he took off in his Messerschmitt for Britain. But there is evidence of a meeting of minds between Hess and Hitler.

Concerning the technical complexity of the flight to Scotland, some British experts considered it doubtful that Hess could have arrived in Britain on his own initiative. The Scottish MP J. J. Davidson said that he had spoken to very experienced airmen who had logged hundreds of hours in the war. 'Every one of them agrees that no one man could have made the flight Hess made without assistance. He had assistance, he must have had assistance. His course was one of the most difficult that could have been undertaken. It was one of the chanciest flights a man could have undertaken unless very careful preparation by experts had been made for that flight.'

In 1990, Wolf Hess, the son of Hitler's deputy, told an interviewer that on the eve of the flight Hess and Hitler had held a four-hour conversation. The younger Hess said that he knew nothing of the content of the talk, but assuming his recollection is correct, there is every reason to believe that the Anglo–German problem – and how to solve it – was at least part of their conversation.

Some evidence that Hitler was aware of his deputy's intentions came from Stalin's chief intelligence agent in Japan, Dr. Richard Sorge.

Sorge received information about Rudolf Hess from the German Ambassador and relayed it to Moscow. After Sorge was arrested he gave a statement to the Japanese police: 'At the time of the Hess affair, I learned from the German Embassy in Tokyo that Hitler had sent Hess to Britain as a last means of reaching a peaceful settlement with the British before waging war against the Soviet Union.'

Other Russian sources say that for some time before his flight to Scotland, Hess had been spotted by friends taking his Messerschmitt up on practice flights.

Additional details of the Hess flight have been supplied by German authorities. Here is what Secretary of State for Foreign Affairs Ernst von Weizsacker jotted in his diary on 19 May 1941: 'The Hess affair is so peculiar that I should like to record what I know about it. I always had the impression that the Führer would have readily agreed to a compromise with Britain on approximately the following terms: The British Empire would remain, but with the continent the British would have nothing to do. It was to this end that he attempted – for the second time, it is said – to end by his personal action the war between "two white nations".'

Russian historian and investigative journalist Lev Bezymensky, who at the end the war acted as an interpreter for General Alfred Jodl and other top-ranking German generals, says that he met two former Nazi officials who claimed that they had knowledge of the Hess affair. One was Fritz Hesse, formerly a subordinate of Foreign Minister Ribbentrop and a specialist on Britain. Immediately after the Hess flight he was questioned by Himmler and Ribbentrop, both of whom wanted to know what chance Hess had of meeting top British leaders.

The other informant was Karl Wolff, a former SS *Obergruppenführer*, who said that on 17 April 1945 Hitler had told him that Hess was acting on his instructions.

Two more entries in the Weizsacker diary are pertinent because they deal with the possibility of making peace with Britain. The first is dated 2 June 1941: 'As long as we will be engaged in a serious war against Russia, the idea of a compromise with Britain will naturally have to be pigeon-holed. But as soon as the military operation is over – and our military leaders expect it to end in four to eight, and at the most 10 weeks – hopes will rise in Britain for a compact.'

A few days before 'Barbarossa', Weizsacker's thoughts were again on securing a separate peace with the West: 'I think that after Germany has turned to the East, there will be, perhaps in September, a greater readiness in the West for peace. In this way victory in the East would be the signal for a compact with the West. It is always necessary to set oneself a new goal.'

After the war Hess was tried by the Nuremberg War Crimes Tribunal. He pretended at first to be a mental case so as to escape punishment. But the ruse didn't work. In his last plea to the tribunal he said:

> 'I am happy to know that I have done my duty as a loyal follower to my Führer. I do not regret anything. If I were to begin all over again I would act just as I have acted.'

Not all of the Hess file has been declassified. A Russian Foreign Office spokesman has deplored the 'stubborn unwillingness' of Britain to release all material on the Hess flight until the second decade of the 21st century.

BATTLES AND ALLIES

★★★ PLAN 'BARBAROSSA' ★★★

Hitler's cocky generals, confident of the superiority of Germany's war machine, had predicted the swift downfall of Russia:

    German General Staff (July 1940)..................9 to 17 weeks.

    German General Staff (September 1940) ......8 to 10 weeks.

As the launch date of 'Barbarossa' (code-name for the invasion), 22 June 1941, drew near, German forecasts of speedy triumph in the East became even more rash.

    Heinrich Himmler (18 June 1941)..........................6 weeks.

    Joachim von Ribbentrop (21 June 1941)................8 weeks.

General Alfred Jodl, Chief of Operations of the Armed Forces High Command, said: 'In three weeks after our attack that house of cards will collapse.'

Hitler and his generals even published a post-victory plan. Known as Draft Directive 32, the plan was entitled 'The Preparation for the Period after the Implementation of the Barbarossa Plan.' Sent to military units on 11 June 1941, the draft stipulated that upon the defeat of Stalin's armies, the conquest of Afghanistan and India was to take place, to be followed by the Mediterranean area, Africa and the Middle East; and, after this, the British Isles.

When the invasion got under way, Hitler told his aides: 'In four weeks we will be in Moscow and that city will be razed to the ground.' The Führer wanted the ancient Russian city and its name to disappear and a lake be created in its place.

Caught up in the euphoria of early triumphs, General Franz Halder, Chief of the German General Staff, jotted in his diary on 3 July: 'It is probably no overstatement to say that the Russian Campaign has been won in the space of two weeks.'

Hitler's generals were certain that the multi-national fabric of Russia would tear apart once the *Blitzkrieg* began. 'Our hopes for victory', wrote German Field Marshal Ewald von Kleist, 'were based to a large extent on hopes that the invasion would trigger a political upheaval in Russia. These great hopes stemmed from the conviction that Stalin's own people would overthrow him after grave defeats. This conviction was disseminated by the Führer's political advisers.'

Western experts also had predicted an easy victory. These included Sir John Dill, Chief of Britain's Imperial General Staff, who said the Germans would drive through Russia 'like a hot knife through butter'. In Washington, Secretary of the Navy Frank Knox said that Hitler would knock Russia out of the war in six weeks and Secretary of War Henry Stimson said that Hitler would 'be busy' with Russia for four weeks, at the most, twelve.

The German invasion of Russia was first code-named 'Restoration in the East', then 'Fritz', and finally, on the Führer's personal order, 'Barbarossa', after the Holy Roman Emperor Frederick Barbarossa. On 18 December 1940, Directive 21 on invading Russia, was signed. The signal for the opening of hostilities was the code-word 'Dortmund'. On 20 June 1941 it was sent to the *Wehrmacht* in a brief cipher telegram: 'Code-word Dortmund 22 June.'

Joseph Stalin had received ample warnings of the invasion, some pinpointing the exact hour of attack, from the offices of President Roosevelt and Prime Minister Churchill, from Moscow's foreign embassies, from his espionage agents in Tokyo and Zurich, from an alleged agent in the German Embassy in Moscow, from a German defector named Alfred Liskow, and from General Filipp Golikov, head of the Intelligence directorate in Moscow. (Two months before the invasion he reported to the Kremlin on the possible directions of the German attack on the Soviet Union.)

Russian archives reveal that Stalin's master spy in Japan, Dr. Sorge, learning that Germany's leaders were completing Plan 'Barbarossa', sent the following warnings to Moscow:

March 1941. 'The German military attaché in Tokyo has declared that immediately after the war in Europe is over war against the Soviet Union will begin.'

May 1941. 'A number of German representatives are returning to Berlin. They believe war against the USSR will start at the end of May.'

19 May 1941. 'Nine armies of 150 divisions will be concentrated against the USSR.'

1 June 1941. 'Flanking manoeuvres and efforts to encircle and isolate separate groups are to be expected from the Germans.'

15 June 1941. 'The war will begin on 22 June.'

In 1990 the Historical–Diplomatic Directorate of the Soviet Foreign Ministry said of the invasion that many warnings were sent to the Kremlin through embassy channels but 'fell on deaf ears' and '[were] ignored until it was too late'.

It taxes belief that Stalin, who had been preparing the country to repel an enemy attack for more than a decade, should be indifferent to these authoritative warnings and oppose the taking of counter-measures. Some observers have wondered why, in light of Stalin's ravaging of the officer corps in the pre-war purges and his invasion-day blunders, his generals continued to rally around him.

Actually, Stalin had counselled the nation to be extremely vigilant. Here, typically, are Stalin's words delivered one year before 22 June 1941: 'We must keep our entire people in a state of mobilisation, so that no enemies abroad can take us unawares.' Why, then, would Stalin, who gave priority to strengthening the armed forces and protecting the country's security, ignore a spate of invasion warnings?

There is some evidence that Stalin had not entirely lost his senses. On 21 June, the eve of the invasion, Stalin ordered Moscow Party officials not to leave town the following day, Sunday. Two hours before the invasion, at 2 a.m. on the 22nd, Stalin telephoned General Ivan Tyulanev, Commander of the Moscow Military District, and gave orders to put the city's anti-aircraft defences at 75 per cent of war readiness.

But a number of Stalin's top generals admit that there were reasons for extreme caution prior to the invasion. Stalin did not wish to give Hitler a pretext for attacking him. Also, the issue of premature mobilisation (discussed in a later chapter) was a difficult one. Moreover Stalin knew that against a huge, well-equipped, combat-tested invasion force, his armies would have to fall back. It is reported that he told a few of his generals that the Red Army would not, in fact, be able to withstand a *Blitzkrieg* attack on the border; and when one of them (Bagramyan) heard this opinion, he was greatly shocked.

Probably nobody knew better than Stalin about Prince Kutuzov's 'formula' for dealing with Napoleon's armies inside Russian territory. Stalin's entire strategy, including the building of war industries deep inside the coun-

try, was based on the eventuality of having to carry on a protracted war with a powerful enemy. Seen in this light, there was realistically not much that could be done at the start of the invasion except to make each day as costly as possible for the invading army, and to thwart the enemy's timetable in bloody 'holding' actions.

It is well to bear in mind that the Red Army probably had at this time – despite the purges – better capability and strength (in manpower, tanks and aircraft) than all other armies except Hitler's *Wehrmacht*; that the loss of preliminary battles, mainly in the first year of the war, was not the disaster for Russia that it would be for most other countries; that the immense early losses were inevitable given the balance of forces in 1941. Neither should the predictions of the Western experts of a quick German victory over Stalin's Russia be forgotten.

In my interviews with Stalin's generals, some of them suggested 'hidden motives', mainly political, for Stalin's seeming pre-invasion impotence. But one Russian military historian, Colonel Vasily Morozov, cautioned against paying 'undue attention' to the early German triumphs. For him it is the increment of German defeats, the final Russian victory that matters, not the first knock-down blows of the struggle.

When Churchill visited Moscow in the summer of 1942, Stalin told him: 'I didn't need any warnings [of invasion]. I knew war would come, but I thought I might gain another six months or so.' Doubtless Russia would have been in a stronger position militarily if Germany had attacked in 1942.

Some writers persist in believing that Stalin trusted Hitler and the non-aggression pact, that 'living corpse that poisoned the air', as one Russian writer dubbed Stalin's August 1939 treaty with Germany. A few experts quote novelist Alexander Solzhenitsyn as saying that, 'Stalin trusted nobody but Hitler!', but the evidence for this is tenuous. While the Hitler–Stalin Pact was in force, there was more acrimony than gestures of goodwill. Stalin, although a fellow dictator, kept aloof from Hitler; he exchanged but one or two perfunctory birthday greetings and messages with him. He declined at least one invitation to visit Berlin with the excuse that he disliked 'unfamiliar settings'.

From memoirs and speeches we know that Stalin had no illusions about Hitler's Germany. Here is what he told Marshal Semyon Timoshenko shortly before the invasion: 'If a provocation needs to be staged, Hitler's generals would bomb even their own cities.' More to the point, he knew that Hitler's appetite for the Ukraine had never abated. While the Führer had at times disavowed what he had said belligerently about France in *Mein Kampf*, he never retracted the part in which he promised the German people the breadbasket of the Ukraine.

Far from trusting Hitler, Stalin had secretly moved sizeable forces up to the border before the invasion. These comprised five Russian armies, according to a former Chief of the General Staff S. K. Shtemenko. In the critical days and weeks before the invasion, the following additional measures were taken to strengthen the armed forces and the border areas. Taken together these steps show, in the words of Marshal Ivan Bagramyan, that a 'titanic effort was made to prepare the nation for war'. The measures:

1. In mid-May as many as 28 divisions started moving to border districts on General Staff directives.

2. On 27 May the General Staff ordered the western border districts 'urgently' to build up front command posts and on 10 June the Baltic, Western and Kiev Military Districts were ordered to move their front commands to the newly built posts.

3. In early June 800,000 reservists were called up for field training and sent to reinforce the western military districts.

4. The Odessa Military District (on the Black Sea) had obtained permission to do this earlier.

5. On 12–15 June the military districts were ordered to bring their divisions closer to the border.

6. On 19 June the military districts were ordered to camouflage airfields, army units, transport, depots and other bases and to disperse the aircraft on the airfields.

7. By mid-1941 Russia's armed forces totalled more than five million, almost three times that of 1939.

8. In June instructions were issued to naval vessels to intensify patrols. Naval bases were moved to safer ports. On the eve of the invasion, the Baltic, Northern and Black Sea Fleets were placed on battle alert.

But because of human failings and the miscalculations by Stalin, there was not enough time to carry out fully the preparations for the coming war.

In a typical Nazi ruse, Hitler said he was 'forced' to attack Russia because Stalin had provokingly amassed large forces on the western border. As a result, a preventive war was necessary to remove this 'dangerous situation'. American correspondent William L. Shirer, who was in Berlin at the time, noted in his diary that Hitler had called his invasion of Russia a 'counter-attack'.

For 'Barbarossa' Hitler amassed on Russia's western frontier almost 200 divisions, including 33 tank and motorised divisions and four air armies, plus those provided by Hungary, Italy, Finland and Rumania. Many of the divisions were bunched in the main, Moscow direction. This invasion force totalled almost 4,000,000 men, and some of Stalin's generals say that it was the then 'most perfect fighting force in the world'. Stalin had just over one million men in the border area, but they were strung out between the Arctic Ocean and the Black Sea.

The invading armies were helped by two facts: the *Wehrmacht*'s prior looting of occupied countries and the exploitation of their economic resources had led to an unprecedented growth in German war production. In the course of the first seventeen months of World War II the Nazis seized in the occupied countries of Europe war supplies, materials and property worth double Germany's pre-war national income. Secondly, according to reliable German and Allied records, on 1 April 1941, the *Wehrmacht* was being armed and serviced by nearly 5,000 factories and other enterprises in occupied lands.

At the outset of invasion, no less than 92 German divisions were using French and other captured vehicles. Rumania was supplying almost two-thirds of the petroleum.

On invasion day the armies rolled into Russia in three powerful columns: A northern group seized the Baltic states, a central group made a pincer movement in the direction of Minsk, in Belorussia, while a southern group invaded the Ukraine.

The streaming lava of attacking troops appeared unstoppable. Within days, major cities were captured and 2,000 aircraft destroyed. Field Marshal Albert Kesselring called the swift destruction by German fighters of numerous 'innocent' flights of Russian aircraft 'sheer infanticide'. In a few weeks more than a million Russian soldiers were prisoners of war and a huge toll in dead and wounded had been exacted.

Stalin's generals do not excuse his miscalculations at the start of the war. But in memoirs, and in other recollections, the generals assert that the blame was not only Stalin's but must be shared with the top military leadership. Marshal Zhukov in his memoirs admits a share of responsibility for the miscalculations on invasion-day.

Except for pockets of heroic resistance like Russia's border fortress at Brest (it held out for more than a month, only a handful of the defenders surviving), Stalin's border troops wilted under powerful frontal assaults and bombing raids. But German losses also mounted. From 22 June to 5 July the Luftwaffe lost 807 aircraft, and from 6 to 19 July another 477. The German General Staff said that this showed that despite the *Blitzkrieg*, the Russians were able to put up a strong resistance.

At Smolensk, 200 miles west of Moscow, on the same soil trodden by Napoleon's armies, the Germans met with unexpectedly stubborn resistance. For the first time a few of Hitler's generals had a foreboding of disaster. On 27 June, five days after the invasion, General Franz Halder, Chief of the German General Staff, wrote in his diary: 'At the front, events are developing not at all as they had been planned by higher staffs.' And on 11 July: 'The [Russian] enemy command shows competence; the enemy fights fiercely, fanatically. Our panzer units suffered heavily both in manpower and *matériel*. The troops are tired.'

On 11 August, Halder wrote despairingly, 'The Russian colossus has been under-estimated by us.'

Later, General Günther Blumentritt, Chief of Staff of the German Fourth Army, said of the attack on Russia: 'From the political point of view, the decision to attack that country was a most fatal decision. Now we had to fight an enemy who was stronger than anyone we had fought before.'

★★★ STALIN IS OUTRAGED ★★★
The Arctic Convoys and the Second Front

The first shots of the campaign in the Arctic were fired on 29 June 1941, somewhat later than in the other theatres of operations. But the Arctic campaign was conducted over boundless expanses in the most difficult conditions. The 'right flank' of the Soviet–German front rested on the chill Barents Sea.

The Germans used the topography to advantage: the great depths of the Barents Sea and the numerous winding fiords gave Hitler's warships, including submarines, which attacked the Allied convoys, room for concealment and manoeuvre.

Thanks to masses of warm water carried by the Gulf Stream from the Atlantic Ocean, the south-western part of the Barents Sea is free from ice all the year round, and open to shipping. The northern and eastern parts of the Barents and White Seas, as well as the Kara Sea, are icebound for a large part of the year.

War supplies to Stalin, known as 'Lend-Lease', from the USA, Britain and Canada, reached Russia mainly through her ports on these icy northern seas, carried by intrepid convoys of British and American ships.

The early failure of Hitler's '*Blitzkrieg* in the north', which aimed to capture Russia's northern ports of Murmansk and Archangel, compelled the Germans to increase their naval strength in the region. At that time Stalin's Northern Fleet had only a few warships: eight destroyers and fifteen submarines. The Fleet's air arm had a total of 116 aircraft, mostly obsolescent types, according to Admiral Nikolai Kuznetsov, who was Commander-in-Chief of Naval Forces during the war. The Russian fleet in the Arctic also lacked adequately equipped naval bases and airfields.

In 1942 Stalin twice protested to Winston Churchill about Allied decisions, one of them suspending Anglo–American convoys to the north because of the threat posed by German bombers and U-boats; the other postponing the Allied invasion of France. Stalin regarded both to be incomprehensible and, in one case, 'intolerable'. He deplored the events surrounding the tragedy of Convoy PQ17 in which 25 transport ships were lost and another half-dozen badly damaged.

The decision to leave unprotected this large convoy *en route* to Russia caused consternation in Moscow. Stalin told Churchill that his experts were dumbfounded by the tragedy. Admiral Nikolai Kharlamov, who was Head of the Soviet Military Mission in Britain during the war, called the order that left the ships naked against the enemy 'criminal'.

In a solemn message to Churchill, Stalin spoke of the high losses Russia was suffering in the war against Hitler and hoped the decision on the convoys would be reversed. He pointed out that a Second Front in 1942 would save the lives of many Russian soldiers. In addition he noted that when the Red Army had successes fighting Hitler, this helped the military positions of the Western democracies.

Stalin's protests to Churchill were couched in unambiguous language. But while blunt and sometimes stinging, they provided room for discussion. Stalin ended one of his protests to Churchill with these words: 'I hope you will not take it amiss that I have seen fit to give you my frank and honest opinion and that of my colleagues on the points raised in your message.'

Averell Harriman, President Roosevelt's special envoy to Russia at the beginning of the German–Soviet war, helped open up a new, safer, supply route to Stalin. He told me:

'We had a very major war – you've probably forgotten it – but the war against German submarines was a tough one. The continued Allied sinkings beginning in 1941 were very serious. And a major effort was made against the subs. We had in the beginning a difficult time getting to the Soviet Union the supplies we had promised. The northern convoys were very vulnerable. And then we opened up the Persian route. I made that arrangement with Mr Churchill in August 1942 when we came through Tehran and Cairo and that turned out to be one of the major supply routes to Stalin.'

In retrospect, experts regard the abandonment of PQ17 by a British naval escort as a 'regrettable folly' of World War II. This ill-fated northern convoy comprised 36 merchant ships.

Since the route of the northern convoys, especially in winter months, passed dangerously near the polar coast of Norway, some losses were inevitable, given the proximity of German naval and air force bases in Norway. But losses in the first dozen or so convoys were not disastrous.

The first twelve convoys had in fact arrived safely. But the thirteenth lost two ships out of nineteen. PQ15 lost three and PQ16 lost seven. The convoys were becoming increasingly risky and expensive, but the British and Americans were determined to do all they could to help their embattled Russian ally. On 27 June, 36 British and American merchant ships loaded with tanks and aircraft, and two Russian tankers, left Hval Fiord in Iceland, bound for the Arctic port of Murmansk. The convoy was code-named PQ17. It was the seventeenth Allied convoy to sail the perilous northern route to Russia. PQ17 was the largest convoy in the history of the war, the estimated worth of the cargo carried being $700 million.

Its immediate escort comprised nineteen warships, including six destroyers and two submarines. There were also two covering forces, one consisting of four cruisers and three destroyers, and another with one aircraft carrier, two battleships, two cruisers and eight destroyers. Sailors in the British and American ships were surprised to learn that in the Russian tankers all the anti-aircraft guns were handled by women.

The German High Command had worked out a plan to destroy as many of the Allied transports as possible. Code-named 'Knight's Move', it is said to have been approved by Hitler. But the Führer was known to oppose a direct engagement with a large British naval task force, fearing to lose his powerful battleships to the enemy. Should the opportunity arise, however, the Germans were ready to throw all their naval and air forces in northern Norway against PQ17.

The British, who remembered with horror the loss of two of their finest naval vessels to the Japanese in 1941, had contingency plans to withdraw their warships in case of a threatened encounter with Hitler's battleships and cruisers. In any event, the British Navy had by now accumulated a wealth of experience in convoy duties in the submarine-infested waters of the Atlantic and Arctic. As a rule losses were not too heavy. But in this case events took an unpredictable turn, and matters were not helped by the onset of the Arctic summer which brought 24-hour daylight.

On 4 July German aircraft, including twenty Heinkel He 115 torpedo-bombers, dubbed 'vultures' by the Russian sailors, located Convoy PQ17 and began to attack the slow-moving targets. Within minutes two transports were torpedoed by the Heinkels; British escort vessels finished them off to prevent their falling into German hands. (This practice outraged Russian naval officers who believed that many such ships could be salvaged. A few Russian crews were decorated by the Allies for refusing to abandon their badly damaged merchant vessels and staying with them until they finally made it into port.)

Suddenly the warships escorting PQ17 received a radio message from London: 'Cruiser force withdraw to westward at high speed.' Another message flashed: 'Convoy is to disperse and proceed to Russian ports.' It was believed by the Admiralty that the main German battle fleet headed by the *Tirpitz* was somewhere near the convoy and intended to attack it. *Tirpitz*, at 52,000 tons, with eight 381mm guns and a speed of 30 knots, was at that time considered to be the world's biggest and most powerful battleship. 'That decision was a fatal mistake,' says German historian Paul Carell.

Next day, July 5, when it became obvious to the Germans that they had nothing to fear from the British Navy, warships under Admiral Karl Dönitz moved against the scattered convoy and sank 25 transports over a period of several days .

Russian naval experts contend that the German attacks could have been successfully repulsed by the powerful forces Britain had put to sea. Admiral Kuznetsov claims that the combined covering force of PQ17 was 'far superior' to Hitler's squadron. But Admiral of the Fleet Sir Dudley Pound believed that the main force of the German surface fleet, including *Tirpitz*, was waiting to attack.

Later it was learned that Hitler's major warships were docked in Norway's Altafiord and had no intention of engaging the Allied convoy the German High Command fearing to risk the large battleships and heavy cruisers operating out of the ports of Trondheim, Narvik and Kirkenes.

When the British escort ships left PQ17 all alone, Stalin's Northern Fleet was put in a tight spot.

Admiral Arseni Golovko, the Fleet's Commander, was one of those who felt that the British decision was unsound. Golovko was one of Russia's best educated naval officers who had been appointed to his post at the age of 34. His submarines patrolled the exit from the fiord in which the German warships had been anchored; so he knew that the German naval squadron had not yet passed the 'patrol zone' of his submarines. Nevertheless, he ordered his submarines to meet the German squadron halfway.

Nikolai Lunin, captain of the Russian submarine *K–21*, observed the German squadron through his periscope. Two of his torpedoes scored direct hits, one on *Tirpitz* and the other on a destroyer, which sank. The Germans were stunned by the audacity of the attack and in the confusion Lunin's submarine escaped unharmed.

Hoping to salvage what remained of PQ17, Golovko sent out his small number of destroyers in search of damaged or abandoned merchant ships. For three weeks the destroyers plied the seas, collaring the merchant vessels that remained afloat. Of the 36, only eleven had survived, and many of these were badly damaged. A total of 3,350 trucks, 430 tanks, 210 bombers and nearly 100,000 tons of general cargo had been lost.

The PQ17 disaster took place during the hard-fought Battle of Stalingrad, which caused one Russian general, S. M. Shtemenko, to exclaim after the war: 'What a difference these supplies would have made to our armies at Stalingrad!'

Admiral Kharlamov says that the Russian tanker, the *Donbass*, performed 'heroic duty' for American sailors during the PQ17 tragedy. Seeing three lifeboats in the water, the tanker's captain was in a quandary. It was dangerous to stop: any moment a U-boat could torpedo the tanker loaded with fuel. But, says Kharlamov: 'The tanker's captain decided it would not do to abandon Allies and comrades-in-arms.' He adds: 'There is hardly a Russian sailor who would ever do such a thing.' The captain called all hands on deck as the tanker approached the boats and brought aboard 51 Americans from the freighter *Daniel Morgan*. All were safely taken to port.

On 18 July Churchill sent Stalin the following message with reference to the suspension of the northern convoys:

'We began running small convoys to North Russia in August 1941, and until December the Germans did not take any steps to interfere with them. From February 1942, the size of the convoys was increased, and the Germans then moved a considerable force of U-boats and a large number of aircraft to Northern Norway and made determined attacks on the convoys.

'By giving the convoys the strongest possible escort of destroyers and anti-submarine craft, they got through with varying but not prohibitive losses. It is evident that the Germans were dissatisfied with the results that were being achieved by means of aircraft and U-boats alone, because they began to use their surface forces against the convoys. Luckily for us, however, at the outset they made use of their heavy surface forces to the westward of Bear Island and their submarines to the eastward.' [Bear Island is about 300 miles north of Norway, between Spitsbergen and the northernmost tip of Norway.]

Churchill said that the British Home Fleet was thus in a position to prevent an attack by enemy surface forces. 'Before the May convoy was sent off, the Admiralty warned us that losses would be very severe if, as was expected, the Germans employed their surface forces to the eastward of Bear Island. We decided to sail the convoy. An attack by surface ships did not materialise, and the convoy got through with a loss of one-sixth, chiefly from air attack.

'In the case of the last convoy, which is numbered PQ17, however, the Germans at last used their forces in the manner we had always feared. They concentrated their U-boats to the westward of Bear Island and reserved their surface forces for attack to the eastward of Bear Island. The final story of PQ17 convoy is not yet clear. At the moment only four ships have arrived [out of 36] at Archangel but six others are in Nova Zemlya harbour. The latter may however be attacked from the air separately. At the best therefore only one-third will have survived.'

Churchill said the British had decided not to risk their Home Fleet closer to Norway where it could be brought under attack by German shore-based aircraft. He said that if one or two of Britain's 'very few' but most powerful warships were lost or seriously damaged, while Germany's largest battleships, *Tirpitz* and *Scharnhorst* remained in action, the whole command of the Atlantic would be lost.

'Besides affecting the food supplies by which we live, our war effort would be crippled; and, above all, the great convoys of American troops across the ocean, rising presently to as many as 80,000 in a month, would be prevented and the building up of a really strong second front in 1943 rendered impossible.'

Finally, Churchill came to the main point:

'It is therefore with the greatest regret that we have reached the conclusion that to attempt to run the next convoy, PQ18, would bring no benefit to you and would only involve a dead loss to the common cause [PQ18, consisting of 40 vessels, sailed on 2 September 1942. Only 27 reached their destination].'

He added: 'I give you my assurance that if we can devise arrangements which give a reasonable chance of at least a fair proportion of the contents of the convoys reaching you, we will start them again at once. The crux of the problem is to make the Barents Sea as dangerous for German warships as they make it for ourselves.' Meanwhile, Churchill said, Britain was prepared to dispatch immediately to the Persian Gulf some of the ships which were to have sailed in the next convoy.

Stalin's second, even stronger, protest was against the Allied decision to delay the opening of a Second Front; he could hardly contain himself:

'23 July 1942
'TO PRIME MINISTER CHURCHILL
'I have received your message of 18 July.

'I gather from the message first, that the British Government refuses to go on supplying the Soviet Union with war materials by the northern route and, secondly, that despite the agreed Anglo–Soviet Communiqué on the adoption of urgent measures to open a second front in 1942, the British Government is putting off the operation till 1943. [The Anglo–Soviet Communiqué, released on 12 June 1942, pointed out that during Foreign Minister V. M. Molotov's London talks with Churchill the two nations had reached agreement on the pressing need to open a second front in Europe in 1942.]

'According to our naval experts, the arguments of British naval experts on the necessity of stopping delivery of war supplies to the northern harbours of the USSR are untenable. They are convinced that, given goodwill and readiness to honour obligations, steady deliveries could be effected, with heavy loss to the Germans. The British Admiralty's order to the PQ17 convoy to abandon the supply ships and return to Britain, and to the supply ships to disperse and make for Soviet harbours singly, without escort, is, in the view of our experts, puzzling and inexplicable.

'Of course, I do not think steady deliveries to northern Soviet ports are possible without risk or loss. But then no major task can be carried out in wartime without risk or losses. You know, of course, that the Soviet Union is suffering far greater losses. Be that as it may, I never imagined that the British Government would deny us delivery of war materials precisely now, when the Soviet Union is badly in need of them in view of the grave situation on the Soviet–German front. It should be obvious that deliveries via Persian ports can in no way make up for the loss in the event of deliveries via the northern route being discontinued.'

As to the second point, namely, the opening of a second front in Europe, Stalin said that he feared the matter was taking an 'improper turn'. He said that in view of the situation on the Soviet–German front, 'I state most emphatically that the Soviet Government cannot tolerate the second front in Europe being postponed till 1943. I hope you will not take it amiss that I have seen fit to give you my frank and honest opinion and that of my colleagues on the points raised in your message. J. STALIN'

Apparently Stalin's frankness, his deep disappointment, but also his firmness, paid off. As Admiral Kharlamov noted, Stalin did not couch his messages and telegrams in 'the usual diplomatic language'. Eight days later Stalin received a reply from Churchill:

'We are making preliminary arrangements for another effort to run a large convoy through to Archangel in the first week of September.' He said that the September convoy would comprise 40 ships. But he added that unless German surface ships in the Barents Sea were prevented from attacking the convoy, there would be little chance of getting even one-third of the ships safely through. He cited the sad experience of PQ17, and said that minimum air cover was indispensable. At the same time, he said that he was willing, 'if you invite me, to come myself to meet you in Astrakhan, the Caucasus, or similar convenient meeting-place. We could then survey the war together and take decisions hand-in-hand. I could then tell you plans we have made with President Roosevelt for offensive action in 1942. I would bring the Chief of the Imperial General Staff with me.' Churchill said that he was setting out for Cairo: 'I have serious business there, as you may imagine. From there I will, if you desire it, fix a convenient date for our meeting, which might, so far as I am concerned, be between August 10 and 13, all being well.'

Stalin sent an answer the same day: 'I am grateful to you for agreeing to sail the next convoy with war materials to the USSR early in September. Although it will be very difficult for us to withdraw aircraft from the front, we shall take all possible steps to increase air cover for supply ships and convoy.'

Stalin kept his word and ordered a large force to help protect the next convoy, PQ18. It included 48 long-range bombers, ten torpedo-bombers and 200 fighters, including 47 long-range fighters. Churchill was pleased.

Stalin also issued a formal invitation to Churchill to visit Moscow. 'I hereby invite you on behalf of the Soviet Government to the USSR for a meeting with members of the government. I should be much obliged if you could travel to the USSR for joint consideration of urgent matters relating to the war against Hitler, who is now threatening Britain, the USA and the USSR more than ever. I think that Moscow would be the most suitable place for our meeting, since the members of the Government, the General Staff and myself cannot be away at this moment of bitter fighting against the Germans. The presence of the Chief of the Imperial General Staff would be most desirable. I would request you to fix the date for the meeting at your convenience, depending on how you finish your business in Cairo and with the knowledge that there will be no objection on my part as to the date.' Next day Churchill informed Stalin: 'I will certainly come to Moscow to meet you, and will fix the date from Cairo.'

Churchill flew into Moscow on 2 August and met Stalin that evening. In the eyes of observers, Churchill appeared agitated while Stalin was calm. Churchill explained that he was overjoyed to be in the 'heroic city' of Moscow. Stalin, recalls an observer, seemed to size up Churchill at a glance, thinking possibly: 'So this is he – a pillar of the British Tories!'

Stalin told his British guest that Hitler's armies were advancing in the direction of Baku and Stalingrad, in some places punching gaps in the lines of the Red Army. Hitler, said Stalin, had apparently pulled in almost all the tanks and troops he had in Europe and put them into a single fist on the Russian front.

Churchill listened. A few minutes later he delivered the most unpleasant news of all; a second front would not be opened in 1942, but another front would be opened, not in France but in North Africa.

The following day Stalin handed him a carefully worded *aide-mémoire* which began:

'As a result of the exchange of views in Moscow on 12 August, I have established that Mr Churchill, the British Prime Minister, considers it impossible to open a second front in Europe in 1942.

'It will be recalled that the decision to open a second front in Europe in 1941 was reached at the time of Molotov's visit to London, and found expression in the agreed Anglo–Soviet Communiqué released on 12 June last.

'It will be recalled further that the opening of a second front in Europe was designed to divert German forces from the Eastern Front to the West, to set up in the west a major centre of resistance to the German Fascist forces and thereby ease the position of the Soviet troops on the Soviet–German front in 1942.

'Needless to say, the Soviet High Command, in planning its summer and autumn operations, counted on a second front being opened in Europe in 1942.

'It will be readily understood that the British Government's refusal to open a second front in Europe in 1942 delivers a moral blow to Soviet public opinion, which had hoped that the second front would be opened, complicates the position of the Red Army at the front and injures the plans of the Soviet High Command.

'I say nothing of the fact that the difficulties in which the Red Army is involved through the refusal to open a second front in 1942 are bound to impair the military position of Britain and the other Allies.

'I and my colleagues believe that the year 1942 offers the most favourable conditions for a second front in Europe, seeing that nearly all the German forces – and their crack troops, too – are tied down on the Eastern Front, while only negligible forces, and the poorest, too, are left in Europe. It is hard to say whether 1943 will offer as favourable conditions for opening a second front as 1942. For this reason we think that it is possible and necessary to open a second front in Europe in 1942. Unfortunately I did not succeed in convincing the British Prime Minister of this, while Mr Harriman, the US President's representative at the Moscow talks, fully supported the Prime Minister. J. STALIN'

At this time Stalin received a message from President Roosevelt acknowledging the huge efforts Russia was making against the common enemy. The President said: 'The fact that the Soviet Union is bearing the brunt of the fighting and losses during the year 1942 is well understood by the United States and I may state that we greatly admire the magnificent resistance which your country has exhibited. We are coming as quickly and as strongly to your assistance as we possibly can and I hope that you will believe me when I tell you this.'

In his reply to Stalin's *aide-mémoire*, Churchill was defensive in addressing each point. He denied that a promise had been broken and then mentioned that another operation would be mounted, namely 'Torch' [the Allied landings in North Africa].

'1. The best second front in 1942, and the only large-scale operation possible from the Atlantic, is "Torch". If this can be effected in October it will give more aid to Russia than any other plan. It also prepares the way for 1943 and has the four advantages mentioned by Premier Stalin in the conversation of August 12th. The British and United States Governments have made up their minds about this and all preparations are proceeding with the utmost speed.

'2. Compared with "Torch", the attack with 6 or 8 Anglo–American Divisions on the Cherbourg Peninsula and the Channel Islands would be a hazardous and futile operation [Hitler had seized the Channel Islands on 30 June/1 July 1940]. The Germans have enough troops in the west to block us in this narrow peninsula with fortified lines, and would concentrate all their air forces in the west upon it. In the opinion of all the British Naval, Military and Air authorities the operation could only end in disaster. Even if the lodgement were made, it would not bring a single division back from Russia. It would also be far more a running sore for us than for the enemy, and would use up wastefully and wantonly the key men and the landing-craft required for real action in 1943. This is our settled view. The Chief of the Imperial General Staff will go into details with the Russian Commanders to any extent that may be desired.

'3. No promise has been broken by Great Britain or the United States. I point to paragraph 5 of my aide-mémoire given to Mr Molotov on 10 June 1942, which distinctly says: "We can, therefore, give no promise." This aide-mémoire followed upon lengthy conversations, in which the very small chance of such a plan being adopted was made abundantly clear. Several of these conversations are on record [Paragraph 5 of the aide-mémoire mentioned by Churchill reads: 'We are making preparations for a landing on the Continent in August or September 1942. As already explained, the main limiting factor to the size of the landing force is the availability of special landing-craft]. Clearly, however, it would not further either the Russian cause or that of the Allies as a whole if, for the sake of action at any price, we embarked on some operation which ended in disaster and gave the enemy an opportunity for glorification at our discomfiture. It is impossible to say in advance whether the situation will be such as to make this operation feasible when the time comes. *We can therefore give no promise in the matter*, but provided that it appears sound and sensible we shall not hesitate to put our plans into effect.

'4. However, all the talk about an Anglo–American invasion of France this year has misled the enemy, and has held large air forces and considerable military forces on the French Channel coast. It would be injurious to all common interests, especially Russian interests, if any public controversy arose in which it would be necessary for the British Government to unfold to the nation the crushing argument which they conceive themselves to possess against "Sledgehammer" [code-name for an operation that American and British forces planned to carry out in the Straits of Dover area in 1942]. Widespread discouragement would be caused to the Russian armies who have been buoyed up on this subject, and the enemy would be free to withdraw further forces from the west. The wisest course is to use "Sledgehammer" as a blind for "Torch", and proclaim "Torch" when it begins, as the second front. This is what we ourselves mean to do.

'5. We cannot admit that the conversations with Mr Molotov about the second front, safeguarded as they were by reservations both oral and written, formed any ground for altering the strategic plans of the Russian High Command.

'6. We reaffirm our resolve to aid our Russian allies by every practicable means. W.CH.'

A few weeks later Churchill addressed the House of Commons and spoke highly of his talks with Stalin. Before making his speech he sent a message to Stalin saying that he retained of his visit to Moscow 'the most pleasing memory of all' and closed with the words: 'May God prosper all our undertakings.'

(Stalin, the one-time divinity student, could also invoke religious images. A few years later, in talking to U.S. Senator Claude Pepper about the difficulties of finding a new basis for friendly ties after the war, Stalin invoked the image of Jesus: 'But Christ said, "Seek, and ye shall find"'.)

NB. Although *Tirpitz* never engaged Convoy PQ17, her suspected presence caused the Admiralty to withdraw British warships from the escort and the convoy was left inadequately defended. She remained at anchor in Kaafiord, repeatedly attacked by the RAF and Coastal Command, before being capsized by Lancaster bombers off Tromso on 12 November 1944.

★★★ THE END OF *BLITZKRIEG* ★★★

In the opening weeks of war, General Pavel Kurochkin's army was caught by a German pincer movement near the historic city of Smolensk, on the same rolling fields where Napoleon had lost his legendary invincibility. After intense fighting, 200 miles west of Moscow, Kurochkin and his staff managed to escape encirclement. The General, who was decorated for bravery, and later became a professor of military science, described his journey to Smolensk.

'A few days before the war I was in Siberia, but on 22 June I had arrived in Moscow and assumed command of the 20th Army. Some days later on arriving at my command centre I received unfavourable news: "Borisov has surrendered." A breach had been formed in the most important strategic line between the border and Moscow, known from time immemorial as the "Smolensk Line".

'In those critical circumstances, I placed all the troops retreating from there under my command and moved one division to the

Borisov area to take up defensive positions and prevent enemy tank and mechanised formations from breaking through across the Berezina. We were ordered to hold the positions for at least four days.'

On 23 July 1941 the German High Command issued Directive No. 33 to Army Group Centre: 'Rout the enemy who is continuing to remain in the area between Smolensk and Moscow, advance with your flank as far as possible eastwards and capture Moscow.'

The crucial Battle of Smolensk was a precursor to the decisive Battle of Moscow. Kurochkin continues: 'I was born near Smolensk. And it was unbearable for me to see the flood of refugees along the Minsk–Moscow road and see German aircraft strafing the roads.'

The Russian General's troops at Borisov swore an oath that they would not retreat from Smolensk where many of their ancestors had fought and routed previous invaders. By their determination to resist they managed to hold up the 'shock divisions' of Hitler's army, an army that had until now won easy victories in western Europe.

But danger lurked at the centre of the Soviet–German front, and Kurochkin's 20th Army as well as 16th Army commanded by General M. F. Lukin found themselves in a pocket, completely enveloped by German forces.

In Moscow, Stalin and his aides, discussing the probable moves of Hitler's army, concluded that the Germans would mount an offensive in all three strategic directions, north, central and south. But the main one would be towards Moscow. Stalin therefore ordered his commanders to concentrate on repulsing the *Wehrmacht* in the centre of the Soviet–German front which included the build-up of German forces at Smolensk.

It was no surprise, therefore, that in July–August 1941, one of the biggest battles in the initial period of Plan 'Barbarossa' took place precisely in the Moscow direction. It has gone down in history as the Battle of Smolensk.

Towards the end of June the success of Hitler's armies in the strategic frontier zone caused the Soviet High Command to deploy four armies (19th, 20th, 21st and 22nd) in an echelon along the Dnieper, and 16th Army in the vicinity of Smolensk. The five armies had a double task: to halt the *Blitzkrieg* and prevent the enemy's march on Moscow.

Hitler's Army Group Centre commanded by Field Marshal Fedor von Bock was the strongest group and was given the task of capturing Smolensk and other key cities, thus opening up the shortest route to Moscow. The *Wehrmacht* had a favourable correlation of forces. Its numerical superiority over troops of Russia's Western Front in the Smolensk direction in manpower, artillery and aviation was 2 to 1, and in tanks 4 to 1. On 10 July 2nd and 3rd Panzer Groups began to drive converging wedges from the Dnieper towards Smolensk.

Fierce fighting raged. On the 16th German tanks broke into Smolensk from the south and north. Street fighting took place day and night, Russian units often fighting to the last man. General Heinz Guderian, who was commanding 2nd Panzer Group, wrote that Frederick the Great had been correct when he said, 'Every Russian soldier has to be shot dead twice, and even then he has to be pushed to make him fall.'

Finding himself surrounded, Kurochkin studied the intelligence reports and looked for the best way out of his predicament. 'Encirclement is not quite defeat. True [he wrote later] our situation called for special tactics. It was impossible for us to stay in one place without dependable channels of supply. So we set up a mobile defensive ring which started shifting gradually eastwards. Every German attack received a vigorous counter-attack. We made 25 miles in ten days. That is how we broke out of the encirclement. Our troops were short of artillery shells and cartridges and had practically no fuel or food. But even in these conditions no one lost his composure. Even while encircled we asked for newspapers to be dropped to us. It was just as important for us to know what was going on at the fronts and in the rear as to have an extra cartridge or a dried crust.'

But Russian losses were high: about 100,000 in killed and wounded and an estimated 300,000 were taken prisoner. In 1812, on the same blood-soaked fields, the Russians lost 10,000 men against Napoleon.

Straight away the Germans announced 'the fall of Smolensk', saying that their troops had almost reached Moscow. But this did not tally with an announcement in the British House of Commons, where Winston Churchill read a report which said that Smolensk was still in Russian hands. An indignant Führer said in a radio broadcast: 'I, Adolf Hitler, question the assertion of Winston Churchill and would request the British Premier to question Russian General Lukin, Commander of the 16th Army, who no longer has control of Smolensk.'

When he was informed of this exchange, Lukin told subordinates: 'Send out a radio message on my behalf. Let Hitler and Churchill know that I am in the northern part of Smolensk with my troops and I'm giving the Germans across the Dnieper a hiding. And with my next artillery assault I'll let Hitler and his troops know where I am, all right!' But a few weeks later, in August, superior German units forced the Russians to abandon Smolensk.

Stalin reportedly was uncertain whether to punish or decorate the generals involved. Discussing the matter with him, Marshal S. K. Timoshenko told Stalin: 'I maintain that by the operations of these days we have completely upset the enemy offensive. The seven or eight tank and motorised divisions and the two or three infantry divisions put into action against us have been deprived of offensive capabilities. Kurochkin and Lukin must be commended as heroes.' Both generals were, in fact, given high decorations.

The Battle of Smolensk had taken place on a front more than 500 miles long and up to 200 miles deep. Russian forces, although badly battered, had upset Hitler's plan for a headlong drive on Moscow. For the first time in World War II, German armies were forced to halt their offensive in the main direction and assume defensive positions. Hitler's *Blitzkrieg* had been halted for the first time.

★★★ THE BATTLE FOR MOSCOW ★★★

In 1970, Marshal Georgi K. Zhukov was asked by a local reporter about the physical demands that war makes on a commander. The interview took place at Zhukov's dacha outside Moscow.

Question: Everybody knows that war is a tough business. Would you please tell us, Georgi Konstantinovich, physically how tough was it for you personally as front commander in the Battle of Moscow?

Zhukov: I'll give you the same answer I gave Eisenhower in '45. The Battle of Moscow was equally trying both for the soldier and the army group commander. During the fiercest fighting (from 18 November to 8 December) I managed to get no more than two hours of sleep a day. To keep going somehow and be able to work, I resorted to brief but frequent physical exercise, drank strong coffee and once in a while permitted myself a 15- to 20-minute workout on skis. When a turning-point in the battle was achieved, I fell so fast asleep nobody could wake me. Stalin phoned twice and was told 'Zhukov is sleeping and we can't wake him.'

Hitler called it Operation 'Typhoon'; it was code-named 'Moscow Cannae'; but in most history books it is known as the Battle of Moscow. It lasted from 30 September 1941 to 20 April 1942, and was the first major defeat for Germany in World War II. Up until December 1941 the Red Army had been almost continuously on the losing end, although more than once by its resistance it had slowed Hitler's 'timetable'.

The Battle of Moscow took place on a front more than 500 miles long and more than 300 miles deep. Together, the two sides fielded a total of 3,000,000 men.

At the end of September, Germany's Army Group Centre consisted of three field armies of which fourteen were panzer and eight were motorised divisions. All told, it had 1,800,000 men, more than 14,000 field guns and mortars, 1,700 tanks and 1,390 aircraft. Its target was the city of Moscow.

Danger confronted Moscow in the early days of October when German tanks were sighted on the city's approaches. There were reports of panic in the city. Stalin recalled Zhukov from Leningrad (the military situation there was also grim) and put him in command of the Western Front. Zhukov's experience and iron will, Stalin hoped, would stabilise the front near Moscow.

On 7 November Stalin surprised the world when the Revolution Day military parade in Red Square took place as usual The participating army units marched straight from the parade ground to the front lines. Meanwhile Stalin dug into GHQ reserves and, within a week, fourteen new rifle divisions, sixteen tank brigades and more than 40 artillery regiments arrived to bolster Zhukov's Western Front.

As German armies closed on Moscow, Stalin created one more defence line almost on the capital's doorstep. About 450,000 residents from Moscow and nearby areas hurriedly built fortifications for the Moscow Defence Zone (MDZ). In Moscow, anti-tank obstacles dotted the streets and squares. At this point, German commanders asked Hitler to give their armies a breathing-space. They now faced a new problem: temperatures had dipped below the freezing mark. No preparations had been made for a winter campaign and German soldiers were freezing to death in their summer clothing. Tanks and trucks were immobilised. But the Führer ordered the troops not to halt their advance. From Berlin, Hitler had taken personal command of the armed forces which, say some experts, was detrimental at times to the smooth running of the army.

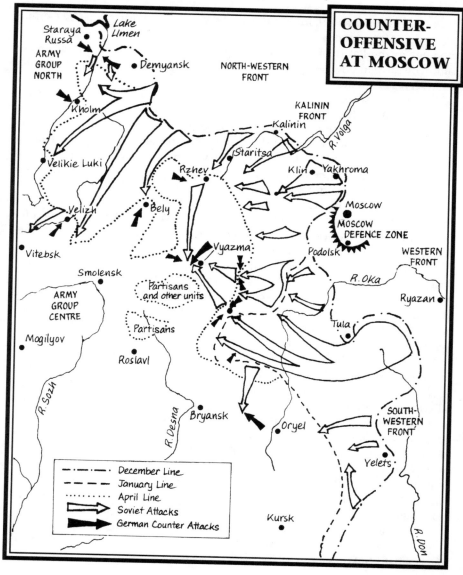

COUNTER-OFFENSIVE AT MOSCOW

- —·—·— December Line
- — — — January Line
- ·········· April Line
- ⇨ Soviet Attacks
- ⬛▶ German Counter Attacks

On 5 December Stalin ordered a powerful counter-offensive and the German forces, suffering heavy blows, retreated. On the 7th General Franz Halder made this diary entry: 'The events of today have been most terrible and disgraceful.'

On 18 December, after ten days of fighting, Zhukov's troops broke through German defence lines, recapturing a number of key towns and villages. The danger to Moscow and its industrial area was eliminated. During the fighting the Soviet troops hurled the enemy back 70 to 200 miles. According to military historian General Pavel Zhilin, German losses totalled 500,000 men, 1,300 tanks and 2,500 guns.

Hitler's Directive 39, in response to the counter-offensive, ordered German troops to adopt a strategic defence all along the Eastern Front. It was a decisive moment in the Battle of Moscow. After the war Field Marshal Wilhelm Keitel said: 'The Russian offensive was most unexpected. We had grossly miscalculated the reserves of the Red Army.'

Hitler was so enraged by the defeat at Moscow that he took reprisals against the German Army leadership. Thirty-five generals were dismissed from their posts, some even being court-martialled. Such a 'pogrom of generals' had not been seen since World War I, according to British military historian J. F. C. Fuller. The Battle of Moscow was Stalin's first significant victory, won at a critical moment. Experts say that it was the beginning of a 'vital turning-point' in the war.

Some German commanders say that their armies waited too long before resuming the offensive. Given other circumstances, they say, they might have taken the Russian capital. Could Hitler's armies have taken Moscow? Not a few German generals say yes. They blame such factors as 'General Winter' for their defeat. Hitler's erroneous decisions are also cited.

When I asked Averell Harriman about this period in the war, the former US Ambassador to Moscow said: 'Stalin told me that the Germans had made a great mistake. They tried a three-pronged drive, remember, one at Leningrad, one at Moscow and one in the south. Stalin said that If they had concentrated on the drive towards Moscow they could have taken Moscow; and Moscow was the nerve centre of the Soviet Union and this would have broken that nerve centre and it would have been very difficult to conduct a major operation if Moscow had been lost. He said the Germans had made that kind of mistake in World War I – by not going to Paris. So Stalin said they were going to hold Moscow at all costs. And Stalin gave us details of his plans and I made up my mind they would be able to do it and reported this to President Roosevelt. That was not the general view. Our military attaché was quite positive that it was only a matter of a few days before the Germans would be in Moscow. And that was the view of all our military attachés. This was no particular wisdom on my part, but Beaverbrook [Lord Beaverbrook, Churchill's special agent, accompanied Harriman to Moscow in 1941] and I did have an opportunity to hear Stalin explain his programme; and we accepted it.'

As to whether German armies could have taken Moscow in 1941, Stalin's generals have a different view from their German counterparts. Here, for example, is what Zhukov said in 1970:

'German troops failed to take Moscow by a *coup de main* in August, as some of their generals had intended. In case of an offensive they would have found themselves in a more tight situation than near Moscow in November–December of 1941. You see, Army Group Centre would have come up against the stiff resistance of Soviet troops directly on the approaches to the capital, and besides a strong counter-blow from our troops in the South-Western direction could have been inflicted as well. That is why all attempts of German generals and some Western war historians to place the blame for the defeat near Moscow on Hitler alone are just as groundless as the entire German strategy.'

The Russian historian-diplomat, Dr. Valentin Falin, calls the Battle of Moscow 'the most important battle of World War II'. Falin, who is also a party functionary, says that after that battle the 'qualitative parameters' that Hitler's armies had enjoyed before the invasion were never restored, the tactics of *Blitzkrieg* were over and done with. After this, Germany waged war to 'save its skin', not to dominate Russia. Also, after the victory at Moscow the world no longer believed in the invincibility of Hitler's armies.

Asked at the Nuremberg War Crimes Tribunal when it was that he began to realise that Plan 'Barbarossa' was failing, Field Marshal Wilhelm Keitel, Chief of Staff of the German High Command, gave one word: 'Moscow'. This first major defeat for Hitler's armies took place 180 days after Hitler had unleashed his *Blitzkrieg*.

★★★ THE BATTLE OF STALINGRAD ★★★

In the next major battle, Stalin's image as war commander soared. This was the battle of Stalingrad whose echoes reverberated around the globe.

It is hard to measure the far-reaching importance of this battle. The defeat and surrender of a large German force and capture of a German field marshal raised the prestige of the Red Army; and, for the first time, the world began to look upon Russia as a formidable Allied power. Stalingrad drastically changed the world's strategic–military situation.

The victory caused jubilation in many countries. In China, Mao Tse-tung, buoyed by this important triumph on the Volga, said: 'This is not only the turning-point in the war against Fascism–Nazism but the turning-point in the entire history of mankind.' Mao saw the victory as helping China's war effort and, thereby, hurting the Japanese invaders.

The West warmly saluted the victory. Prime Minister Churchill called the triumph at Stalingrad 'a wonderful achievement' and President Roosevelt said that it 'stemmed the tide of invasion' and was the 'turning-point' in the war. At the Tehran Conference in late 1943, Churchill presented as a gift from King George VI to the defenders of Stalingrad a Sword of Honour. Stalin put the sword to his lips and kissed it.

(But memories fade. Ten years after Stalingrad, the victory that was once hailed throughout the democratic world was now seen in some political and academic sectors as a disaster. US Senator Joseph McCarthy said in a book published in 1952: 'It can, I believe, be safely stated that World War III started with the Russian victory at Stalingrad.' Walter Rostow, a US economics professor and government official, claimed in 1960 that the Cold War could be dated from the time it became clear that the Russians would hold Stalingrad, that is, roughly from the beginning of 1943.)

Founded on the Volga in the 16th century, Stalingrad became an important industrial centre with a population of 600,00 in the 1930s, and was a key communications junction linking the central regions of European Russia with the Caucasus. Baku oil for the defence industries in the Urals was transported along the Volga. Hitler was determined to capture the eponymous city at all costs because of its far-reaching strategic significance. By holding the Stalingrad region Stalin's armies could at any moment strike in the rear of Hitler's forces in the Caucasus.

The German High Command knew that unless they captured Stalingrad they could never possess the entire Caucasus region. And the Caucasus meant oil for German industry; the possibility of linking up with Turkish forces and cutting off the Trans-Iranian Railway along which Moscow maintained overland connections with its British and American allies; and the heady prospect of being able to advance into Iraq, Iran and India.

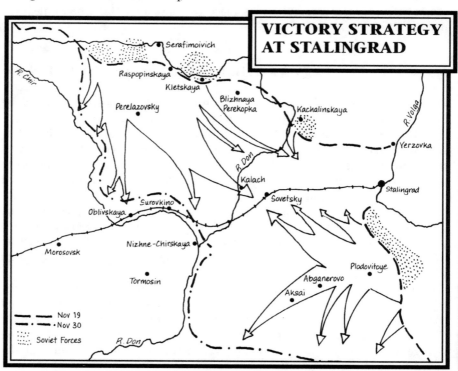

The battle on the Volga lasted more than six months, from 17 July 1942 to 2 February 1943, and covered an area of nearly 80,000 square miles, the length of the front extending up to 600 miles. At times more than two million men were engaged.

Hitler's troops began their 'decisive offensive' of the 1942 campaign at the end of June. A few days before the attack the Führer assured his generals that Russian resistance would be negligible. But Stalin, who had helped defend the city during the Civil War (it was known then as Tsaritsyn), had seen the danger of a breakthrough along a broad front to the Volga and the Caucasus, and held nothing back. By comparison with defensive engagements of 1941, the defence of Stalingrad was characterised by greater troop mobility, stability of positions and the greater skill of Stalin's generals.

Stalin was in constant touch with his commanders, often conferring with his deputy Zhukov, and Vasilevsky of the General Staff. At critical moments in the battle he sent them to the front to work out details of operations on the spot. In July strong German forces drove a wedge into the right flank of the 62nd Army. Stalin demanded that the Front Commander eliminate the wedge: 'You have the strength for this and you must do it. I categorically forbid any withdrawal from the indicated line of defence.'

On 25 July, after German units had broken through in several sectors, Stalin ordered Vasilevsky to issue a stern directive to the Front: 'The actions of the Stalingrad Front are evoking indignation at the General Headquarters of the Supreme Command.' A few days later Stalin issued what some generals consider the most important document of the war, No. 227. Stalin dictated its basic paragraphs which said that troops must hold their positions under all conditions. It contained the memorable phrase 'not a step back' – which is said to have inspired officers and men alike, but which, after the war, elicited adverse comment from critics. The order, they said, was too harsh and caused unnecessary casualties.

On 7 September Stalin asked Zhukov and Vasilevsky whether their forces were strong enough to defeat the German armies at Stalingrad. They replied: 'The forces that the two Fronts have at Stalingrad are obviously not sufficient for the complete defeat of the enemy. An additional group must be concentrated so that a harder blow can be struck at the enemy as soon as possible.' Dramatic events were being prepared that would change the shape of the war.

On 9 September the Supreme Commander expressed dissatisfaction over the failure of his armies to advance north of Stalingrad and concern over the worsening situation in the city itself. An offensive was tried but without success. Then, on the 12th, Stalin agreed with plans drawn up by Zhukov and Vasilevsky to choke off the German spearhead on the Volga. The spur to victory was to be a counter-attack on the southern flank of the Russo–German front.

By mid-September German forces at Stalingrad could no longer attack – had in fact been halted. Meanwhile, in far-off Siberia and Central Asia, the formation of massive GHQ reserves was nearing completion, including large tank units that would be a decisive factor.

At the beginning of October bitter street battles were raging in Stalingrad with widespread house-to-house fighting. The German General Friedrich Paulus massed his large infantry and tank forces near the city's sprawling tractor works. On 4 October troops of Russia's 37th Guards Division under General Viktor G. Zholudev arrived there. An official history says that on 14 October German troops made 2,000 sorties against positions held by Zholudev's men. During the second half of the day the three-mile front of the division was attacked by several German infantry divisions using some 200 tanks as battering-rams. Zholudev's troops dug in and received reinforcements. The official history says that those German troops who broke into the tractor works and reached the banks of the Volga were dealt with by individual 'shock teams' and not one of them lived to tell the tale. On that day, General Vassily Chuikov, one of the heroes of Stalingrad, remarked: 'Paulus has petered out. He will never be in a position to muster enough forces to repeat a blow of such might.'

By a coincidence, while Stalin was suggesting the launching of a powerful counter-offensive, Hitler and his generals were conferring at the same time; Hitler claiming that the Russians were on the verge of exhaustion and no longer capable of broad strategic operations. But on 24 December the counter-offensive began.

The Russians quickly breached the German defences and advanced 20 to 30 miles, trapping the enemy in a giant pocket. On New Year's Eve the outer front of the encirclement was 150 to 200 miles west of Stalingrad. The surrounded Germans totalled about 250,000 officers and men, 300 tanks and assault guns, more than 4,000 field guns and 100 combat aircraft. Inside the ring the Germans tried in vain to set up an effective defence.

The task of destroying them was assigned to troops of the Don Front under General K. K. Rokossovsky who had at his disposal seven armies with up to forty divisions. Hitler meanwhile demanded that the troops of General Paulus's Sixth Army fight to the last cartridge.

Unsuccessful efforts were made to extricate the army, and a rescue attempt by von Manstein from the south-west also failed. On 31 January 1943 Paulus received a telegram informing him that Hitler had promoted him to the rank of field marshal. Said Paulus: 'This, evidently, means an order for suicide. However, I shall not give him such a pleasure.'

After having refused several demands from Rokossovsky to stop fighting, Sixth Army's Commander finally declared his readiness to end hostilities. In the evening of 31 January Paulus and his staff officers arrived at Rokossovsky's headquarters to agree on surrender terms. In all, 92,000 men were taken prisoner including 24 generals. It was the first time a German field marshal had been taken prisoner.

In Germany there was mourning. One German general, Siegfried von Westphal, commented: 'Never before in Germany's history had so large a body of troops come to so dreadful an end.'

Commenting on the victory, US General Douglas MacArthur, a student of military history, said: 'During my lifetime I have participated in a number of wars and have witnessed others, as well as studying in great detail the campaigns of outstanding leaders of the past. In none have I observed such effective resistance to the heaviest blows of a hitherto undefeated enemy, followed by a smashing counter-attack which is driving the enemy back to his own land. The scale and grandeur of the effort mark it as the greatest military achievement in history.'

After Stalingrad, German General Hans Doerr, who had fought in that battle, had a new regard for Moscow's strength. He says in his memoir that at the historic Battle of Poltava (1709), which resulted in a complete defeat of a Swedish army, Russia won the right to be called a great European power. At Stalingrad, the world saw Russia turning into 'one of the two greatest powers'.

Battlefield casualty figures vary. Official Soviet sources have in the past said that the total losses at Stalingrad for Germany and her Axis partners in killed, wounded, missing and taken prisoner totalled more than one million officers and men, approximately 25 per cent of all German troops operating on the Eastern Front. German losses included 3,000 tanks, almost 4,400 aircraft and more than 12,000 artillery pieces. Russian losses in manpower were similarly high. (But in 1992 a member of the Russian Institute of Military History said that the Red Army had lost 1.1 million men and the Germans, fewer, about 800,000.)

The extreme brutality of the fighting and the enforced discipline is shown by a harrowing statistic. At Stalingrad, according to a recently released Russian Defence Ministry document, 13,500 Russian soldiers were executed for desertion.

The extent of the physical destruction at Stalingrad can hardly be imagined. One Western scientist, Dr. Philip Morrison, estimated that to equal the damage the German armies inflicted on Stalingrad and the surrounding cities and villages would take more than a hundred atomic bombs of the type that levelled Hiroshima.

On 15 March 1995 the Russian State Duma, or Parliament, rejected a Communist proposal to restore the name of Stalingrad to the city (it had been renamed Volgograd after Premier Nikita Khrushchev denounced Stalin in 1956 for his repressive rule).

★★★ THE BATTLE OF KURSK ★★★

Some historians refer to the Battle of Kursk as 'the Waterloo of German Fascism'. One Western military expert calls it a 'titanic battle of modern war'. For Stalin, it was one of the most important victories of the war.

At Kursk there occurred another gigantic clash of armies. Each side committed an army more than a million strong. In no other battle of World War II were more tanks, guns, mortars and aircraft engaged. The Kursk battle was noteworthy for the complete defeat of German tank formations. One titanic duel on 12 July involved a combined total of at least 1,200 tanks. Hitler never recovered from his defeat at Kursk.

For this battle Stalin and his generals chose a strategy of waiting for the Germans to attack, stopping them short and then launching a powerful counter-offensive. Russian military experts say that the Battle of Kursk broke the back-bone of Hitler's Germany. After the battle, the German High Command failed to regain the strategic initiative and was forced to assume the defensive on all fronts.

Hitler's generals based their plans for Operation 'Citadel' on the particular situation that had arisen at Kursk as a result of battles in the region during the winter of 1942/3. The front line had assumed contours which have gone down in history as the 'Kursk Bulge' – or 'Kursk Salient'. This was a huge area of 65,000 square kilometres and was held by Stalin's troops. Both in the north and south of the bulge were two wedges held by powerful German forces.

Wehrmacht generals were eager to exploit the situation and launch pincer attacks at the base of the salient, using the element of surprise. After their antic-ipated victory, they hoped to advance on Moscow and Leningrad.

The main Soviet defences were commanded by Generals Rokossovsky and N. F. Vatutin. Other Russian commanders included I. S. Konev, A. I. Eremenko and R. J. Malinovsky. The key commanders on the German side were Erich von Manstein and Günther von Kluge.

Although the Germans intended their attack to commence on 5 July, the battle began in an unexpected fashion. At 2.30 a.m. on that day, German troops concentrated in the assembly areas for the assault were suddenly struck by a hail of Russian artillery fire. Having learned the day and hour of the enemy opera-tion, the Soviet forces unleashed an artillery bombardment that delayed the attack up to three hours. Hitler's troops had lost the element of surprise.

The main attack forces numbered more than 400,000 officers and men with about 6,000 guns and mortars and more than 1,000 tanks and assault guns. Large formations of bombers flew over in successive waves. Hundreds of aircraft filled the sky at all times.

The Russian forces met the advance with heavy fire from artillery and anti-tank rifles, grenades and incendiary bottles, known as 'Molotov cocktails'. The German pincers, slowed by minefields and fierce resistance, advanced less than ten miles.

On the evening General Rokossovsky, Commander of the Central Front, who had won fame in the battles of Moscow

NAZI
ATTACK
FOILED
AT
KURSK

and Stalingrad, decided to deliver a counter-blow at the main attack force the following morning to weaken the enemy's pressure. The counter-attack was executed under difficult conditions, in a very short period of time, on heavily mined ground and under harassment from German aircraft. After two hours of fierce fighting the Russian troops managed to push the Germans back a short distance to the north.

On July 7 and 8 Hitler's armies tried to break through the Soviet defences on the northern flank of the Kursk Salient, but the attempts failed. Crippling losses were sapping German strength. Fighting was also strenuous on the southern flank of the salient with little success for German commanders.

The Battle of Kursk lasted almost two months. A Russian Defence Ministry report says that from the beginning of the battle until the end, a total of 6,000 tanks and self-propelled guns saw action at Kursk, many of them at Prokhorovka. This unprecedented clash of armour and fire from self-propelled guns lasted for weeks. Aerial combat was also fierce.

A key role in the frustrating of 'Citadel' had been played by tens of thousands of civilians who built trenches and other fortifications. The Russian military historian Dr. Leonid Yeremeyev says that the total length of trenches dug at the Kursk Bulge 'equalled the distance from San Francisco to Washington to Montreal'.

On 9 July the Germans were compelled to halt the offensive and regroup for a new attack. The offensive was renewed next day but again without success. But the entire situation in the Kursk Salient was soon to be rapidly changed. Two Russian reserve armies had been brought up close to the rear of the front line to prepare for a counter-offensive.

Stalin, who was directing the day-to-day operations of the fronts, was now asked his view on the exact moment for launching the counter-offensive. He replied:

'Let the Fronts decide that themselves, depending on the situation that has developed. The General Staff is responsible only for seeing that co-ordination does not break down, and that there is no long pause during which the enemy can consolidate on the lines they have reached. It is also very important to throw in the GHQ reserves at the right moment.'

The counter-offensive began 72 hours later (on 12 July) with artillery preparation lasting two hours and 45 minutes. After this 'softening-up' barrage against the German front lines, artillery fire was shifted to the depth of the enemy's defences. This was followed by an infantry and tank attack Despite fierce German resistance, the offensive was successful, and the Russians took 25,000 prisoners as they surged westwards.

This day also saw the greatest tank battle of the war near Prokhorovka, about 70 miles south of Kursk. This ferocious clash of armour has been vividly described by Chief Marshal of the Armoured Forces, Amazasp Babadzhanyan:

'In a few hours hundreds of tanks were turned into scrap. The earth groaned from exploding shells and bombs and from the roar of the tanks. There were several hundred aircraft overhead all the time. Fierce air battles were being fought. The clouds of black dust raised by the tanks, bursting shells and bombs, and the black smoke rising from the burning tanks and vehicles turned the soil and sky a grim grey colour. The horizon disappeared. The sun too was dimmed. Its red disk could hardly be seen through the murk.'

During the battle, Russian tanks from the Fifth Guards Tank Army under General Pavel Rotmistrov drove full speed into the German attack formations, and the units of both sides were now intermingled. At close quarters the German 'Tiger' tanks could not use the advantages of their armament and were put out of action by the Red Army's T-34 medium tanks, the appearance of hundreds of which came as a surprise to the Germans. At Prokhorovka the Germans lost about 400 tanks and sustained heavy losses in manpower. German historian Walter Görlitz has written of the battle that the last units capable of offensive operations had 'burned to a cinder'.

During the Battle of Kursk a group of French pilots belonging to the 'Normandie-Niemen Regiment' fought their first engagements against the Luftwaffe, shooting down more than 30 German aircraft in July and August.

Both sides suffered heavily at Kursk. In 50 days, says an official Soviet history, the Germans lost 3,700 aircraft. Stalin's air force is said to have won strategic superiority at Kursk. In addition, Hitler's armies lost more than 500,000 officers and men, 3,000 guns and 1,500 tanks. Russian losses were also heavy, reportedly close to the German figures.

The Russian commander of an artillery battery no doubt expressed the truth when he said of his fellow soldiers, 'They conquered death by death.'

An important event occurred while the Kursk Battle was raging: Anglo–American forces invaded Sicily. Russian historians deny claims that the landing in Sicily in July 1943 influenced the course of the Battle of Kursk. They say that, on the contrary, it was the fierce fighting in the Kursk Bulge that prevented Hitler from reinforcing his army in Sicily and thereby contributed to the success of the Allied campaign. According to Russian military historian General Pavel Zhilin, nine Italian and two German divisions were defending Sicily when the Anglo–American troops landed, while on the same day in the Kursk Bulge 50 German divisions were in action.

Despite the importance of the Battle of Kursk, considered by many experts as one of the greatest land battles ever fought, some Russian historians claim the battle is slighted in the West. An official Russian history of the war laments the fact that General Dwight D. Eisenhower's war memoirs, *Crusade in Europe*, 'has not one word' about the historic Kursk battle. Eisenhower's grandson, David, supports this view. In a book about the Supreme Allied Commander in Europe, David Eisenhower says an important omission in his grandfather's memoirs was the vital bearing on his thinking and actions of the Russo–German War on the Eastern Front. The Russians say that to under-estimate the interdependence of

Stalin acknowledges spectators at a military exercise. (HAA)

Above: Tsar Nicholas II reviewing his troops at the beginning of World War I. (HAA)

Below: Georgi Malenkov, a member of the State Defence Committee, 1941–5, became Prime Minister after Stalin's death in 1953; and Lavrenti Beria, Commissar for Internal Affairs and Chief of Security during the war and until Stalin's death. (HAA)

Right: From left to right: Lazar Kaganovich; Stalin; Vyachlesav Molotov, Deputy Chairman of the State Defence Committee and Foreign Minister during the war, taking a stroll on 1 May 1939. (HAA)

Below: From left to right: Anastas Mikoyan, a deputy Prime Minister and member of Stalin's 'inner circle'; Joseph Stalin; Lazar Kaganovich, a member of the State Defence Committee and Minister for Transport during the war, watching air force manoeuvres on Army Day 1939. (Hermann Axelbank Archives)

Left: German prisoners of war at Stalingrad early in 1943. (HAA)

Left: German soldiers surrendering in Russia. (HAA)

Left: German prisoners in Moscow in the summer of 1944. (HAA)

Right: German prisoners in Moscow in the summer of 1944. (HAA)

Right: A German officer in custody in Russia. (HAA)

Right: The grim, apprehensive expressions on the faces of German captives. (HAA)

Left: A column of German prisoners weaving its way through a Moscow street in the autumn of 1944. (HAA)

Lower left: Churchill flanked by Anthony Eden, is toasted by Stalin while celebrating his 69th birthday in the drawing-room of the British Legation in Tehran. President Roosevelt was also present. (IWM A 20731)

Below: A portrait of Stalin in 1944. (IWM HU 57225)

Above: Stalin with President Roosevelt at the Tehran Conference. (IWM NYP 10913)

Below: Stalin arrives for a dinner-party with Churchill and President Truman on 23 July 1945. (IWM BU 9292)

the Eastern and Western Fronts was to overlook the fact that without a resurgent Russian front, including a simultaneous offensive by the Red Army at the time of the Allied invasion of France in June 1944, this invasion of Europe might have been impossible, or might not have been undertaken at that time.

In any case, Stalin's successes at Stalingrad and Kursk in 1943 had created a new military-political reality. At the same time, Stalin did not fail to salute American and British successes against Italy and Japan. Partly as a consequence of Stalin's victories at Stalingrad and Kursk – and his continued daily involvement in Red Army strategy – Roosevelt and Churchill agreed to hold a summit close to Russia (in Tehran) at the end of 1943.

★★★ OPERATION 'BAGRATION' ★★★

As Stalin had promised at the Tehran Conference at the end of 1943, the Red Army launched a powerful offensive timed to coincide with the Allied landing in France. On 23 June, when the battles for Cherbourg and Caen – in northern France – were still going on, Stalin's armies began Operation 'Bagration' in Belorussia. In many Western history books and some encyclopedias this battle is ignored, but it dwarfs almost every other battle of World War II and was to prove more devastating than anything the Germans had so far experienced.

Siegfried von Westphal, one of Hitler's leading generals, wrote of Operation 'Bagration': 'During the summer and autumn of 1944, the German armies suffered the greatest disaster of their history which even surpassed the catastrophe of Stalingrad ... Only scattered remnants of thirty divisions escaped death or Soviet captivity.' (*Fatal Decisions*, London. 1965)

The German historian, Paul Carell, writing about 'Bagration', asks: 'Who in 1941 would have thought it possible that the proud armies of Army Group Centre [the spearhead of Operation 'Barbarossa' with two panzer groups and three powerful infantry armies] would suffer the greatest disaster in military history within a mere three years, a battle of annihilation, a Cannae without parallel?' [At the Battle of Cannae in 216 BC. the Roman legions of Terentius Varro were wiped out by a Carthaginian army commanded by Hannibal.]

At the time of 'Bagration', Hitler had twin objectives in mind: to put up a stiff resistance; and try to derail the 'unnatural' Anglo–American alliance with Moscow. Stalin had one central aim: to drive the invader from Belorussian soil. Hitler was unable to break the alliance, but his troops resisted fiercely.

Behind artificial obstacles built by the Germans in Belorussia were deep firing and communications trenches, open machine-gun emplacements and dugouts, and many mortar and gun-firing positions. The German High Command had created a very strong, well-organised system with several defence lines and zones extending to a depth of more than 200 miles. The defences were erected along the western banks of important rivers such as the Dnieper, Drut and Berezina, with their broad, swampy flood plains.

The German commanders hoped that the wooded and swampy terrain interspersed by lakes would significantly help their defence and hinder Russian manoeuvrability, forcing the Russians to attack along the roads where powerful positions had been set up. Vitebsk, Orsha, Mogilev and Rogachev were turned into major strong-holds reinforced with systems of trenches, pill-boxes and block-houses.

Operation 'Bagration' began on Friday, 23 June 1944 on the fields of Belorussia (White Russia) and lasted 67 days and nights. This campaign was one of the largest offensive operations of the war and fundamentally changed the strategic situation on the entire Eastern Front. After 'Bagration', the next most important objective was Berlin. 'Bagration' was also one of the most outstanding encirclement operations of World War II, came close to knocking out Hitler's once 'invincible' war machine.

Stalin was active in the original planning of this operation that would require the closest co-operation between adjoining Fronts. He himself had named the operation after Pyotr Bagration, a general who came from a noble Georgian family and died a heroic death while engaged against Napoleon's army in 1812.

To defend the Belorussian salient, the German High Command had 63 divisions and three infantry brigades, totalling 1,200,000 men. They were equipped with 900 tanks and assault guns and 9,500 field guns and mortars. At their disposal were 1,350 combat aircraft.

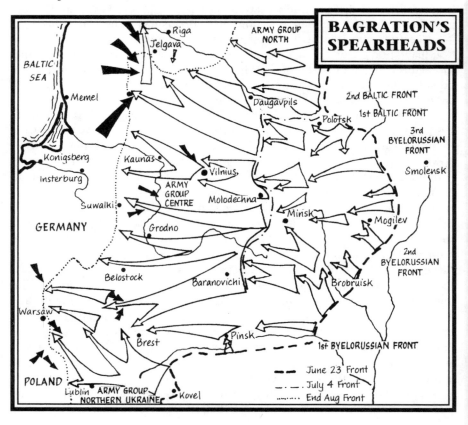

On battle alert for Stalin were 2,400,000 men, 36,000 guns and mortars, 5,200 tanks and self-propelled guns and 5,300 combat aircraft. So the Russians were superior in manpower and weapons.

The principal Russian commanders were Marshals Zhukov, Vasilevsky and Rokossovsky, Marshal of Artillery Voronov, and Generals Ivan Bagramyan, Pavel Batov, Alexei Antonov and Ivan Chernyakovsky. The German commanders included some of Hitler's best generals: Field Marshal Ernst von Busch, Field Marshal Walther Model, Colonel-General Hans Reinhardt and General Werner von Tippelskirch.

On 12 April 1944, Stalin had instructed the General Staff to work out a master plan for a strategic offensive operation in Belorussia, and to start deploying troops and *matériel*. The immediate aim was to liquidate the large 'Belorussian salient' and to do this it would be necessary to rout the major forces of Army Group Centre. In the process, Belorussia and its capital, Minsk, would be cleared of Hitler's armies.

Later, after destroying the enemy's reserves, the task of the Russian armies was to create conditions for new offensive operations in the eastern areas of the Ukraine, the Baltic area, East Prussia and Poland. These operations would 'open the road' to Berlin.

The Belorussian bulge had developed during the previous winter campaign of the war. At that time, when Hitler's armies on the flanks of the Eastern Front had been crushed, there developed a vast salient in the central sector, the apex of which faced eastward. This bulge was held in a tight grip by the Germans who called it 'the Balcony'. It was of enormous strategic significance to the German High Command because it protected the shortest routes to East Prussia, Warsaw, Berlin and the vital centres of the Third Reich.

By mid-May the planning for 'Bagration' had been completed. From 22 to 24 May the draft plans were discussed in detail at a conference of the GHQ Supreme Command attended by Stalin and the commanders of the respective Fronts. On the first day of the conference an argument broke out between Stalin and Rokossovsky that became known throughout the army.

The tall, highly popular army commander wanted to envelop the German armies in a powerful pincer movement. Stalin and some of his General Staff officers demanded a single offensive thrust. A number of generals including Rokossovsky himself have described the incident.

When Rokossovsky would not agree with him, Stalin ordered the marshal to go to the next room and think over Stavka's [General Headquarters] proposal. After 20 minutes he came back. He said there was nothing for him to think over and he stuck to his view. Again Stalin sent him back to the next room to 'think' for twenty minutes. During this second interval (Rokossovsky calls it 'confinement') Foreign Minister Molotov and Stalin's right-hand man Georgi Malenkov joined him, saying that they disapproved of his quarrel with the Supreme Commander and suggesting that he accept the Stavka proposal. But Rokossovsky replied that he was convinced of the correctness of his view and that if Stavka ordered him to mount an offensive according to its own plan, he would ask to be relieved of his Front command. He returned to the conference room but again failed to convince Stalin and his advisers. So for a third time Stalin asked him to 'think it over' in the next room, alone. But when he returned this time with his mind unchanged, Stalin went along with him. In acceding to Rokossovsky, Stalin said: 'When a commander is so determined he probably knows what is best.'

On 30 May the basic plan for 'Bagration', after some amendments, was approved by Stalin and the next day directives were issued to prepare the Fronts for combat. On 6 June Stalin informed Roosevelt and Churchill: 'The summer offensive of the Soviet troops will begin in mid-June in one of the vital sectors of the front. The general offensive will develop by stages, through consecutive engagement of the armies in offensive operations. Between late June and the end of July the operation will turn into a general offensive.'

At the beginning of the campaign but separate from 'Bagration', the Russians pierced powerful deeply echeloned German defences, then crushed the enemy in southern Karelia and the Karelian Isthmus. By coming up to the state frontier with Finland, the Russians caused that country to withdraw from the war.

Because of the scale and topography of Belorussia, 'Bagration' came up against many difficulties. Hindering the Russians and helping the *Wehrmacht* were the Pripet Marshes, a great natural barrier of forests and swamps, 38,000 square miles in area. At the same time, the closer the Red Army got to Germany the fiercer became German resistance. Distances for the Luftwaffe got shorter, and while German supply lines shortened, those for Stalin's armies lengthened.

Of outstanding importance was the use by the Russians of three cavalry corps – in addition to twenty infantry armies, two tank armies, five air armies, and twelve separate tank and mechanised corps. 'Bagration' saw the last major cavalry attack in World War II, and perhaps for all time.

No previous strike by the Red Army against Hitler's armies had been prepared more carefully.

Here is what Marshal Rokossovsky says: 'Planning was preceded by extensive work in the field, especially on the forward lines. Men learned to swim, cross swamps and rivers by any available means and find their way through woods. They made special "swamp shoes" to cross bogs, and built boats, rafts and platforms for trundling machine-guns, mortars and light artillery. The tankmen also underwent training in the art of marsh warfare. Helped by engineers, the crews provided each tank with anchoring fascines, logs and special triangles for crossing wide ditches.'

And General Shtemenko: 'Before launching the offensive we carried out many training sessions and headquarters practised carrying out the actual task the troops would be called upon to perform in battle. Action by infantry, artillery and tanks was carefully co-ordinated. The infantry learned how to keep advancing just behind the shell bursts of their own artillery, and the gunners how to concentrate or shift their fire in accordance with the movements of infantry and tanks. A real fighting friendship grew up between the various branches of the army.'

In the penetration sectors, there was a dense concentration of firepower: 150 to 204 field guns and mortars per half mile of front line. Much attention was paid to the 'surprise factor', all preparations being carefully concealed from the enemy. Only five members of the top command knew the plans relating to 'Bagration'. All correspondence and discussion by telephone and telegraph were strictly forbidden. New code-names were given to the top commanders: Stalin, Supreme Commander-in-Chief, was called Semyonov, Zhukov became Zharov and Vasilevsky – Vladimirov.

In order to create the subterfuge that the Russians were preparing for defence rather than offence, on 29 May Stalin ordered the several Belorussian Fronts to build three defensive lines up to 25 miles deep. Troops were regrouped 300 to 600 miles away from the concentration areas, with full observance of camouflage and other 'precaution regulations'. Major formations were concentrated in the breakthrough sectors only at night. Dummy field guns and tanks were placed in simulated positions. In the daytime trainloads of dummy tanks and field guns were going from the front to the rear.

As it turned out, many of Hitler's generals failed to determine the direction of the main Russian attack in the summer offensive, although General von Tippelskirch, who was commanding Fourth Army in Army Group Centre, said that he noticed the first signs of a Russian offensive two weeks before it occurred. Top-ranking German generals mistakenly believed the attack would come from a southerly direction.

Alfred Jodl, Operations Chief of the German High Command (OKW), said at the Nuremberg Trials that he thought the blow would come from the direction of the Rumanian oil wells, and OKW Chief of Staff Field Marshal Wilhelm Keitel also thought that the Russians would concentrate their main forces on the southern sector of the front.

Although the German forces did not expect the Red Army to launch an offensive in this sector very soon, they were fully aware of its strategic significance. One year earlier, in August 1943, they had begun to build the 'Eastern Wall'. Some Germans claim that it was much superior to the 'impregnable Atlantic Wall'. Its purpose was to block the Soviet Army's way to the west. The Belorussian 'Balcony', a component of the Wall, was to protect the shortest routes to Germany and secure the Nazi forces' main lines of communication along the whole of the Eastern Front. Their military supplies and troops moved to the front mainly through Belorussia and that was why the Wehrmacht High Command ordered its forces to defend Belorussia – and later Poland – as stoutly as they would defend Germany itself.

On 22 June the Russians carried out a reconnaissance in force along a 300-mile front. As a result, Stalin's headquarters was able to verify data on enemy defences and make necessary corrections to artillery and air strike zones.

In 'Bagration', the partisans were of major help to the regular armies. A German officer, Hermann Gackenholz, has noted: 'The beginning of Army Group Centre's downfall began with the operation launched by 240,000 Belorussian partisans who, within one night (19/20 June) blew up all the railway lines west of Minsk in 10,000 places.' This action is said to have nearly paralysed the German transport network. The partisans were given other concrete tasks, for example, preventing German troops from blowing up industrial plants and bridges.

Launching of the big offensive by four Russian Fronts was announced by thunderous shell explosions in the rear of the German defence lines. Russian General Kuzma Galitsky was an eye-witness:

> 'At exactly 0600 hours we heard the roar of the first salvo of Katyusha rocket-launchers. The air trembled. More than 1,800 guns and mortars of the 11th Guards Army launched a hail of fire at the enemy's defences. Our softening-up bombardment kept to the following pattern: a five-minute attack by all our artillery, a 30-minute pause. Then aimed fire for 85 minutes to destroy enemy covered positions, to be followed by 20 minutes of direct fire to destroy enemy gun emplacements, and finally 40 minutes of fire to neutralise defences in the forward line and immediately behind it in the sector earmarked for penetration and in adjacent areas. To avoid a pause between the end of the bombardment and the start of the attack our batteries began gradually to shift their fire, without diminishing its intensity, only three minutes before the infantry and tanks rushed the enemy positions. This enabled the units carrying out the attack to follow the fire barrage 75 to 100 yards behind the shell-bursts.'

German troops resisted stubbornly. Counter-attacks followed one after another. Bloody battles took place up and down the line. Many positions and inhabited areas changed hands repeatedly. In some sectors of the vast front the enemy was taken completely by surprise. In others the Russians were unable to make full use of air power because of bad weather. In certain areas the Russian forces advanced further than had been originally planned for the first day, in others complications arose. But on the whole resistance was broken and the German defences penetrated.

Having encircled and destroyed large enemy forces, the Russians pursued the Germans and expelled them from the territory of Belorussia, the greater parts of Lithuania and Latvia, and some eastern areas of Poland, getting as far as the Vistula and the border of East Prussia. Forcing the river, they captured two important bridgeheads which would be used as launch sites for the future strategic blow directed at Berlin.

Polish and French units took part in 'Bagration'. The Poles belonged to the 1st Polish Army under General Zygmunt Berling; the French were pilots attached to the Russian 1st Air Army.

Six days after the offensive, the Russians captured the city of Bobruisk and 8,000 prisoners including the commandant of the city, General Hamann, who was included in a list of war criminals by the State Commission for Investigation of Nazi Crimes. On his orders, said the indictment, 'children were forcibly taken from their mothers and sent off as chattels to Germany; and it was he who ordered that children's blood be used for transfusions for wounded German troops'.

Belorussia suffered untold damage. Along the route of the German retreat the Russian soldiers saw only chimneys standing among ruins – and gallows from which were hanging local citizens. In their capture and occupation of Belorussia the Germans had partially or totally destroyed several hundred villages. In the capital city of Minsk 300 factories were destroyed, only a handful remaining. The *Wehrmacht* set the torch to 78 schools, the State Art Gallery, the Ballet and Opera House, and all the city cultural centres and libraries.

By 5 July the main elements of German Fourth Army were cut off and more than 105,000 men encircled. They tried but could not break out of the ring. Elimination of the enemy grouping was done by splitting it up into small isolated pockets.

Some German generals, like Friedrich Wilhelm Muller, commander of 12th Army Corps, ordered their men to stop fighting: 'Our situation has become hopeless. Our best avenues of escape have been cut off. Our units are scattered and in disorder. A tremendous number of wounded have been left behind without any assistance. Therefore I order an immediate end to all resistance.'

General Heinz Traut, commanding 78th Assault Division (he was taken prisoner), said: 'Our defensive front was no longer able to resist the onslaught. It began to roll back under continuous attacks by the Russians who relentlessly mopped up the weakened front-line troops and their reserves.'

When 'Bagration' ended Hitler's forces had lost more than 1,000,000 men, 6,700 tanks, 28,000 field guns and mortars and more than 2,000 combat aircraft. Two Army Groups – Centre and Northern Ukraine – had been routed. Two dozen of Hitler's divisions had been destroyed and many others had lost up to 70 per cent of their manpower.

By the end of the battle German losses on the entire Eastern Front amounted to almost one-third of their original strength. These losses sharply aggravated Hitler's manpower problem. No longer could they be replaced by 'total mobilisation'.

At last Stalin's armies had reached the state frontier, even somewhat beyond. Now they were poised to invade Germany on a broad front and approach Berlin. Operation 'Bagration', which ended on 29 August, was regarded as a complete success. But the story would not be complete without mention of a Polish tragedy: the Warsaw Uprising.

In late summer of 1944 the world heard of the uprising in which more than 20,000 Poles rose in arms against the German occupiers. They had received their instructions from the Polish Government in Exile in London, which appeared to be as opposed to Stalin as it was to Hitler.

Although Russian armies had already entered parts of eastern Poland, the Polish insurgents received no substantial aid from them. Stalin has been accused of holding back on purpose, of being indifferent to the fate of the Poles who without outside help were cruelly suppressed by Hitler's troops.

That the Polish insurgents made a critical error is no longer in doubt. Taking their orders from London, they failed to co-ordinate their uprising with Moscow, which was probably tantamount to suicide. Moscow learned about the uprising after it had started and Stalin dissociated himself and the Soviet Command from it. On 16 August he sent a message to Churchill: 'The Warsaw action is a reckless and fearful gamble, taking a heavy toll of the population. This would not have been the case had Soviet headquarters been informed beforehand about the Warsaw action and had the Poles in London maintained contact with them.'

The approximately 40,000 insurgents went into action with less than 10,000 weapons (including rifles, machine-guns and pistols) and less than five days' supply of ammunition. Nevertheless the fighting lasted two months. To be fair, the Russians did make efforts to assist the Poles. Some aid supplies were airdropped, and small groups of Russian liaison officers were parachuted into Warsaw; most of them lost their lives.

One Russian parachutist who survived, Ivan Kolos, recalls meeting several Polish officers in Warsaw who bluntly told him: 'Our command does not expect aid from Russia. London will assist us.'

Marshal Rokossovsky makes this comment on the tragedy in Warsaw: 'Starting 13 September we had begun to supply the insurgents by air with weapons, ammunition, food and medical supplies. We used Po-2 night bombers. From 13 September to 1 October 1944, Front aircraft flew 4,821 sorties in aid of the insurgents, 2,535 of them with various supplies.'

An official military history published in Moscow says that Russian aircraft parachuted to the Polish insurgents 2,667 submachine-guns and rifles, 41,780 grenades, 3,000,000 rounds of ammunition, 113 tons of rations and about 1,000 pounds of medicines.

But by 18 September it was already too late. During the uprising, American, British and Polish air commanders became involved in a separate Warsaw supply mission from Italian bases, but found that dropping loads from high altitudes was a complete waste because of the small area of the drop zone and high winds that swept the parachutes on to German positions.

Air Marshal Sergei Rudenko, one of the Russian officers involved in helping the Warsaw Poles – he was chief of 16th Air Army – maintained that it was simply not possible for the Red Army to rush effective aid to Warsaw in late August 1944. He said Russian air bases were too far away. He blamed the tragedy on the Polish emigré government in London.

B. H. Liddell Hart, viewing the tragic events, says that it was 'natural' that the Polish underground forces felt that the Russians had deliberately held off. But he points out that, while controversy will remain, the German forces that the Russians had still to confront were powerful enough to cause military factors to outweigh political considerations.

In mid-August, while the Warsaw Uprising was in progress, Russian troops launched unsuccessful actions against German forces in eastern Poland. An official military history published in Moscow says that at the beginning of August the German High Command had brought large forces into action against the 1st Belorussian Front and were putting up serious resistance. It adds that Soviet forces during the course of almost six weeks of continuous fighting suffered heavy losses, with supplies and artillery lagging far behind.

Of some interest in discussing the Warsaw Uprising is the fact that fighting alongside the Russians was the 1st Polish Army under General Berling. The Poles ran into trouble in their attempt to attack Warsaw from a bridgehead along the west bank of the Vistula. The plan failed when three full-strength German divisions, including the crack 'Hermann Göring Division', were moved in to prevent the bridgehead from being expanded.

In the 1980s, declassification of pertinent British documents adds to the evidence that Moscow was not notified in advance of the Warsaw Uprising. A commission appointed by the British General Staff reported on 31 July 1944, on the eve of the uprising: 'It would be politically and militarily unacceptable to undertake any such measures without the approval and co-operation of the Russians.'

A Moscow document, approved by Stalin, stated at that time that no army command in the world, American, British or Russian, could tolerate 'an uprising being organised in a large city ahead of the front lines of its troops without its knowledge and contrary to its operational plans. There is no question that if, before the uprising in Warsaw began, the Soviet command had been asked about the expediency of staging an uprising in Warsaw in early August, it would have argued against.'

When Winston Churchill asked his military staff in August why the Soviet offensive on Warsaw had halted and whether this had been prompted by political considerations, British General Staff officers gave this reply: 'The Germans are making great efforts to hold this nodal point in their communications and they have surrounded and annihilated Russian armoured forces which were advancing on that city.' Russian historian Lev Bezymensky comments: 'You can't help admiring the insight and honesty of these British General Staff officers.'

★★★ THE JASSY–KISHINEV OPERATION ★★★

In the summer of 1944 Stalin's armies were poised to drive a wedge into Rumania and enter the 'powder keg' of the Balkans.

The Jassy–Kishinev Operation required high levels of military strategy and diplomacy. Political relations in the Balkans have long been considered among the most complicated in the world. Before the battle, Stalin offered an armistice to the pro-Hitler regime of General Ion Antonescu. It was rejected. Later there was an uprising in the capital, Bucharest. The Kremlin also had to deal with the problem of royalty: what to do about Rumania's King Michael?

In view of Rumania's political and strategic importance, the Jassy–Kishinev Operation was among the most important campaigns carried out by Stalin's armies in World War II. Also, Russia's allies, particularly the British, were showing a keen interest in the Balkans. Winston Churchill, on a visit to Moscow on 9 October, attempted to 'bargain' post-war spheres of influence with Stalin, pitting Rumania against Yugoslavia. At one of their meetings, Churchill handed 'U.J.' (Churchill referred to Stalin as 'Uncle Joe' in some of his correspondence with Roosevelt) a piece of paper on which he had written figures, suggesting for example that Russia hold a 90 per cent post-war hand in Rumania, and Britain a 90 per cent hand in Yugoslavia. Stalin dismissed the idea and, rather than keep the incriminating scrap of paper offered to him by Churchill handed it back. (Churchill writes in his memoirs that prior to the Allied landing in Sicily he sent a cable to General Harold Alexander imperatively demanding that he prepare his troops for the seizure of the Balkans.)

Rumania was a vital source of supplies for Germany, and Hitler wanted the country defended stoutly. If Stalin's forces could defeat Germany's powerful Army Group South Ukraine in Rumania, it would have vital political, military and economic consequences. As a German satellite, Rumania provided raw materials and manpower. According to official Rumanian and German documents, in the period from 1939 to August 1944 Rumania delivered to Hitler more than 13,000,000 tons of oil. From 1940 to 1944, 1,300,000 tons of grain and seed, 75,000 tons of meat, 126,000 tons of vegetables and fruit and a large quantity of timber. This constituted a large percentage of the total material resources that Germany consumed during the war.

Rumania was also a source of manpower: it furnished 16 –18 army divisions for Hitler's invasion and occupation of Russia.

At the Soviet General Headquarters in July 1944 Stalin repeatedly emphasised the significance of the forthcoming Jassy–Kishinev Operation, named for two strong-points in east Rumania. Hitler's High Command realised that if Russian forces were successful in eastern Rumania it would greatly endanger the

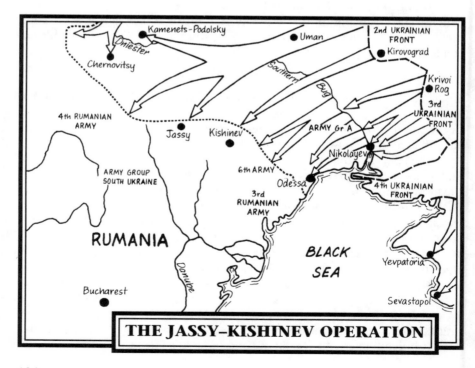

THE JASSY–KISHINEV OPERATION

defence of vital strategic routes, and that Stalin's armies would thereby gain access to Central Europe and the Balkans. Furthermore, the Germans knew that if Rumania fell, Germany would probably also lose her Bulgarian and Hungarian allies. So it was decided to defend the country with a large force consisting of more than 80 divisions.

In anticipation of the Red Army offensive, the German High Command concentrated troops in the Jassy–Kishinev area, namely Army Group South Ukraine under General Johannes Friessner, an officer of considerable experience who had earned the reputation of being a 'cunning fox'.

A few months earlier Stalin's armies had advanced towards Rumania. On the night of 26 March 1944 the men of 2nd Ukrainian Front under Marshal Ivan Konev reached the Russian–Rumanian frontier. Moscow saluted this victory with 24 salvoes from 320 guns. At this time the Rumanian army had 31 divisions including an armoured division, but seven of them were fighting against the Red Army in the Crimea. The German Army Group which was covering the Balkan theatre at the end of March consisted of more than 60 of the 250 divisions deployed on the Eastern Front.

By mid-May the Red Army had advanced about 70 miles into Rumania and reached the foothills of the Carpathians and the town of Jassy. In his offer of an armistice to Rumania, Stalin demanded a complete break with the German forces and a joint struggle against the Nazis, the return of all prisoners of war and reparations for the destruction caused by Rumanian military action and occupation of Soviet territory. Rumania rejected these demands.

Consequently, the Soviet High Command concentrated a large group consisting of four armies and parts of two other armies in a relatively small area of Rumania. The German High Command, which had assembled a strong force against 2nd Ukrainian Front, north of Jassy, ordered a series of counter-attacks. It was just before the summer of 1944.

Especially heavy fighting took place in May and early June as the Germans mounted an offensive in an attempt to hurl the Russians back across the River Prut. They concentrated a powerful force at Jassy, and on 30 May, after a strong artillery barrage and a massive air strike, attacked the Russian forces in fierce battles over seven days but failed to achieve their objective. At high cost the Germans pressed the Red Army back in some sectors. An important role in the fighting was played by 3rd Ukrainian Front commanded by General Rodion Malinovsky, which captured key positions from which it later mounted an offensive against the *Wehrmacht*'s Jassy–Kishinev grouping.

On the political front, in May and June 1944 an anti-Hitler group was formed in Rumania and, later, a similar bloc of resistance forces gained strength in other Balkan countries.

The summer of 1944 was a time of sweeping victories for Stalin. The Russians successfully carried out large-scale offensive operations on the Belorussian and Finnish fronts. Advancing on the central, Warsaw–Berlin sector, Soviet forces early in August reached the River Vistula in Poland on a wide frontage, seriously weakening German Army Groups Centre and North Ukraine. These were two of four German army groups operating on the Soviet–German front.

The loss of the Crimea had had a harmful effect on the position of German forces on the southern flank of the Eastern Front. After this, the Black Sea Fleet of the Red Navy deployed to Sevastopol and Odessa and posed a serious threat to the Rumanian coast. During the Jassy–Kishinev Operation the Black Sea Fleet under Fleet Admiral F. S. Oktyabrsky and the Danube Naval Flotilla under Rear-Admiral Sergei Gorshkov attacked enemy shipping supporting the German armies, landed troops near Akkerman close to the estuary, and bombarded the ports of Sulina and Constanta. At the same time, ships of the Black Sea Fleet intercepted German ships on passage through the Bosporus and Dardanelles. By the middle of August the Red Army had reached the main routes leading to the Balkan states.

The aim of the new Red Army offensive was to encircle and destroy the main body of the German and Rumanian forces comprising Army Group South Ukraine, and prevent the withdrawal of the enemy to the Focsani Gate, a plain extending from the East Carpathians to the lower reaches of the Danube. (The plain is about 100 kilometres long and 80 kilometres wide.)

The Soviet High Command carefully chose the point of the main attack. Marshal Sergei Biryuzov, who took part in the operation as Chief of Staff, 2nd Guards Army, writes:

'We spent a long time, carefully discussing the advantages and disadvantages of every direction. The map favoured an attack in the direction of Kishinev. It seemed as if the terrain were specially created for attack. It afforded plenty of space for the tanks, it abounded in hills that would provide cover for troops in an assault position. The River Prut protected our forces from an enemy attack on our flank. But this was not the main point. We were facing Hitler's crack troops in dense concentrations. In the course of preliminary shelling they were bound to suffer heavy losses. Moreover, a main strike from this area afforded possibilities of closer co-operation with the 2nd Ukrainian Front which would most probably launch an offensive toward Jassy and then make a drive towards the Focsani Gate.'

Nevertheless, the Soviet forces chose a less favourable location for the main attack, and one the Germans least expected. This was north of Kishinev, close to Lake Botna and the River Dniester. It should be borne in mind that the strategic importance of Rumania and other Balkan states was enhanced by their mountains and hills which provided good conditions for organising defence.

In the opinion of the German generals several factors ruled out the possibility of an attack from this location: the steep banks of the Dniester; the marshy floodlands around Lake Botna; the vulnerability of the area to surveillance. The Germans expected no surprises here. But they were mistaken. And subsequent events show that they were unable to repel the blow struck from this direction.

To achieve rapid penetration of the main line of defences, the Soviet GHQ had decided that the foremost divisions should receive the maximum reinforcement of tanks, whose commanders were ordered to deploy them *en masse*, not dispersed. To mislead the German High Command, a 'leakage' of information was organised by the Supreme Command of GHQ to 'convince' the Germans that the Russians were going to attack only towards Kishinev. The German commander, General Friessner, believed for a long time that they would strike at no other place, and was apparently also deceived as to the scale of the operation.

The Germans had a powerfully echeloned system of defence lines, up to 20 kilometres deep in the most vulnerable sectors. In the Jassy sector, for instance, there were four lines extending to a depth of 80 kilometres. The lines between the Carpathians and the Danube consisted of thousands of permanent emplacements, and a ramification of trenches, minefields and anti-tank traps. Many inhabited localities were turned into strong-points, there were powerful defences along the Dniester, and there were other water obstacles and the hilly terrain.

Friessner's army of 47 divisions (25 German, 22 Rumanian), five Rumanian brigades and several dozen separate regiments and battalions, had a total strength, including logistic support units, of 900,000 men, the Germans numbering 565,000. It was heavily equipped with guns, mortars, tanks and aircraft.

In planning this giant operation, the Soviet High Command assigned the attack to two Fronts, 2nd Ukrainian and 3rd Ukrainian. They were commanded by Generals Rodion Malinovsky and F. I. Tolbukhin. (Both were promoted to the rank of marshal in September 1944.) The two Fronts were to be co-ordinated by Marshal Semyon Timoshenko.

On 31 July 1944 at GHQ the High Command met to discuss the forthcoming operation. Stalin showed keen interest in the density of artillery to be used by Malinovsky's forces. According to military historian Colonel M. M. Malakhov, Malinovsky said that he could concentrate 220 guns per kilometre on the 22 kilometres of the German front that was to be breached. In Stalin's opinion even this high density was not enough to soften up the enemy.

But no resources were to hand in the area to increase it . The solution was to reduce the front to be breached to sixteen kilometres, thereby achieving a density of 240 guns, or even slightly more, per kilometre. This was a guarantee for the troops that the German forces would be suppressed, their defences penetrated, and that a drive could be made in the direction of the Focsani Gate to the south. It was Stalin's opinion also that powerful blows against the defences of Hitler's ally would influence the policies of the Rumanian monarchy and thereby help bring about the country's withdrawal from hostilities.

A few weeks before the off, the Red Army Front commanders were summoned to GHQ to discuss details, and on 2 August GHQ signed the orders to go ahead.

The 2nd Ukrainian Front's attack would be aimed at the weakest point in the German lines, avoiding major fortified areas. The attacking troops would be able to break up the German defence in a very important sector, cut off German Sixth Army from Eighth Army and bypass the rugged East Carpathians from the south.

The echeloned order of battle of the Russian divisions would make it possible to build up the strength of the blows, rapidly push into the defences, surround the German reserves and smash them. It was planned that during the offensive the Russian infantry would advance from 20 to 25 kilometres and the mobile units from 30 to 35 kilometres daily. This rapid pace would enable the troops to capture the Focsani Gate (in east central Rumania) on the eighth or ninth day and then push swiftly into the central regions of the country.

From here they could take the shortest route to the Bulgarian and Yugoslav borders and also enter the Hungarian Plain in the rear of the German Carpathian Group. Great secrecy surrounded the coming offensive, the Germans learning little or nothing of it until 18 August, two days before it began.

The two Russian Fronts together had thirteen armies, including two air and one tank army. These included more than 90 divisions, six tank and mechanised corps, and three brigades. The 2nd Ukrainian Front included the Rumanian Tudor Vladimirescu Volunteer Division and a Yugoslav brigade. The two fronts had 930,000 combatant troops (1,250,000 including logistical units), 16,000 guns and mortars, more than 1,870 tanks and self-propelled guns, and almost 2,200 aircraft. Powerful naval units were also involved.

The Soviet Command had a 1.8-fold superiority in divisions, 1.4 in manpower, more than twofold in artillery and aircraft, and 4.5-fold in tanks. The superiority of the Russian armies in the breakthrough sectors was even greater, from four to six times.

Because the army was operating outside Russia, it was felt necessary to issue an 'educational directive' which said: 'It should be explained to the troops that we are now fighting on alien territory and that every officer and man should display a high degree of vigilance and discipline and resolutely suppress any manifestations of negligence, gullibility and indiscipline.' It added that the Rumanian civilian population should not be subjected to any arbitrary acts.

On the morning of 20 August the battle commenced.

At 0605 hours the sun rose slowly from behind the hills of Moldavia. Five minutes later 4,000 Russian guns and mortars of various calibres heralded the start. The sound of Katyusha rockets joined the roar of the guns. The Russian guns positioned for direct fire destroyed targets detected in the forward areas as well as the barbed-wire entanglements. At the same time a squall of fire of unprecedented power struck the defence works. One report says that the shells literally lifted the German positions into the air.

The 90-minute barrage inflicted heavy losses on the defending troops. German and Rumanian prisoners said that they had been virtually overwhelmed by the gunfire whereas their own fire system had been disorganised, their fire and communication trenches destroyed, and the troops demoralised by the heavy losses in manpower and equipment.

On the first day the 2nd Ukrainian Front pierced the entire tactical zone of the defence positions and advanced sixteen kilometres to reach the third, or rear line. Five German divisions were routed and 3,000 officers and men captured. The 3rd Ukrainian Front completed the breakthrough to a depth of 10 to 12 kilometres, and in places wedged into the second line and routed four divisions.

The Order of the Day of the Soviet Supreme Command dated 22 August says that the forces of 2nd Ukrainian Front 'after three days of offensive battles, advanced 60 kilometres, widening the breach to 120 kilometres;. General Friessner, the commander of the German Army Group South Ukraine, acknowledged serious losses. Later he wrote that by the close of 23 August 'encirclement of Sixth Army was already an accomplished fact'. That not a single unit or formation of Sixth Army had managed to break out is evident from an entry made in the logbook of Army Group South Ukraine:

'The surrounded army corps and divisions of Sixth Army should be regarded as irrevocably lost. There is no longer any hope that any of the surrounded formations will break out of the ring. This is the worst disaster the army group has ever experienced. It has lost five army corps staffs (of Fourth, Seventh, 30th, 44th and 52nd Army Corps) and eighteen divisions (9th, 15th, 62nd, 79th, 106th, 161st, 257th, 258th, 282nd, 294th, 302nd, 306th, 320th, 333rd, 370th, 376th and 384th Infantry Divisions, and 153rd Field Training Division). Only negligible units remain of 10th Motorised and 13th Panzer Divisions.'

Meanwhile the 3rd Ukrainian Front widened the breach to 350 kilometres and advanced 110 kilometres.

General Kurt von Tippelskirch commented that Russian forces rolled over the German units 'like huge waves and swept over them from all sides'. He added that the ring around several divisions became so tight that they had to surrender. While Hitler's forces sustained heavy casualties, the Rumanian army was also staggered. General Friessner admitted that the results of the fighting on 20 August were catastrophic: 'In Combat Group Dumitrescu the two Rumanian divisions completely disintegrated. Five Rumanian divisions of Combat Group Wohler were totally smashed.'

The German command made a futile attempt to stop the Red Army's drive by transferring one panzer and three infantry divisions to the Jassy area. In turn, the Russians moved large tank units into the breach which exploited the success and initiated pursuit of the battered enemy units that were retreating in disorder. A vast number of Red Army infantry, 1,000 tanks, 3,000 guns and mortars, hundreds of rocket-launchers supported by bombers and fighters swept to the south.

The Russian land forces had the assistance of 5th and 17th Air Armies whose pilots flew more than 6,000 sorties in two days. Also, aircraft of the Black Sea Fleet attacked enemy ships and bases, dropping bombs on the port of Constanta.

On 21 August the Soviet General Staff telephoned the Front commanders for details of the situation. General M. V. Zakharov, 2nd Ukrainian Front's Chief of Staff, was optimistic, believing that the offensive would soon be advancing rapidly and that Jassy would soon be taken – and it was. General Staff officers rushed to the Kremlin to report to Stalin. Examining the map attentively, he demanded that the Front commanders be reminded emphatically that their main task was to encircle the German forces as quickly as possible:

'At present the principal task of the forces of 2nd and 3rd Ukrainian Fronts is by joint efforts to close the ring of encirclement around the enemy in the Husi area [south of Kishinev] as soon as possible. Afterwards the ring is to be drawn in, with the aim of destroying or taking prisoner the enemy's Kishinev troop concentration. GHQ demands that both Fronts deploy their main forces and matériel for the accomplishment of this paramount task, without drawing off forces to achieve other ends. Success in destroying the enemy's Kishinev concentration will open to us the road to Rumania's chief economic and political centres.'

The GS officers whose job it was to see that Stalin's instructions were carried out, listened closely to his concluding remarks: 'Your two Fronts are facing about 44 enemy divisions, six of which have already been destroyed. You have 87 divisions, and also a significant superiority in artillery, tanks and aviation. Thus you have everything needed for the accomplishment of the task indicated, and you must accomplish it.'

Marshal Timoshenko, who represented GHQ at the front, was ordered to ensure that Stalin's directive was carried out to the letter.

By nightfall on 21 August the German defences had been overrun and the German High Command had exhausted all their operational reserves. The two Ukrainian Front armies still had 25 uncommitted infantry divisions at their disposal and were in an advantageous position to surround the German forces in the Kishinev salient. That evening GHQ ordered the ring to be closed without delay.

On 22 August Hitler sanctioned the withdrawal of his troops from the salient, but by nightfall they had been almost completely encircled. On this day too, sailors of the Danube Flotilla joined a commando from 46th Army and forded the 11-kilometre-wide Dniester lagoon and freed Akkerman, thereby helping in the encirclement of Rumanian 3rd Army.

The two Soviet Fronts pushed on: one advanced 60 kilometres, widened the breach up to 120 kilometres and overran 200 large inhabited areas; the other advanced 70 kilometres and widened the breach up to 130 kilometres. By nightfall, said General Friessner, the encirclement of Sixth Army was an accomplished fact.

By the 24th eighteen German divisions were trapped. Those Rumanian soldiers who refused to fight surrendered *en masse* while the remnant of Rumanian 4th Army retreated in disorder to the south, and another Rumanian army of four divisions and one brigade was encircled and laid down their arms.

The investment of this large German force brought an end to what the Russians call the 'first phase'.

According to German sources, in the evening of 23 August King Michael told the German Embassy that Rumania was withdrawing from the Axis.

Stalin appears to have handled the question of the king's status with marked sophistication.

In August and September 1944 it became necessary for the Supreme Command to formulate a policy for dealing with young King Michael who had retained his throne. (According to some sources he proved himself a shrewd monarch by reportedly making contact with both the OSS – the forerunner of the CIA – and the Soviet Legation in Turkey.) Generals Antonov and Shtemenko had warned Stalin that the royal court would become a nest for anti-Moscow elements. To counter this they urged 'energetic measures' for removing the king.

Stalin listened attentively, pipe in hand. As was his habit when deep in thought, he took his time in lighting it. Then he said: 'Somebody else's king is not our affair.' He went on to say that a tolerant attitude towards the king would help promote good relations with Britain and the United States and, no doubt, with the Rumanian people who saw the royal court as a force opposed to the pro-Hitler dictatorship of General Antonescu.

Thus, says Shtemenko, 'we were given a lesson in elementary politics. King Michael', continues Shtemenko, 'devoted much of his time to leisure activities and little to affairs of state'. (When it was learned that the king was an amateur pilot, the Russians presented him, in Stalin's name, with a de luxe version of a light, single-engined Russian aircraft.)

Having finally surrounded the German group of armies, 2nd and 3rd Ukrainian Fronts began to reduce it, using a part of their forces, while the rest launched a swift offensive into the interior of Rumania, freeing it of German troops. The Russians call this the beginning of the 'second phase'.

For five days, from 25 to 29 August, the Russians were locked in bloody battles. The German commanders made a desperate effort to pull out Sixth Army, which was trying to reach the crossings on the Prut, but it was hopeless, so they abandoned their troops and fled to the Carpathian mountains.

The intensity of the fighting is shown by the fact that on 25 August alone, 3rd Ukrainian Front wiped out up to 30,000 soldiers and took more than 20,000 prisoners. Only a small number of German troops was able to cross the Prut, but they too were surrounded and had been destroyed by nightfall on the 29th. Scattered groups of German soldiers who had remained in the forests and managed to cross the River Siret were mopped up during the next few days, but by 4 September the remnant of the German forces had been completely eliminated. Eighteen of the 25 divisions of Army Group South Ukraine had been destroyed.

While some of the troops of the two Ukrainian Fronts were fighting at Kishinev, their main forces were driving into the interior of Rumania in three prongs, heading for the Carpathians, Focsani and the sea.

The *Wehrmacht* continued their desperate efforts to slow down the pace of the Russian offensive and win time to reconstitute their front. The German High Command wanted its forces to defend Bucharest, Ploesti and other cities and areas, but this was impossible because Army Group South Ukraine now had only the remnants of seven German divisions under command. The 3rd Ukrainian Front, advancing along the Danube, routed scattered groups of German troops and prevented them getting to Bucharest where an anti-Nazi uprising was in progress.

This had begun on 23 August and resulted in the overthrow of the Antonescu dictatorship. Under a pre-arranged plan the royal guards arrested dictator Antonescu and his followers at the palace and kept them in custody pending their being handed over to the Soviet Command. A new government was formed which announced, first, Rumania's withdrawal from the Axis and, secondly, its acceptance of the terms of armistice. It ordered Rumanian troops to cease operations against the Red Army.

Meanwhile Rumanian patriotic groups were occupying government buildings and strategic points in Bucharest and beginning to disarm German troops in the city. The old regime was crumbling.

Hitler ordered his troops to crush the uprising, arrest the king and his court and install a government headed by a general friendly to Berlin. In the morning of 24 August 1944 the Luftwaffe bombed the city. At the same time a hastily assembled group of 6,000 German troops mounted an offensive against the Rumanian capital with orders to link up with the German units stationed in the city and unleash reprisals against the population.

At first the balance of forces was in favour of the Germans who had about 8,000 troops in the city and about 6,000 in the suburbs. The German commanders intended to call in the 25,000-strong force stationed near the Ploesti oil fields, and troops from other parts of the country. They pinned great hopes on the paramilitary organisations of Rumanian Germans which had about 40,000 members.

They also planned to bring in troops from Yugoslavia and Bulgaria. But as more and more disaffected Rumanian troops arrived in the city, the balance of forces began to change. By the 28th the numbers of anti-Nazi Rumanian troops in Bucharest had reached 39,000 and the total strength of the armed civilian groups had risen to 2,000. By the end of the month Rumanian patriots had cleared the city and its environs of German soldiers and held it until the arrival of Russian units. In the course of the fighting the insurgents took prisoner about 7,000 German officers and men, including their commanding officer.

But not all the Rumanian troops turned against the *Wehrmacht*. What actually occurred is a complex affair and it provided an additional headache for Moscow. Although the top Rumanian general had been obliged to turn his guns on the German occupying forces, a large number of Rumanian soldiers chose to lay down their arms and surrender to the Red Army instead of continuing to fight against the Germans. Five Rumanian divisions surrendered on 26 August. The rapidity of the Soviet armies' advance had helped thwart the German High Command's attempts to suppress the Rumanian uprising.

Military historian Colonel Malakhov says that an important factor contributing to the success of the Rumanian insurgents was the defeat of the Germans in the oil-rich region of Ploesti and the entry of Russian troops into Bucharest. The Germans tried to stop the Russians in the outlying suburbs, employing their anti-aircraft guns against Red Army tanks, but their resistance was soon crushed, and by the morning of the 30 August 5th Guards Tank Corps and 3rd Guards Airborne Division, operating in conjunction with elements of the Rumanian 18th Infantry Division, which had withdrawn from the front, plus the Rumanian units sealed inside the city, had routed the Germans at Ploesti, 60 kilometres from Bucharest. Together, Russian and Rumanian troops overpowered the German groups and freed the entire oil-bearing province of Ploesti. Militarily and economically the fall of Ploesti was a decisive blow for Nazi Germany.

The entire operation had cost the Russians dearly. Total casualties were 286,000 officers and men, including 69,000 killed. The Rumanians also sustained considerable losses: 58,000 killed, wounded and missing.

The Jassy–Kishinev Operation was one of the most significant military campaigns of World War II. The defeat sustained by the *Wehrmacht* sharply altered the entire war situation on the southern wing of the Eastern Front and led to the collapse of the German defences in the Balkan strategic sector. The Russian victory opened the gates to Bulgaria and Yugoslavia where the next set of strategic tasks for Stalin's armies awaited.

★★★ STALIN'S JEWISH GENERALS ★★★

General Lev Mikhailovich Dovator, the son of a peasant, graduated from a cavalry school in 1926 and then attended the Frunze Military Academy in 1939. After Hitler's armies invaded Russia, Dovator commanded a cavalry group that made daring raids behind German lines at Smolensk in August and September, 1941. He later displayed gallantry during the defence of Moscow. Before the year was out he was killed in action.

Infantry General Yakov Grigorevich Kreizer graduated from infantry school in 1925, commanded the 1st Motorised and 1st Tank divisions from June to August 1941, and took part in the major battles of the war. His battle decorations included five Orders of Lenin and four Orders of the Red Banner.

Both Dovator and Kreizer excelled as military commanders and are applauded in the memoirs of Stalin's most famous marshals. Both were among the highest Jewish officers in Stalin's armies.

Colonel-General David Dragunsky, who was wounded four times during the war and achieved fame as a tank commander, told me that during the war more than a hundred generals of Jewish ancestry served in the Red Army. This figure is also mentioned in an official booklet, *Jews in the USSR – Figures, Facts, Comment*, published in Moscow in 1982. The existence of these generals complicates the conventional impression of Stalin as anti-Semite. A look at Red Army rosters shows that many soldiers who were members of minorities, including Jews, Georgians and Armenians, were able to climb to the top of the ladder of command.

Like many young Russian Jews, Dragunsky had entered the army in the early 1930s when Hitler and his National Socialist Party were threatening Europe with a new war. Before that he had worked as an agronomist on a collective farm. In the army he was promoted to general before Stalin died in 1953.

He first saw action in 1938 when Japanese troops invaded Russian territory at Lake Khasan, near Vladivostok. He then commanded a tank company. As a tank brigade commander, he fought at Moscow, Kursk, Kharkov and Kiev; and then in Poland, Germany and Czechoslovakia. For gallantry in action he received two gold star hero medals, the highest military combat decoration. When the war ended, he relinquished his command of the 55th Guards Tank Brigade and, shortly afterwards, was appointed chief of a higher infantry school, called 'Vystrel'.

I first met Dragunsky at an American Embassy reception in Moscow. He told me that during a visit to the United States, some people, unaware that Dragunsky was not a rarity in Russia, dismissed him as a 'token Jew'. Later, I met several other generals of Jewish origin, including Boris Sapozhnikov, who commanded a division at Stalingrad and, afterwards, fought in the Far East against Japan; and Lev Skvirsky, who served in Karelia, on the Finnish border.

Dragunsky has written a book of memoirs entitled *A Soldier's Life*. In it he recalls a balmy day in May 1941, just before the German invasion, when there was a happy gathering of his relations at his birthplace, the village of Sviatsk in the Ukraine. Sviatsk is small, picturesque and friendly. But in those grim days the village had a fatal drawback: it was situated too close to the state border.

Remembering that day, the stocky, broad-shouldered general said that he and his two brothers were especially attentive to their mother. 'She came up to us repeatedly and spoke special tender words to each of us.' The parting was solemn, he said, because 'in her heart she could feel the impending disaster'.

It was the last time he saw his mother and most of his family. The invaders put to death 74 of his relatives, including his parents and sister. He was told that his mother died heroically. Seized from her home early in 1942, she refused to obey a Gestapo order to profane her three army sons and was shot.

Dragunsky lost his two brothers in the war, both killed in the fighting at Stalingrad.

In the battles of Kursk, Berlin and Prague, Dragunsky, then a colonel leading a tank brigade, seemed always to be in the thick of the fighting. On three occasions his tank was hit and 'brewed-up' but always he managed to get out. Although wounded four times, he always returned to the front as quickly as possible.

At the Battle of Kursk, where more than 1,200 tanks were locked in battle, Colonel Dragunsky's commanding officer was General Semyon Krivoshein. David had recently been discharged from the hospital where army surgeons 'beat the odds and saved my life'. A few months earlier a piece of German shrapnel had pierced his liver.

Now, back at the front, Dragunsky was eager for action but was without a command. He appealed to General Krivoshein who wrote to a subordinate: 'I'm sending you Lieutenant-Colonel D. A. Dragunsky. He's a brave officer, but is rather too hot-headed. He fights well. He will make a useful tank brigade commander. Try him – you won't regret it. Semyon.'

Dragunsky got his own tank brigade and was soon fighting the panzers.

In the final weeks of war he took part in the race for Berlin: 'I was proud that the main ring of encirclement within Berlin had been closed by General

Krivoshein's troops and by my 55th Tank Brigade. My teacher had met his pupil in the capital of Nazi Germany."

After the war Dragunsky never thought that he'd make the army a career. His hobbies were swimming, fishing and writing and he looked forward to settling down as a civilian. 'I felt that the profession of soldiering would no longer be needed in a world at peace.' Before he joined the army he had thought of a writing career. 'I liked to read and write and thought of myself as a literary person, or a journalist.'

When I met General Boris Sapozhnikov he was poring over Chinese and Japanese texts in preparation for a book on Japanese warfare in China. As a youth, Sapozhnikov had decided to make the army a career. He said that his father probably would have been astonished to see his general's uniform: 'No doubt he would have wanted me to be a Talmudic student, not an army officer.'

In the thick of the Battle of Stalingrad this scholar-general took over command of a division after his superior officer was killed.

Sapozhnikov: 'I had early in life decided on an army career because I thought one member of our family – me – must help defend the country. In the army I could also learn a technical speciality. I chose signal communications.'

After victory over Hitler, Sapozhnikov quickly entrained for the Far East to join the war against Imperial Japan. Fluent in the Japanese language, he acted as interpreter for a number of captured Japanese generals.

During the war Major-General Lev Solomonovich Skvirsky, who served on the Finnish front, often skied to the front line despite a leg injury from a Japanese grenade. In the summer of 1939 he had fought against invading Japanese troops in Mongolia. When Hitler invaded Russia, Skvirsky was Chief of Staff of 14th Army near Murmansk. German troops tried but failed to capture this key Russian port in the Arctic. For most of the war Skvirsky fought on the Karelian Front where Russian forces kept Finnish–German troops at bay.

Three or four inches over six feet, Skvirsky had joined the Red Army when he was only 14. ('I was big for my age and passed for 17.') Military life, especially its discipline, was to his liking. Displaying an aptitude for learning, he was sent to various military schools. When he first entered the army he was, he says, the only literate person in his company.

Skvirsky's 14th Army distinguished itself guarding the Moscow–Murmansk railway and the port of Murmansk where Lend–Lease supplies arrived from the USA and Britain carried by Allied convoys that had to brave packs of U-boats and bombers based in occupied Norway.

Skvirsky was often on the telephone to Stalin during the war. 'Stalin didn't like beating around the bush. He had no patience with too much talk. In my experience, I saw that he wanted frankness and no varnishing of the facts. Also, he favoured commanders who applied themselves and carried out their assignments well.'

On the subject of anti-Semitism, the three generals had almost identical views. They hadn't encountered bigotry in the military; all the men they mixed with in the Army were impervious to prejudice. Dragunsky said that after the Berlin operation was completed in mid-1945 only a handful of military persons were awarded the country's highest decoration – the Gold Star Hero Medal. 'I, a Jew, was one of those few. Stalin himself approved the order, knowing I was a Jew.' According to Dragunsky, political indoctrination in the Army had weeded out bigotry.

Sapozhnikov: 'I'm a Jew. I never concealed it. And everybody knows it.' Pointing to snapshots of his children, he said: 'My daughter Ada has a Jewish husband, my son Grisha has a Russian wife.' He said the fact that he was a general – and that he had many high-ranking army friends who also had Jewish backgrounds – showed that a minority nationality could rise to the top in the army.

Skvirsky claimed that in forty years of army life he hadn't encountered anti-Semitism. Sapozhnikov, when asked if Stalin was an anti-Semite, replied: 'No, I don't think so, and besides, Stalin was himself a member of a minority people.'

On the other side of this controversy there are those who hold that anti-Semitism in the army was not frozen in wartime Russia. Stalin critic Roy Medvedev gives examples of Stalin's anti-Semitism in the army, including the discharge of 'many Jewish political officials' during the second half of the war; and, also, Stalin's reported rejection at the beginning of the war of a list of editors for Army newspapers, on the grounds that many of the nominees were Jews. But there is ambiguity: some of the best-known Soviet war correspondents were Jews, such as Ilya Ehrenburg and Vasily Grossman, both of whom wrote highly acclaimed novels. Meanwhile, there was the presence of over 100 Russian Jews who attained the rank of general in Stalin's army.

Sviatsk, the small village where Dragunsky was born, is situated near the junction of the Russian Federation, the Ukraine and Belorussia – now Belarus. Its residents include Russians, Ukrainians, Jews and Poles. In 1951 in the village centre a bronze bust surrounded by lilac bushes was erected in honour of 'twice hero of his country' David Abramovich Dragunsky. He is the only native of Sviatsk to have received this honour.

★★★ THE DEATH OF STALIN'S SON ★★★

On the day war broke out, Lieutenant Yakov Djugashvili, Stalin's eldest son, rang up his father before leaving for the front. Stalin was laconic: 'Go and fight!' One month later Yakov was taken prisoner by panzer troops.

After lining up the Russian POWs, an SS officer barked: 'All commissars, communists and Jews, step forward!' A few men left the ranks. The SS man stepped up to one prisoner and stuck a pistol in his belly. 'Why don't you step out? You're a Jew.' 'I'm not,' was the reply. Then some men in the ranks shouted: 'That's Stalin's son. He's a Georgian.'

(German historian Hans-Adolf Jacobsen points out that of the nearly four million Russian soldiers who perished in Nazi POW camps, tens of thousands fell victim to execution squads either because they were circumcised – like Muslims – or had 'certain facial features' that doomed them.)

As a prisoner, Yakov's position was hopeless. He believed, according to some accounts, that by becoming a POW he had failed his father and therefore could never return home even if the Germans released him. The very idea of surrender was anathema to Stalin whose military commissars instilled 'fighting spirit' and self-sacrifice in the men when necessary. Stalin had issued Order No. 270: 'Those who surrender to the enemy shall be considered traitors who have violated the oath of duty and betrayed the Motherland.'

When surrounded by the enemy, many Russian soldiers rather than be captured used their last bullet or grenade on themselves.

In an attempt to persuade Stalin's soldiers to defect, the Germans had dropped propaganda leaflets over Russian lines urging troops not to lose their lives for nothing: 'Avoid senseless bloodshed in the interest of Jews and commissars! If you abandon the defeated Red Army and cross to the side of the German Armed Forces, German soldiers and officers will render assistance to give you a good welcome, feed and arrange a job for you.'

After Yakov's capture, the Nazis, experts in guile, prepared a new leaflet:

'To Red Army soldiers. Follow the example of Stalin's son! He has surrendered and is a prisoner. He is alive and feels fine. Why do you want to die when already the son of your leader gave himself up and is our prisoner? Peace to your tormented Motherland! Stick your bayonets in the earth!'

When Yakov was taken prisoner, a German officer who interrogated him wrote: 'Yakov Djugashvili knows the English, German and French languages and gives the impression of being a highly intelligent person.'

The following is a verbatim record of an interrogation of Stalin's son conducted by Major Walter Holters on 18 July 1941:

Holters: Did you surrender of your own accord or were you taken by force?
Yakov: I was taken by force.
Holters: In what way?
Yakov: On 12 July our unit was surrounded. There was heavy bombing. I tried to reach my men but was stunned by a blast. I would have shot myself if I could.
Holters: Do you believe that your troops still have a chance of reversing the war?
Yakov: The war is still far from ended.
Holters: And what if we shortly get hold of Moscow?
Yakov: You will never take Moscow.
Holters: Why are there commissars in the Red Army?
Yakov: To raise the fighting spirit and give political guidance.
Holters: Do you believe that the new government in Russia is better suited to the needs of workers and peasants than the Tsar's government?
Yakov: I have no doubts at all about that.
Holters: When did you last speak to your father?
Yakov: I rang him up on 22 June 1941. Upon hearing that I was leaving for the front he said, 'Go and fight'.

Yakov rejected a suggestion that he write to his family and also refused to send a radio message. A photograph, showing him in conversation with two German officers, was widely used as propaganda. The Germans also forged a letter and quickly circulated it: 'Battery commander Senior Lieutenant Yakov Djugashvili has written to his father Joseph Stalin: "Dear father, I'm in a prison camp. I am well. I will soon be transferred to an officers' camp in Germany. I'm treated well. Wishing you good health, regards to everyone. Yakov."'

A second interrogation was conducted by intelligence officer Wilfred Strick who said that all attempts to win Yakov over to the German side failed. Strick described Yakov: 'He has a fine intelligent face with sharp Georgian features. He is self-possessed and carries himself well. He last spoke to his father over the 'phone before leaving for the front. He flatly rejected any compromise between capitalism and socialism. He refused to believe in Germany's final victory.'

The Germans took Yakov to Berlin and apparently handed him over to Dr. Joseph Goebbels' propagandists. But attempts to 'turn' him were fruitless. In December 1941 he was sent to a camp for ordinary POWs.

In the archives can be found the recollections of an ex-prisoner of the camp, Alexander Uzinsky: 'Yakov had lost weight, was black in the face and a heavy dismal look came from his sunken eyes. He was wearing a much worn greatcoat and a torn army shirt. One of the camp guards came up to him with a bucket of red paint and began to paint the letters "SU" on his chest, back, shoulders and even on his trousers. Stalin's son said for all to hear: "Let him paint. The Soviet Union is my motherland!" This was a shock to the guards. Such words were punishable by death.'

Yakov was next sent to a camp in Nuremberg, then to one in Lübeck where a large number of Polish officers were held. The Poles good-naturedly shared some of their Red Cross food packages with Yakov once a month. The Germans denied to Red Army officers and noncoms any of the privileges granted under the Geneva Conventions, but some Polish orderlies made him a pair of boots and coat. A Polish officer remembers Yakov saying that if he never saw his country again to get word to his father that he never betrayed him.

Early in 1943 came the Russian victory at Stalingrad and the surrender of a German field marshal. The tide of war was turning. The facts are difficult to document, but from various accounts it appears that Berlin offered to exchange Stalin's son for Field Marshal Friedrich Paulus. It is reported that Stalin sent a terse reply via the Swedish Red Cross: 'Soldiers are not exchanged for marshals.'

Yakov's death was witnessed by Harry Naujocks, a German Communist and prisoner at the Sachsenhausen prison camp:

'Yakov Djugashvili (Stalin) was haunted by his hopeless position. He was often depressed and refused food. He was terribly affected by Stalin's statement that there were "no prisoners of war, only traitors to their homeland" which was repeatedly broadcast over the camp radio. Maybe this prompted him to the fateful act. He began looking for a way to die – and found it. After dark on 14 April 1943, Yakov refused to go back to the barracks and started running into the "dead zone" (where the guards had orders to shoot without warning). The sentry fired. Yakov died instantly. Then his body was thrown on to the electric fence. They said that the prisoner had "Attempted to escape". The remains of Stalin's son were taken to the camp crematorium.'

Information about Stalin's son and the other prisoners is kept in the documentation office at Sachsenhausen.

In her memoirs, Svetlana Alliluyeva, Stalin's daughter, says that her father broke silence over Yakov in the summer of 1945 just after the war. He told her that the Germans had 'shot Yasha' and that he received a letter of condolence from a witness, an officer who had been a POW with Yakov. Svetlana says Stalin spoke with much effort and was unable to say more than a few words.

INTERVIEW: THE GENERALS SPEAK
MISCALCULATIONS

Admiral of The Fleet Sergei Gorshkov — Admiral M. M. Ivanov — General I. G. Pavlovsky — General S. P. Vasiagin — Colonel Y. B. Andronikov

(The admirals, generals and colonel in this interview, which took place on 23 January 1987 at the Institute of Military History in Moscow, all served in the Great Patriotic War. The late Admiral of the Fleet Gorshkov has been called the 'father' of the modern Russian Navy. Pavlovsky commanded a division and fought on various fronts. After the war he was Deputy Minister of Defence and Commander-in-Chief of Ground Forces. Vasiagin, a military commissar, was Deputy Commander for Political Affairs of a rifle division. Andronikov is a military historian.)

Author: Could Stalin have done more to build up the army and navy between August 1939 and June 1941?

Gorshkov: No. The maximum was done to build up our armed forces. Everything possible was done.

Pavlovsky: Yes. And our entire industry worked around the clock.

Author: Before the war started?

Pavlovsky: Yes. To supply equipment and arms to the armed forces, our industry worked three shifts per day before the war broke out. Reserves were constantly formed and trained to increase the armed forces.

Gorshkov: I would add this: Stalin and other military leaders drew many conclusions from the war that was being waged in the west. As a result, important steps were taken to improve the quality and organisation of our forces. Based on our observance of how the war had been fought in western Europe, we created more mechanised corps. That's why I confirm that everything was done by the political and military leadership of our country to prepare for hostilities.

(A voice in the background: And don't forget: We had only 15–17 years of peace after the end of the Civil War which ravaged our country. It is a very short time.)

Author: Admiral, if everyone in the military and civil spheres, including that of diplomacy – did everything humanly possible before 22 June 1941 to prevent the German invasion and to prepare for it, was there anything in addition that could have been done to face the coming danger?

Gorshkov: It was necessary to strengthen the forces on the western border of the country and keep them on full military alert. I wish to add in this connection that our Navy, thanks to a decision by Admiral Nikolai Kuznetsov, was kept in a state of highest military alert. To tell the truth, we were at battle stations even several hours before the attack. Because of that we avoided big losses to our navy.

Author: Admiral, when did you personally go into action?

Gorshkov: We went into action immediately. I was awakened during the night. All our naval ships were alerted and at 3 hours 15 minutes on 22 June 1941 we began firing at German warplanes that attacked the Crimean naval base of Sevastopol. I was then commander of a cruiser in the Black Sea.

Author: Did you expect the German attack on 22 June?

Pavlovsky: After 1939, especially after Hitler attacked Poland and France, our political and military leaders understood that we would also be attacked. Hitler's intention was to destroy our country and our political system. And, naturally, Nazi Germany was preparing for this attack. Our leaders were getting the country ready for defence. Our first task was to create an industry that would give us first-class weapons; and during the pre-war five-year plans, since the 1930s, we built up such an industry.

Author: Was the pact with Hitler of much benefit to your armed forces?

Pavlovsky: Consider this: Between 1939 and 1941, while the pact was being honoured, our industry supplied the armed forces with 17,750 aircraft, 7,000 tanks, more than 100,000 ordnance pieces and other military equipment. As you see, we were preparing in earnest to defend our country against Germany. But when precisely would Hitler attack? We didn't know. There were various suppositions. But the state, the political and the military leadership, could not be certain when the attack would occur.

Meantime, the troops were being drilled in combat operations. First of all, we developed a system of defence called 'operation in depth'. We conducted manoeuvres. We began training our civilian population to defend the country. But while doing this we did not seek to provoke a conflict with Germany after Hitler occupied part of Poland in late 1939, and became our neighbour. It was a very difficult time for us because at the border we had only fortified areas and border guards and, for the reasons mentioned, we were hesitant to bring up much larger forces to augment the border defences.

Author. What were you commanding when the war began?

Pavlovsky: I was commanding a battalion in a fortified area near the Dniester River. And on 22 June I was in Moscow at the Frunze Military Academy, writing my examinations. It was a correspondence course. On the same day – it was a Sunday – we left the academy and I 'passed my examinations' on the battlefield.

Gorshkov: I would say it this way. From the political position, from the military-strategic position, there was no surprise at all about the war with Germany. Stalin and our highest military men understood perfectly that sooner or later there would be war between our country and Nazi Germany. And our leaders took every measure to delay the outbreak of war. This was necessary for us because our armed forces were in the stage of reorganisation; and our industry had not yet finished building up a military base. However, if you look at Germany's attack from the point of view of actual front-line readiness, from the standpoint of operations, then the invasion came as a surprise.

There were, it is true, miscalculations as to the probable time of attack. This was partly a miscalculation by the military, including Defence Minister Marshal Timoshenko and Chief of Staff General Zhukov. And because of that our forces at the border areas were less powerful than our enemy's. We had half as many troops as the Germans. Of course, the surprise attack gave a certain advantage to the aggressor. But we must say – and you should stress this because it is often overlooked – that the extraordinary courage of all our people, military and civilian, even at the time of the surprise attack, caused far greater war casualties to Hitler's armies than they had suffered previously on the Western Front.

Author: Was it a disadvantage that you had to have naval forces in the Far East facing Japan?

Gorshkov: No, the distribution of our Navy in the various theatres of operations was, in my opinion, correct. You, as a former navy man, will understand that because of our geography it was very difficult to move our ships between the different operational theatres. This was so even though our 'four sea theatres of operations' were related to one another. Of course, on the rivers in the war zones we could only use small naval vessels.

Author: How about the distribution of troops?

Pavlovsky: Our land forces were distributed in such a way, taking into account the expanses of our country, as to be able to fight the enemy in the west and the east. In the east we had enough forces to defend the country if Japan attacked. We were facing three Axis powers: Berlin, Rome, Tokyo. Our political and military leadership reckoned that not only would the Germans attack us but the Japanese too. And, then, the Axis bloc had satellites – including Finland, Hungary and Rumania. All were at our threshold and all were threatening us. So we had difficulties in manoeuvring our forces.

Andronikov: Germany at the beginning of the war had 8.5 million men under arms. The Germans had approximately half that many soldiers on 22 June at the border. We had 2.9 million soldiers on the western border and slightly over 5 million all told, including the other forces deployed against Turkey, Afghanistan and against Japan, in the Far East. That's why we were in a very disadvantageous position at the time of Hitler's attack. Besides, our forces were still in the stage of advancing to our western border while the German Army was concentrated in full at our borders. Hitler's armies had experience in conducting military operations in the west. They were fully armed. Yes, we called up large contingents of our own people but they had to be trained before confronting the enemy.

Author: Would you call the beginning of the war, the huge losses of men and territory, the big successes of the *Wehrmacht*, as a catastrophe for Russia?

Gorshkov: Some specialists say that the heavy losses of the Red Army were unavoidable at the beginning of the war.

Pavlovsky: I want to stress that there was no catastrophe. There were difficult conditions, hard conditions, but no catastrophe, not like the British and French faced at Dunkirk or, towards the end of the war, as the Anglo–American armies faced in the 'Battle of the Bulge'. Excuse me, there was no catastrophe.

Author: You mean there was no catastrophe on the scale of the surrender of France?

Pavlovsky: That's right. Or for American and British troops in the Ardennes forest in 1945. That came close to catastrophe. It would have been so, because if the Germans had had enough fuel during the Ardennes Battle they could have broken through to the sea! And if Stalin had not started our big offensive in the East, earlier than planned, to help our American and British allies....

Andronikov: The war against the Axis powers was our common victory with America and Britain, with the decisive battles fought on the Eastern Front.

Vasiagin: I don't want to create the opinion that we under-estimated Hitler's army. That army was very strong, had plenty of modern armaments and had considerable combat experience. To fight against the German armies was not easy. Another thing was that we had to fight their allies: Italians, Finns and others, even if they were not as strong as the Germans. As for German generals, they were well trained.

But in our defence against the unexpected and lightning attack, we made some success even in 1941, in the first six months of the war. When the enemy came up to Moscow, a counter-offensive was launched and the celebrated *Blitzkrieg* offensive was buried right there. And Hitler's armies were pushed back, up to 250 miles. Then in 1942, at Stalingrad, a huge German grouping was surrounded and destroyed. At the Kursk Battle, in 1943, German army groups were encircled and destroyed. In Operation 'Bagration', in 1944 in Belorussia, another giant encirclement occurred, one of the biggest of the war. And in the Jassy–Kishinev Operation, and the Baltic. That is, starting in 1942, from Stalingrad onward, the German forces were often being surrounded. They were also encircled in the Berlin operation, and in the final Prague operation.

These facts clearly indicate the effectiveness of the Supreme High Command and the quality of our military science.

Author: Admiral, how do you assess Joseph Stalin's role in the war?

Gorshkov: Stalin's good point was that he could choose very talented military leaders. Stalin was of course also an outstanding political, state and military leader. This is not only my opinion but that of Churchill and Lord Beaverbrook and many other prominent foreign personalities. Stalin had a broad understanding of military matters. And he was able to find solutions and make decisions in the most difficult situations.

Author: So, you would say that Stalin was the Supreme Commander not just in name?

Gorshkov: Yes. For example, Zhukov always reported his draft plans of operations to Stalin for approval. I took part a number of times in military councils during the war in the presence of Zhukov. For example, during the Jassy–Kishinev Operation on the Danube in the last ten days of August 1944, I was present when Zhukov reported to Stalin his detailed proposals, and Stalin examined them thoroughly, slightly amended them, and affixed his signature to the plans.

Author: Many people in the West say that Stalin was responsible for huge mistakes in the early part of the war...

Gorshkov: And Zhukov bears responsibility for some mistakes that he made.

Author: Actually, many persons in the West do not give Stalin credit for his role in the defeat of Hitler's Germany; and there are books by experts, and an encyclopedia or two, that say that Stalin 'interfered' with his commanders in the field...

Gorshkov and Pavlovsky: That is not correct.

Author: But what about criticisms of Stalin for his failure to order mobilisation in time?

Pavlovsky: That was not only Stalin's mistake. The military commanders failed to convince Stalin that it was necessary to mobilise the army and keep it on the alert. They should have proved their case to Stalin! It was their responsibility. So it is their mistake as much as his. Also, keep in mind that mobilisation was a tricky thing because it could provoke war when Stalin was trying by diplomatic means to delay it.

Author: What, in your view, was the main difficulty in the Red Army at the beginning of the war?

Pavlovsky: Stalin knew very well the condition of the armed forces before the war and at the beginning of the war. Admiral Gorshkov said to you earlier that the army was in a state of reorganisation. Many troops did not get new armaments in time.

(*Another general's voice: 'The supply of new armaments to our armies, according to the plans, was to be finished in 1942.'*)

Pavlovsky: (Replying) But can we call that a mistake by Stalin — if there are not enough armaments, if the army is not brought up-to-date in time?

Gorshkov: Stalin's words in the early days were very well known by everybody. 'Our cause is just. We will win!' They were so well understood by all personnel that we remember them even now.

Author: Can Stalin and Zhukov be compared?

Pavlovsky: Stalin was the Supreme Commander. He was also the political leader of our country. Zhukov was the Chief of the General Staff. He was also at times First Deputy Supreme Commander and Commander of the Western Front, the Ist Ukrainian Front, and Ist Belorussian Front — several Fronts. Naturally all operations were developed at Headquarters over which Stalin presided. It is necessary to repeat that Stalin looked into all operations, offensive and defensive, and at the many details of these operations. For example, he was interested in how artillery is used for offence and defence. He knew what industry was doing, our aircraft design bureaux, and so on in order to produce better artillery, better aircraft, and other armaments. He was present on the field during the testing of many new weapons. Stalin knew every single Front, army and corps commander, especially in the tank and aircraft units. And he received daily reports from the commanders, sometimes two and three times a day, and he knew the names of all the deputy commanders, too.

Author: And Zhukov?

Pavlovsky: Of course Zhukov was a great military leader. We may say the best among the best. He contributed much to the common victory. But we had twelve Front commanders at the end of the war. All of them were good military commanders. However, Zhukov was outstanding among them. They recognised this themselves.

Author: To rephrase my question, could you have had a better Supreme Commander-in-Chief than Stalin?

Gorshkov: I think the question is incorrect. You are trying to counterpoise Zhukov against Stalin. You cannot do that. Stalin was a leader of the state and armed forces.

Pavlovsky: And the Party.

Gorshkov: In the West, Zhukov is considered the victor at the Battle of Moscow. But Zhukov credits Stalin's role in that battle. Stalin was in Moscow organising forces for the defeat of the enemy. It's necessary to give him his due. He was head of the State Defence Committee and did very careful work. He created the necessary strategic reserves and technical means for assuring the counter-offensive near Moscow. 'By his unrelenting demands, he reached the almost impossible.' Zhukov used these words in his memoirs.

Author: Why did the British–French–Russian military talks in Moscow in the summer of 1939 fail?

Pavlovsky: They [Britain and France] made a very big mistake. But the West was afraid of the existence of a country with a socialist system.

Author: Getting back to June 1941, did Stalin and the Soviet General Staff under-estimate the threat from Nazi Germany?

Pavlovsky: Stalin and the General Staff estimated correctly the threat of a German attack but they tried to delay the war in order to prepare our armed forces for defence.

Gorshkov: They miscalculated the time of attack. It was a serious mistake in defin-ing the time of Hitler's invasion.

Author: (A question for Admiral M. M. Ivanov, a veteran of many sea battles and a decorated hero.) I heard that you were one of the survivors when your mine-sweeper was sunk in the Black Sea by German aircraft.

Ivanov: Yes. It was the worst day of my life and it occurred one year before Victory Day. Our fleet was sailing back in June 1944 to Sevastopol, its main base. I was in a mine-sweeper, the 5,000-ton *Kharkov*, which was armed with powerful guns. And our three minesweepers had attacked and destroyed German transports in the ports of Feodosiya and Yalta, where Hitler was stockpiling bombs to throw at us. Probably our reconnaissance was poor. Anyway, we didn't take German aviation into account and we found ourselves beyond the range of our own aviation – the range of the fighters that were covering us. And after performing our tasks we were attacked by German dive-bombers. For hours we were bombed and we had no air cover. All attempts to help us were in vain because, as I said, our aircraft were unable to reach us. And my ship was sunk, the ship that I had sailed in from the very first day of the war. This was my biggest day of grief – when I lost my ship and my comrades. My ship had taken part in many operations but we had never lost a single seaman up to that time. This was the saddest and most difficult day in my life. Later I found myself in a base hospital. I had been picked up unconscious by a torpedo-boat.

General Boris Vyashin (who served as a senior officer in a rifle division in the war): All of us had days of great joy and days of grief. I was wounded early in 1945. It was in Germany. I was hit by shrapnel. I fell down, feeling I was dying. It was a terrible moment for me. The war was coming to an end, and I didn't want to die at that time. But in spite of my being sure that I would die, I survived.

★★★ STALIN: 'WHO WILL TAKE BERLIN FIRST?' ★★★
C-In-C Joseph Stalin — Marshal Ivan Konev — Colonel S. M. Shtemenko

Berlin was more than a victor's prize for Stalin. The Allied army that arrived first would be able to control a large part of post-war Germany and Eastern Europe. Thus, in addition to Berlin's strategic value, political considerations were also behind the storming of the Reich capital. There was of course an overwhelming desire by Stalin's soldiers to be the first to enter Berlin. No other army or people had paid such a high price in blood to overcome Nazi depredations. No other country still fighting had had so large a part of its territory under the heel of the enemy. No one waited so impatiently for victory.

Two years earlier, President Roosevelt had raised the subject of Berlin's future. On 19 November 1943, aboard the US battleship *Iowa*, en route to an Anglo–American conference in Cairo, he had given his views to US military chiefs on the future Allied occupation of Europe. He wanted the USA, together with Britain, to occupy as much of Europe as possible. Britain was to 'have' France, Belgium, Luxembourg and south Germany. 'The United States', Roosevelt said, 'should take north-west Germany. We can get our ships into such ports as Bremen and Hamburg, also [the ports of] Norway and Denmark, and we should go as far as Berlin. The Soviets could then take the territory to the east thereof. The United States should have Berlin.'

In early April 1945, with Russian armies poised outside Berlin waiting to strike, Stalin summoned Marshals Zhukov and Konev to the Kremlin. Entering Stalin's study, they saw the country's greatest military heroes, Suvorov and Kutuzov, staring down at them from the walls. After an exchange of greetings, the following dialogue took place:

Stalin: Are you aware how the situation is shaping up?

Konev and Zhukov: Yes.

Stalin: (turns to Colonel Shtemenko of the General Staff) Read the telegram to them.

Shtemenko: (reading) 'The Anglo–American Command is staging an operation to capture Berlin with the aim of taking the city before the Soviet Army can do it. The main forces are being organised under the command of Field Marshal Montgomery. The direction of the main attack is being planned north of the Ruhr, via the shortest road between Berlin and the main British forces. There are preliminary measures including the organisation of an assault group and concentration of troops. The plan to capture Berlin before the Soviet Army is regarded in the Allied headquarters as quite feasible and the preparations to carry it out are proceeding apace.'

Stalin: Well, then, who is going to take Berlin, we or the Allies?

Konev: It is we who will be taking Berlin, and we shall take it before the Allies.

Stalin: (A faint smile on his lips.) So that's the sort you are. And how will you be able to organise forces for it? Your main forces are at your southern flank, and you'll apparently have to do a good deal of regrouping.

Konev: You needn't worry, Comrade Stalin. The Front will carry out all the necessary measures, and we shall organise the forces for the offensive in the direction of Berlin in due time.

Zhukov: (He reports that the troops are ready to take Berlin and says his First Belorussian Front, with plenty of troops and equipment, is now aimed directly at Berlin via the shortest route.)

Stalin: All right! The two of you must work out your plans right here in Moscow, at the General Staff, and as soon as they are ready, say, in a day or two, report them to General Headquarters, so that you can go back to your fronts with approved plans.

Konev records that on the morning of 3 April he and Zhukov showed their plans to General Headquarters and discussed the starting date of the Berlin operation. Stalin agreed. While making his proposals Konev asked Stalin to give the First Ukrainian Front additional reserves so as to extend the operation in depth. Stalin replied that since the fronts were beginning to shorten in the Baltic areas and in East Prussia he would give Konev two armies – the 28th and 31st – from those fronts. Konev says:

> 'According to the initial plan, Berlin was to be captured by Zhukov's
> 1st Belorussian Front. But the right flank of my 1st Ukrainian Front,
> on which the main assault group was concentrated, was just south of
> Berlin. Who could at that time say how the operation would develop,

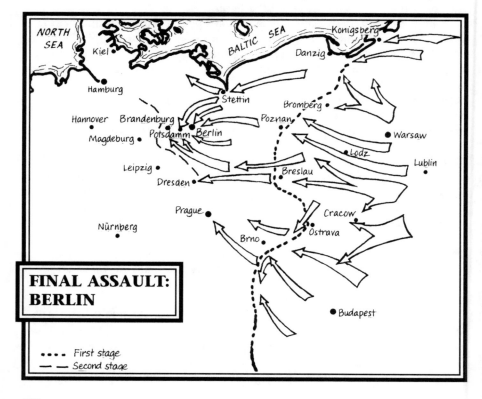

FINAL ASSAULT: BERLIN

•••• First stage
— • — Second stage

what surprises were in store for us in the different directions and what new decisions or corrections we might have to make in the course of events? At any rate, I did then have an idea that, owing to a successful advance of the troops of the right flank of our front, we might find ourselves in an advantageous position for a manoeuvre and attack against Berlin from the south. I felt that it was premature to give voice to these considerations, although I had the impression that Stalin also, without saying it beforehand, thought such a variant possible.

'My impression grew stronger when Stalin, while approving the composition of the groups and the direction of the attacks, began to pencil on the map a boundary between 1st Belorussian and 1st Ukrainian Fronts. In the draft directives this line ran through Lübben and then somewhat south of Berlin. While pencilling this line, Stalin suddenly halted it at the town of Lübben, which was about 80 kilometres south-east of Berlin, and then stopped short. He did not say anything, but I think Marshal Zhukov also saw a certain implication in this.

'The line of demarcation was cut short at about the point we were supposed to reach on the third day of the operation. Subsequently [apparently depending on the situation], it was tacitly assumed that the commanders of the fronts could display their own initiative.'

After studying the matter, Konev raised a question: 'Could this halting of the boundary at Lübben have suggested emulation between the two Fronts? [Author's note: In the Communist lexicon emulation is used to mean competition.] I admit that could have been the case. At any rate, I do not exclude this possibility. This becomes all the more plausible if we think back to that time and recall what Berlin meant to us and how ardently we all, from soldier to general, wished to see that city with our own eyes and capture it by the force of our arms.'

The planned Russian offensive began on time.

Reeling under the impact of powerful blows, Hitler's army was being driven to the wall in the spring of 1945 but it still had powerful forces defending Berlin.

In January–March Stalin's armies liberated Nazi-occupied Poland, a large part of Hungary and Czechoslovakia, and were deep into German territory in the provinces of Pomerania, Brandenburg and Silesia. By April they were only 60 kilometres from the German capital. The Soviet forces now faced their final task – the crushing of the German army which, four years ago, had mounted the *Blitzkrieg* against Russia.

The aim of the Berlin operation was to wipe out the German defences by a series of crushing blows in several sectors simultaneously, then encircle the last-ditch defences in Berlin, split them up and destroy them in detail. After that the Red Army would join up with the Americans and British at the Elbe, and the victory over Hitler's Germany would be complete.

This final assault was assigned to the forces of three Fronts: 1st Belorussian Front under Marshal Georgi Zhukov; 2nd Belorussian Front under Marshal Konstantin Rokossovsky; 1st Ukrainian Front under Marshal Ivan Konev.

The goals were: stage one – penetration of the German defence positions on the Rivers Oder and Neisse; stage two – encirclement of German forces in the Berlin area; stage three – the storming of Berlin. Despite the near collapse of the *Wehrmacht*, the penetration of the defences on the Oder and Neisse and the capture of Berlin were a formidable task. Hitler's troops were determined to defend Berlin.

The Oder–Neisse defence system had an overall depth of 20–40 kilometres. The Soviet armies had to cross several major waterways including the Oder, Neisse and the Spree. Hitler had turned all the cities, towns and villages into powerful strongholds and centres of resistance.

Berlin was defended by three exceptionally strong perimeters – outer, inner and city The city was divided into nine sectors, eight arranged in a circle around the central sector. The streets were barricaded and the buildings turned into strongholds. There were more than 400 ferro-concrete weapon emplacements each manned by a garrison numbering from 300 to 1,000 officers and men. The streets, squares, parks, boulevards and buildings were crammed with weaponry. The Luftwaffe too had made careful preparations, with fighters constituting a large component of the air defence system.

In their turn, the Soviet forces had been very thoroughly prepared for the assault, the High Command having elaborated a detailed schedule. The 1st Belorussian Front would rout the German forces on the eastern approaches, capture the city and reach the Elbe on the 12th–15th day. First Ukrainian Front would advance in a north-westerly direction, rout the enemy forces south of Berlin, and reach a line, Beelitz–Wittenberg, on the 10th–12th day of the operation – which would be extended farther along the Elbe to Dresden. The ultimate aim being to isolate the main body of German Army Group Centre from the Berlin grouping , thereby protecting 1st Belorussian Front from the south.

Second Belorussian Front would cross the Oder, rout the enemy around Stettin and reach a line, Anklam–Wittenberg, on the 12th–15th day, thereby protecting 1st Belorussian Front from the north. As the operation progressed, the Berlin defences would be enveloped from the north and north-west by the main strike forces of 1st Belorussian Front, and from the south and south-west by the right wing of 1st Ukrainian Front. The encircled German troops would then be split apart by a powerful attack from the left flank of 1st Belorussian Front, driving towards Brandenburg, a southern suburb of Berlin.

Forces and *Matériel*	Soviet	German
Troops	2,500,000	1,000,000
Guns and mortars	42,000	10,400
Tanks and SP guns	6,250	1,500
Aircraft	8,300	3,300

On the night of 16/17 April the forces of 1st Belorussian and 1st Ukrainian Fronts went into action simultaneously, 2nd Belorussian Front taking the offensive on 20 April. At 0300 hours the artillery and air force of 1st Belorussian Front struck a double blow at the defending German troops in complete darkness. The artillery preparation lasted for only 20 minutes, but during that time about half a million artillery and mortar shells were fired.

As the artillery shifted its fire into the depths of the enemy defensive positions, Russian infantry and tanks went into action. At that moment the beams of 143 powerful anti-aircraft searchlights illuminated the battlefield, blinding the enemy. According to the attackers, the artillery fire, air bombardment and bright illumination by the searchlights was so powerful that for a time the German troops seemed to be virtually paralysed.

As soon as they had got over the shock they began to resist strongly but were unable to stop the onrush. In fierce fighting one stronghold after another was taken and heavy casualties inflicted. After piercing the defences of the Oder and Neisse, the Soviet offensive gained momentum and, Hitler's main reserves having been used up, the German troops found it impossible to contain the mounting pressure of the assault.

Having crossed the Spree, the tank armies of 1st Ukrainian Front made rapid progress towards Berlin. On the 20th they reached the approaches to the outer perimeter and struck in rear of German Ninth Army's right flank. While the Soviet forces were engaging the enemy in the suburbs of Berlin, the Military Council of 1st Belorussian Front appealed to the officers and men to take Berlin as quickly as possible so as not to let the enemy recover: 'Let us bring down on his head the entire might of our combat equipment; let us mobilise all our willpower and mind to secure victory. We shall not disgrace our honour as soldiers or the honour of our colours.' 'Storm Berlin!' became the catchword on every soldier's lips.

Air power gave continuous support to the ground troops, striking the Germans both on the ground and in the air. On 16 April alone, 1st Ukrainian Front's aircraft flew 3,376 sorties against tanks, infantry, airfields, strong-points and centres of resistance, with cannon and machine-gun fire, rockets and bombs, paving the way for the advancing infantry.

On 23 April the main body of the Russian Front reached the River Spree and in some sectors effected crossings. Late on the 25th troops of 1st Belorussian and 1st Ukrainian Fronts reached the central districts of Berlin. Ferocious fighting went on round the clock, German officers and men putting up a stubborn resistance in the face of overwhelming forces. Every building in Berlin was defended by a garrison of up to company – and sometimes battalion – strength. Many buildings, air-raid shelters and pillboxes were connected by underground passages. These and the underground railway tunnels were used to shift units from one neighbourhood to another and even to strike in the rear of Soviet troops.

Berlin was burning. The streets were cluttered with rubble. Combat was hampered by smoke, dust from demolished houses, piles of broken brick, road blocks and fires.

On the night of 1 May, having sustained 300,000 casualties and taken 480,000 prisoners in two weeks of fighting, the Russians raised their victory banner over the dome of the Reichstag. The roar of artillery stopped and no more blasts from bombs or shells could be heard. Suddenly there was silence.

★★★ SIBERIANS AND SAMURAI ★★★

One of Stalin's trumps in the war were the Siberian divisions.

Afanasy P. Beloborodov is probably Stalin's best-known Siberian general. Wiry, energetic, pink-cheeked, this officer fought numerous battles against Germany and Japan, finishing the war with ten rows of campaign ribbons and his country's highest combat awards. His exploits are recorded in the memoirs of some of Stalin's famous marshals. He is one of the few generals to be honoured with a life-sized portrait in the war museum that is a part of Moscow's mammoth new Victory Monument. Most of the others so honoured are marshals.

Beloborodov's men often amazed other generals by their daring and resourcefulness in battle. One of their first successful assaults took place in November 1941 at the Battle of Moscow. Less than 150 days after Germany's invasion, this Siberian unit, the 78th Rifle Division, suddenly burst upon Hitler's troops, annihilating 12,000 officers and men who had tried to storm the Russian capital.

Observing the strike, Marshal Rokossovsky was astonished to see Beloborodov's Siberians cross a roaring icy river under enemy fire, in a makeshift flotilla of logs, boats and rafts made of straw. The exploits of Beloborodov's division, and later army, are prominently mentioned by top commanders in their war memoirs.

After victory over Hitler, Beloborodov flew to the Far East to join the war against Japan ('I didn't even have time to pack,' he told me.).

On 9 August 1945 Stalin's armies attacked Japanese-occupied Manchuria in what was to be the shortest campaign the Russians fought throughout the entire war. In two weeks all major objectives were accomplished. But, says an official Russian war history, 'in scale, scope, dynamics and end results' it was a very important battle in World War II, operations in the Far East spreading across a 3,000-mile front.

From 9 to 20 August about 80,000 men of the Kwangtung Army – Japan's strongest – were killed and 600,000 taken prisoner. (Russian losses were 8,000 dead and 22,000 wounded.) Twenty-two Japanese divisions were routed. Captured were 600 tanks, 861 aircraft, 1,565 guns and 2,139 mortars and grenade-launchers. So intense was the fighting that the Japanese Imperial Army lost more fighting men in those few August days than it had lost on all its other fronts during four years of war.

'Our task', says Beloborodov, 'had been to rout Japan's most powerful forces, the Kwangtung Army, and we are convinced that it was this that predetermined the surrender of Japan.'

Japan's leaders hesitated to surrender. The US Air Force dropped an atomic bomb on Hiroshima (6 August) and one on Nagasaki (9 August). But Japan waited five days before capitulating. Beloborodov's view – which is also the official view of the Russian General Staff – is that Tokyo's leaders admitted the impossibility of continuing the war only after Russia had opened hostilities against Japan. They point to the fact that on the same day (August 9) that Russia entered the war against Japan, Prime Minister Kantaro Suzuki said: 'The entry into the war of the Soviet Union this morning puts us in an utterly hopeless situation and makes further continuation of the war impossible.'

In the opinion of Beloborodov, Japan would have surrendered even without the atomic bombs. In any case, five months before the 'revolutionary weapon' was used, Japanese cities were being flattened one after another by conventional bombs. On the night of 9 March hundreds of B-29 bombers raided Tokyo, killing 97,000 people, wounding 125,000 and leaving 1,200,000 homeless. Beloborodov says: 'It's hard to understand what was in the minds of those Americans who said that Japan might have to be invaded.'

Throughout Stalin's war with Hitler there had been an uneasy truce between Russia and Japan. In 1944, for instance, Moscow accused Japan of violating the Soviet Far Eastern border 144 times. Despite the existence of a non-aggression treaty, the Japanese Navy sank eighteen Russian transport ships, and between 1941 and 1944 Japan detained 178 Russian merchant ships.

Beloborodov gave me details of a dialogue he had with an officer who at first refused to surrender. This 'Samurai' was Lieutenant-General Noritsumi Shimizu. 'I questioned him when he was captured and we had quite an interesting talk. First I asked him to tell me how many soldiers there had been in his army. He said 85,000. I then asked how many he had left. He said about 45,000.'

Beloborodov: Then your army is crushed?

Shimizu: No, it is not crushed.

Beloborodov: Where is the other half of your army, the other 40,000?

Shimizu: The answer is that some were killed, some of them were wounded and some deserted.

Beloborodov: Do you confirm that your army is crushed? You must understand that as a military man you do not have enough men to attack the enemy.

Shimizu (thinking for some time): Yes. I agree, my army is crushed.

Beloborodov: Then, okay, accept the conditions of unconditional surrender.

Shimizu: In our language, in the Japanese language, there is no such word as surrender.

Beloborodov: You are sitting in front of me. You are captured. My men have taken prisoner another five Japanese generals. Your troops are throwing away their rifles. In Russian we call it surrender.

Shimizu: The word does not exist in the Japanese language.

Beloborodov: Why do you personally surrender then?

Shimizu: That was the order from the Emperor.

Beloborodov: What did the Emperor order you to do?

Shimizu: He ordered us to surrender our arms.

Beloborodov: That is unconditional surrender, what you are doing, whether you have the word for it or not. If you didn't have the word before in the Japanese language, now you'll have to add it.

In comparing Japanese and German soldiers, Beloborodov said that the Japanese army lacked the military experience of the German Army and was not so well armed. 'It was weaker. We had good military equipment and much experience by 1945, and also a high morale among our troops.'

Beloborodov said that General Shimizu was sent to a POW camp in Khabarovsk, north of Vladivostok. He said that in the short, swift Russian offensive 148 Japanese generals were taken prisoner.

★★★ MUTUAL CRIES FOR HELP ★★★

Given the disproportionate scale in fighting between the Eastern Front and action elsewhere during World War II, it is not surprising that Stalin sometimes, when he felt the Allies were not pulling their weight, pointed to their 'insignificant' sacrifices compared to the Russians. He is quoted as having said at one time: 'The United States gives money, Britain gives time, and Russia gives blood.'

This of course was unfair. But to the Russians, who pleaded long for a 'second front', the waiting seemed endless; they had been slugging it out with the *Wehrmacht* for three years before the Anglo–American landings in France.

But Stalin also saluted the Allies. His messages to Churchill and Roosevelt, particularly in 1944, conveyed high praise to the American and British Armies. For example, in June 1944 he sent this message to Churchill: 'I congratulate you on the taking of Rome – a grand victory for the Anglo–American troops. The news has caused deep satisfaction in the Soviet Union.' And on the Allied invasion of France the same month: 'It is a source of joy to us all and of hope for further successes.'

There is no doubt that the Allied 'Lend–Lease' shipments of badly needed equipment and raw materials which began in August 1941 helped Russia in her ordeal with Nazi Germany. But on the other hand, a consensus among Russian historians holds that the giant Red Army counter-offensives saved thousands – even 'hundreds of thousands' – of American and British lives, and that many Russian lives would have been spared if the Allies had invaded France in 1942, or even 1943 (as Stalin pointed out in wartime messages to Churchill and Roosevelt).

There is no argument, however, that the large-scale operations by Stalin's armies pinned down the bulk of Hitler's divisions, thereby making it easier for the Allies to contend with his forces on the Western Front.

Discussing the war in Europe, historian Dr. Oleg Rzheshevsky makes this point: The June 1944 success of the Allied landing in France was 'ensured in decisive measure' by all the preceding actions of the Russian armed forces. To support his claim, Rzheshevsky says that in the winter and spring of 1944 the huge operations on the Eastern Front made it impossible for Hitler to rush reinforcements to foil the cross-Channel invasion.

With many Anglo-American military operations going on during the last year of the war, probably insufficient attention has been given in the West to Moscow's contribution to the Allied cause in 1945, when Stalin's armies were pushing from the Vistula to the Oder. One example is Stalin's decision in January 1945 to advance the date of a major offensive in order to help American, British and Canadian soldiers who were being hard pressed in the celebrated 'Battle of the Bulge' in the Ardennes. Most Western accounts of this battle ignore the Anglo–American appeals to Stalin for assistance.

Hitler hoped by his Ardennes offensive to cause a split among the Allies. A German document gives some details.

The time: 12 December 1944. A few miles from the Headquarters of Field Marshal Gerd von Rundstedt, Hitler is conferring with his senior commanders of the Western Front. He has a plan to launch a powerful military strike against American and British troops – to present them with a 'second Dunkirk'. If faced with a catastrophe, America and Britain will sue for peace, Hitler believes, and thus break with the Russians.

These were Hitler's words: 'Never before in history has there been a coalition like that of our enemies, consisting of such heterogeneous elements with such contradictory aims. On the one hand – ultra-capitalist states, on the other – ultra-Marxist. Each of the coalition members joined it with the hope of attaining its own political ends. This coalition is already rent by the most acute contradictions and I, like a spider sitting in the centre of a cobweb, see that the antagonisms between then are growing with every hour. If we can deliver a few heavy blows now, then this artificially created united front will crumble with a thunder clap at any moment.'

(Two months later Joseph Goebbels' newspaper, *Das Reich*, announced on 23 February 1945: 'There will be a Third World War in 1948.' Hitler's chief propagandist said that Stalin would betray Washington and London after Germany's defeat and occupation, by pouncing on British forces in Germany and, later, on the Americans. Hitler, according to Goebbels, counted on support from Winston Churchill who 'hates the Bolsheviks almost as strongly as I do'.)

Although defeat for the Germans was only five months off, they still had the manpower to field powerful forces: 9,420,000 men, 110,100 guns and mortars, up to 13,200 tanks and assault guns and more than 7,000 combat aircraft.

The German strike had initial success. Hitler's troops broke through the Allied lines, assaulting Anglo–American forces with fourteen infantry and ten tank divisions, and during ten days of fighting advanced on a wide front. They forced the US First Army back in disarray, meanwhile pressing stubbornly towards the Ardennes.

Sizing up the danger, General Eisenhower appealed for more troops and equipment and, also, for Russian help: 'The tension of the situation could be largely relieved if the Russians undertook a major offensive.' Meanwhile, on 1 January 1945, Hitler launched 1,000 aircraft in a surprise attack on 27 Allied front-line airfields and depots. Alarmed at the outbreak of heavy fighting, US General George Patton jotted in his diary: 'We can still lose this war.'

135

On 6 January Churchill sent a message to Stalin: 'I shall be grateful if you can tell me whether we can count on a major Russian offensive on the Vistula front, or elsewhere during January. I regard the matter as urgent.'

On the 7th Stalin replied: 'We are mounting an offensive. GHQ of the Supreme Command has decided to complete preparations at a rapid rate and, regardless of weather, to launch large-scale offensive operations along the entire Central Front not later than the second half of January. Rest assured we shall do all in our power to support the valiant forces of our Allies.'

Eight days earlier than planned, on 12 January, the Russians began a new offensive, one of the greatest of the war, on a broad front stretching from the Baltic to the Carpathian mountains. (According to historian William L. Shirer, Stalin threw in more than 180 divisions.) During this offensive 60 German divisions were routed, Poland was freed and the stage set for the final blows against Berlin. But the cost was heavy; in Poland alone the Russian toll in killed and wounded was 500,000.

Berlin's reaction was swift. The High Command ordered the transfer to the Eastern Front of large numbers of German troops from the west. According to German General Siegfried Westphal, one-third of military forces were moved to the East between 12 and 31 January.

Meanwhile the Allied troops regained the positions they had lost in the area of the Ardennes and General Eisenhower was delighted: 'The Russian offensive has achieved major success and the enemy has been forced to begin troop withdrawals from the Western Front.' Roosevelt told Stalin: 'Your heroic soldiers' past performances and the efficiency they have already demonstrated in this offensive give the high promise of an early success to our armies on both fronts.' Earlier, Roosevelt had sent this note of thanks to Stalin: 'I have a full appreciation of the effect your gallant army has had in making possible a crossing of the Rhine by the forces under General Eisenhower.'

As to the Pacific Theatre, a Russian military historian, Colonel M. I. Semiryaga, is categorical: 'By smashing Japan's Kwangtung Army and forcing Japan to surrender, our country saved hundreds of thousands of Allied soldiers from inevitable death and millions of Japanese from terrible privations and suffering.' (This statement is based on the very contentious point of view that Japan surrendered primarily because of Russian intervention in the Pacific War.)

Siberian General Beloborodov, who fought against both Nazi Germany and Imperial Japan, strains belief with his allegation that Russia 'saved our British and American allies from defeat in the Pacific Ocean'. (To support his claim, Beloborodov points out that Moscow's stationing of an entire self-contained army in the Far East – up to forty divisions on the border with Manchuria – 'deterred Japan and helped the Allies, especially the United States, to find new forces after the defeat at Pearl Harbor.')

'We kept enough military forces in the Far East to deter the Japanese. You can say that, in a way, the Japanese throughout World War II were fighting on two fronts.' There is, however, no doubt that Japan's rulers respected Stalin's armies. An article published as far back as 1936 by a Japanese foreign affairs specialist, Toda Ishimaru, says frankly: 'We must have Russia as an ally whether we fight England or America. We would be rendered powerless if we make her hostile.' Five years later, Yosuke Matsuoka, the Japanese Foreign Minister, told the Diet: 'An understanding with Russia will be a counterweight against Anglo–American efforts to encircle Japan.'

At the end of the war a jubilant Stalin sent greetings to Roosevelt: 'The peoples of the Soviet Union greatly appreciate the part played by the friendly American people in this liberation war.' He saluted the 'gallant US Armed Forces' and said that the 'joint effort of the Soviet, US and British Armed Forces against the German invaders' would 'go down in history as a model military alliance between our peoples'.

Simultaneously Stalin congratulated the 'gallant British Armed Forces and people of Britain' and, with an eye to the future, said he hoped for a 'happy development in the post-war period'.

★★★ TRAGEDY IN A CENSUS ★★★

If Stalin's armies were fighting not only for the Russian Motherland, but indirectly to save the Allies from disaster, the huge Russian losses are the more understandable and the more heroic. Some Western experts say that to these losses must also be added the millions that were never born because of the war, and post-war when there was a huge nation-wide shortage of men.

A census taken in Russia fifteen years after the war found that the population based on official projections should have been 257 million, but was in fact 209 million. The missing population – almost 50 million – could be accounted for by the ravages of war, but not only to those men and women who fell on the battlefield or died in Hitler's POW camps. According to Professor Alexander Kvasha, a scientist studying the problems of population growth, 'indirect losses' accounted for more than half the missing population.

Compare: in 1940, six million babies were born in Russia. In 1943: about three million.

There were additional reasons for the decline in post-war population growth: poor health, grief, over-exertion and the resulting lower life expectancy. In post-war demographic studies, the missing population always showed up.

Using demographic tools we are able to look inside one generation that fought in World War II. Its cries at birth were first heard early in the 20th century. In the year 1906 nearly seven million births were registered in Russia, more or less evenly divided between the sexes. This was eleven years before the Revolution.

In 1906 more than three million Russians were suffering from malaria. In that year infectious diseases carried off almost 800,000 people. Most of the 1906 babies – about 5½ million – were born to poor families living in dark, overcrowded houses, little more than hovels. Few midwives had any notions of hygiene, and millions died in infancy. In 1906 too, about 150,000 babies were born to wealthy families and another million to well-to-do peasants (*kulaks*), tradesmen and professional people.

Of the total of nearly seven million births, more than 1,800,000 died before the year was out. Hundreds of thousands of children aged one year and older died of smallpox, scarlet fever, diphtheria, typhus, dysentery, tuberculosis and other diseases.

At the time of the Revolution in 1917, three million of the seven million children born in 1906 had perished before the age of eleven years.

By the age of twenty more than half the girls born in 1906 had married. At thirty more than 80 per cent had families.

Women of this generation were 38 and 39 when the war ended – an age when many of them could possibly have resumed the child-bearing disrupted by the war. But they were not destined to do so because a huge number of men of their age and several years older had fallen in the war. Most of the women had become widows. At the age of 52, only 49 per cent of them were married.

For men in the post-war period it was different, that is, for those lucky to have returned in reasonable health and without serious injury.

About one-third of the men born in 1906 were married at 20; some 89 per cent of them were married by the age of 32; and after the war those who were married made up 96 per cent of the total male survivors. Thus the war caused the percentage of married women to drop and the percentage of married men to rise.

By the age of 25 women of the 1906 generation had given birth to 2,500,000 children. In the 25–34 age group the birth rate was still significant, although it dropped somewhat.

Those women aged 34 or over spent the next five years in the grim conditions of the war, and when the men returned their wives were approaching 40. Like most Russian women, they were so exhausted by the war that most of them who still had husbands refused to take on the burden of bringing up small children in the fifth decade of their lives.

Over the years 1.7 million of the women born in 1906 gave birth to 6.2 million children, including three million girls – or 175 per cent of their own number. Allowing for child mortality before the Revolution, this means that the 3.3 million females born in 1906 produced only three million females. The number of girls born in 1906 was 10 per cent more than the number of girls they themselves produced.

Regeneration was therefore incomplete.

When World War II broke out, of the people born in 1906 there still survived 1,560,000 men and 1,580,000 women. That is, more than half had died before they were 35. After Germany attacked Russia in June 1941 hundreds of thousands of women saw their husbands off to war.

At the age of 34 or 35, the men were mobilised in the first days of the war. At the front half a million men born in 1906 were killed. The number of widows rose sharply. About 80 per cent of the men born in 1906 never reached the age of 60.

Other generations – for example, those born in the years 1920, 1921, 1922 and 1924 – were struck down by the war, so that some villages were without men or had very few men.

In addition to the half million men born in 1906 who died on the field of battle, 130,000 women of that generation were killed or wounded.

138

★★★ STALIN: A PERFECTIONIST? ★★★

Stalin's generals and other officers, particularly those who saw him on a daily basis, saw him as a demanding chief who exacted the utmost in effort from everyone holding a responsible job. No excuses were accepted for slipshod work and penalties could be severe.

According to Marshal Vasilevsky, Stalin worked very hard himself but he also made sure that others worked to capacity. The highest standard was insisted on in all matters involving the armed forces, extending to the drawing up of documents. The Marshal says that Stalin even paid attention to improving the literary quality of documents: 'Stalin never forgave carelessness in work, or failure to finish a job properly, even if this happened with a highly indispensable worker without a previous blemish on his record.' His demands were in most cases just, the Marshal goes on: 'His directives and commands showed Front commanders their mistakes and shortcomings [and] taught them how to deal with all manner of military operations skilfully.'

Other generals recall that Stalin looked into day-to-day problems of the army, ranging from conjugal visits of officers to the writing of war manuals. When General (later Marshal) Meretskov told Stalin that officers stationed close to Moscow had no place to meet their wives except in the nearby woods, he issued instructions for buildings to be made available to the couples. Informed that, after a German bomb had fallen on the General Staff building, damaging the kitchen, there was no longer food available for staff members, Stalin ordered that sandwiches be delivered to them in baskets three times a day, three sandwiches per person.

In mid-war, one of the daily summaries of reports from the Voronezh Front said that 100 enemy guns had been captured in a successful counter-attack by the Red Army. The report was sent to GHQ (Stalin). The next morning Stalin telephoned the General Staff and asked if together with the captured guns, shells had also been taken. No one knew.

'Look into it and let me know,' said Stalin.

Hasty calls were made to the Front's chief of staff. He didn't know either but promised to find out and call back. Hours passed. Again, Stalin called and this time said:

'If we've got shells, too, it will be possible to form nearly 20 batteries with the captured guns. Isn't this true?'

General Shtemenko, who answered the telephone, said yes.

'But you don't know how many shells we've got?'

'Not yet.'

Stalin hung up abruptly, displeased.

Shtemenko put through a call to the Front and this time learned that it was not 100 but ten guns that had been captured and only four of them were in working condition. An investigation began to find out who had made the mistake.

Sensing that a storm was coming, Shtemenko conferred with his chief, Marshal A. I. Antonov, who said they should wait until the evening report to tell Stalin: 'But if he asks before that, we won't hide the truth.'

In the evening, as expected, there was an uproar. Stalin berated the General Staff, staffs in general, and spoke of unreliability, slipshod work, blundering and slackness.

The Chief of the General Staff was ordered personally to find out who was responsible for the error. It was learned that the figure 10 had been distorted to 100 by the telegraph operators when sending the report from the Front to the General Staff. In future, Stalin was told, stringent measures would be taken to prevent such errors.

Stalin, listened, puffing his pipe as he walked back and forth.

'Certainly, the girls at the telegraph office should be warned but they can't be held responsible,' he said. 'They don't understand what the telegrams are about. But the officer who received the report should have checked the figures. It was not a matter of one cannon or two. This was probably one of the few occasions since the war began that such a large number of guns had been captured.'

Stalin then asked Shtemenko:

'Who took the report?'

Shtemenko said that it was the chief of the sector in charge of the Voronezh Front.

'Then he's the one to get rid of,' said Stalin. 'Have him moved to a less responsible job, but not on the General Staff.'

Another sample of Stalin's exacting nature involved war manuals. Here, the highest generals in the army were involved.

A year into the war, Stalin and the General Staff wanted those with combat experience to put it in writing for the benefit of others, and a new unit was set up at GHQ in the autumn of 1942, its task being to recruit the best men to write articles on combat operations.

Before being published, each collection of articles was sent to Stalin for approval. When a new infantry manual was being prepared in 1942, Stalin insisted that the job be done with great care. For this purpose groups of officers were sent to the Fronts to gather detailed information. With the help of company, battalion and regimental commanders, all chosen for their talent and experience, a first draft of the manual was compiled. In Moscow, a special body was formed to examine the draft and make suggestions.

Next, the manual was discussed at a two-day meeting at GHQ with Stalin in attendance. Also on hand were front-line commanders. Only then did Stalin give his approval for publication.

But a breach of these guidelines occurred in 1944 and resulted in sharp reprimands for Stalin's deputy, Marshal Zhukov. The incident lingered in the memory of General Staff officers.

General Shtemenko says that after a routine meeting one day, Stalin asked top General Staff officers how the new section on war manuals was doing. The Chief of Operations said that it was 'working well', that everyone was being diligent and that the Supreme Commander would be provided with all the results of their work.

Stalin disagreed.

'It seems to me, though, that it is not doing its job properly, and that you are not keeping an eye on it,' he said. 'Is it known to the General Staff that two artillery manuals, both with serious departures from the established rules, have been published this year?'

The generals and other officers present were at a loss.

Stalin demanded they make an inquiry and report back to him in two days. It was learned that the Chief Marshal of Artillery, N. N. Voronov, had in fact compiled two manuals without the knowledge of the General Staff; that the two manuals, one for anti-aircraft artillery and one for regular artillery, had been approved by Marshal of the Soviet Union Georgi Zhukov, Stalin's deputy.

At the next meeting Stalin listened while pacing up and down the room. Finally he spoke:

'An order should to be issued about this. It would probably be awkward for the General Staff to do it, since two very high-ranking officers are involved. So we shall write it ourselves.'

Stalin began to dictate:

'On 29 May 1944, Chief Marshal of Artillery Voronov, without obtaining approval from the General Headquarters of the Supreme High Command, submitted a manual for the anti-aircraft artillery of the Red Army (in two parts) for the approval of the Deputy People's Commissar for Defence, Marshal Zhukov.'

Looking at the dates on the manuals, which were on his desk, Stalin added: 'On 18 October 1944, Voronov also submitted a Red Army artillery manual for the approval of Marshal Zhukov, also without any presentation or report to GHQ of the Supreme Command. The manuals were approved and put into effect by Marshal Zhukov without sufficient verification, without summoning and consulting officers from the front, and without making any report to GHQ.'

Stalin paused, puffed at his pipe, and continued.

'An investigation has shown that these manuals, because of their hasty confirmation, contain serious flaws. They do not take into account new ordnance systems, and are not in keeping with the plan for adopting manuals for the Red Army artillery.'

Stalin then explained the reasons behind his order.

'The People's Commissariat for Defence [Defence Ministry] holds that a manual is not an order, which is in force for a short time only. A manual is a code of laws to be followed for years by the Red Army. For this reason a manual, before it can be confirmed, must be carefully gone over with comrades from the front. This was the procedure followed with the field manual for infantry. The same procedure should have been followed in presenting for confirmation the two manuals mentioned above, so that mistakes could be avoided, and so that military personnel would not have to be punished to no purpose for violating defective regulations. It must be stated that Comrade Voronov disregarded this method for working out field manuals and submitting them for confirmation, and that Marshal Zhukov forgot about it.'

Stalin now came to the conclusion of his order. He spoke slowly. All present, says Shtemenko, listened raptly. 'In connection with this:

'First: I countermand the [previous] orders [he glanced at the manuals again] Numbers 76 and 77, dated 29 May 1944, and Number 209, dated 18 October 1944, issued by Deputy People's Commissar for Defence of the USSR Marshal Zhukov, which confirm and put into effect the field manual for anti-aircraft artillery and the field manual for the Red Army artillery.

'Second: I reprove Chief Marshal of Artillery Comrade Voronov for showing carelessness in regard to regulations for artillery.

'Third: I make it incumbent upon Marshal Zhukov not to permit this sort of haste in deciding important questions in the future.

'I order that two commissions be set up to read and correct the manuals mentioned above:

(a) a commission to review and check up the field manual for anti-aircraft artillery;

(b) a commission to review and check up the field manual for the artillery.

'Deputy People's Commissar for Defence of the USSR Comrade [Nikolai] Bulganin is to draw up lists of members for these commissions and submit them for my approval.

'This order is to be circulated among all commanders of Fronts [Military Districts] and armies, heads of main and central departments, and commanders of various arms of the services under the People's Commissariat for Defence of the USSR.'

Stalin's order impressed the General Staff as an exercise in precision. According to Shtemenko, all those present, as well as those who were affected by Stalin's order, learned a lesson they would never forget.

INTERVIEW: THE GENERALS SPEAK
'WHAT WE UNMASKED'
General Alexei G. Zheltov
(Colonel-General Alexei G. Zheltov, a military commissar, took part in the defence of the Russian Arctic region and later served on the southern front. After the war he was for a time chairman of the War Veterans' Committee. The interview took place on 31 January 1985.)

Author: Some people blame Stalin for the losses at the start of the war. Do you agree?
Zheltov: A person who does not do anything is always right. This is the attitude of people who do not know the burden of war. The aim of Plan 'Barbarossa' which Hitler had drawn up was to try to strangle us by using masses of tanks and aviation, first of all, and secondly, to divide our country, the peoples who live in our country, our different republics; to destroy the bond between countryside and cities.

We had to mobilise everything and we had to suffer great losses at the beginning of the war because we were fighting for our land. But we also felt we were fighting for all people, for civilisation. We lost more than 20 million people. But our losses were not only on the battlefield. Nazi Germany also lost millions of soldiers.

Author: Would you have wanted to 'exchange' Stalin, to get another Commander-in-Chief in his place?

Zheltov: That's a question that only comes from the imagination. Stalin, after Lenin, was leader of this state for 30 years. As C-in-C he led this country to victory. We did not think of finding a substitute for Stalin. Not at that time, and not now. This question is very tricky.

Author: Let's turn to the war. Could Russia have defeated Hitler's Germany if the Allies had not invaded France?

Zheltov: I have written an article for one of our magazines in which I state that we were able to defeat Hitler ourselves. And after three years of severe battles on the Eastern Front, our Allies decided to occupy France because they wanted to get to Berlin as soon as possible.

Author: In your opinion did Moscow's victories over Hitler prevent a German invasion of Britain?

Zheltov: Hitler considered our country to be the number one enemy. And he thought that – you remember those rockets sent across the Channel – he thought his rockets were enough to put an end to Britain. To add to my answer to your previous question, I want to stress that I don't want to belittle the importance of those battles which our Allies fought in France.

Author: General, what would have happened if the Soviet Union had entered the war not in 1941 but in September 1939, two years earlier, when Germany invaded Poland?

Zheltov: At that time we considered that Germany was fighting another bourgeois state, Poland. We saw it as an imperialist war. But Poland, as you know, had military assistance agreements with Britain and France. So the question was: where to defend Poland? But you remember that when the military delegations from France and Britain came to Moscow, just before Hitler attacked Poland, they came without the right to decide anything. They lacked what are known as 'plenipotentiary powers'. During the consultations in Moscow, the leader of those talks on our side was Marshal Klementi Voroshilov together with Boris Shaposhnikov, the Chief of the General Staff at that time. Voroshilov made it clear to the British and French that we were ready to deploy 125 divisions for battle. But it was necessary for them to do the same. And that was the essence of their policy – to turn Germany against us, to force us to fight alone. That was what we unmasked. And, afterwards, the Nazis invaded our country.

Author: On the Russo–German Non-aggression Pact of 1939 – would you say that most Russian generals and military men looked at this pact as giving the Red Army two more years to prepare for war?

Zheltov: I can't speak for all our generals.

Author: Please speak for yourself.

Zheltov: Many people in the West say that we betrayed Britain and France. But actually those two countries were guilty of betrayal at Munich. After that conference which effectively eliminated Czechoslovakia as an independent country, we were face to face with Hitler's Germany and we were not ready to fight against them. Our armies were being trained in new combat techniques and learning how to use newly acquired military equipment, including new tanks and aircraft.

Author: General, did you ever meet Stalin?

Zheltov: Yes.

Author: And what was your opinion of him?

Zheltov: I believe Winston Churchill evaluated Stalin highly, and I agree with this opinion. Our soldiers fought shouting the words 'Motherland' and 'Stalin' because Stalin was our C-in-C and leader of the state at that time. Our troops had a very high morale and this assisted us in our victory over Hitler's Germany.

Author: Did you participate at the link-up with the Americans at the Elbe in Germany?

Zheltov: I haven't yet fully answered your question about Stalin. Yes I met Stalin. Stalin, I found, was very conscious of the way the military lived and functioned at that time. He gave close attention to such things as how they were equipped, how they were dressed and what they ate.

And when Stalin learned that there were complaints from the officers and men on one of the Fronts, he notified all the commanders involved that the problem must be taken care of immediately and to inform him of the outcome.

Author: On the Elbe meeting...

Zheltov: I was in the south and can't say much about it. But, by the way, Russian and American troops also met in Austria, in Linz and Graz and other places.

STALIN'S HEROES

★★★ TOASTING THE RUSSIAN CHARACTER ★★★

When speaking to Roosevelt and Churchill during World War II, Stalin often began with the words, 'We Russians'. To inspire soldiers in the war, Stalin peppered his speeches with the names of legendary heroes of Russian history such as Alexander Nevsky, Dimitri Donskoi, Alexander Suvorov and Mikhail Kutuzov. Stalin called them 'our heroes'.

In turn Stalin was hailed by eulogisers as heroically Russian. This is seen, for example, in the wartime best-seller, *The Last Days of Sevastopol*, in which the author Boris Voyetekhov calls Stalin 'the most Russian of all Russians'.

For Stalin, Russians were the country's cohesive force, the most loyal and self-sacrificing in the multi-nation state, the least ethnocentric. For Russians, Stalin – a Georgian – was accepted as one of their own.

So it raised few eyebrows at the end of the war when, at a glittering reception for more than a thousand senior officers in the Kremlin's Georgiyevsky Hall, Stalin raised his glass and toasted the Russians as the 'most outstanding' people in the country.

Thunderous applause broke out.

At post-mortems on the toast, some observers branded it as 'insulting' to the millions of non-Russians who had fought in the war.

Insulting? Yes, says British scholar Alex de Jonge who writes that Stalin made no secret of his lack of faith in the fighting abilities of non-Russians. Yes, says Russian expert Alexander Werth who says that the toast 'slighted' Ukrainians.

But as far as is known none of Stalin's non-Russian generals and Marshals, including Ukrainians, Armenians and Jews, has ever protested about Stalin's admiration for the Russian people, or about his 'victory toast'.

Stalin was no novice where nationality problems were concerned. In the first government after the 1917 October revolution he had the post of Commissar of Nationalities. A few years earlier, apparently under Lenin's guidance, he wrote a tract, *Marxism and the National Question*, which is still cited in Marxist–Leninist literature published in the West. In 1929–30 he wrote at least two articles dealing with the complex 'ethnic problem' in Yugoslavia.

Here is Stalin's victory toast (given at a reception to honour the Commanders of the Red Army on 24 May 1945):

'Comrades, allow me to propose one more, last toast. I should like to propose a toast to the health of our Soviet people and, above all, to the health of the Russian people. (Cheers and ovation.)

'I drink above all to the health of the Russian people because they are the most outstanding nation of all the nations who compose the Soviet Union.

'I propose a toast to the health of the Russian people because they have deserved in this war general recognition as the leading force of the Soviet Union among all the peoples of our country.

'I propose a toast to the health of the Russian people not only because they are the leading people but also because they have a lucid mind, staunch character and patience.

'Our government made quite a number of mistakes. We had some desperate moments in 1941–2, when our army was retreating, and abandoning our native villages and towns in the Ukraine, Belorussia, Moldavia, the Leningrad region, the Baltic lands, the Karelo–Finnish Republic, abandoning them because there was no other alternative. Another people might have said to its government: "You have not justified our expectations. Get out. We will install another government that will make peace with Germany and assure our safety." But the Russian people did not take that step because they believed in the correctness of their government's policy, and they undertook sacrifices in order to ensure Germany's defeat. And this trust of the Russian people in the Soviet government was the decisive force that ensured the historic victory over the enemy of mankind – over Fascism.

'Thanks to them, the Russian people, for that confidence!

'To the health of the Russian people!'

General S. M. Shtemenko said that when Stalin concluded his toast a five-minute ovation from a thousand guests vibrated under the building's palatial ceiling.

The 'Kamikaze Pilots'

'If machine-guns jam in the air, if cartridges are spent prematurely, if the enemy is out to destroy an important state object, go and destroy the enemy by ramming.' – Combat directive to pilots of the 6th Air Corps during the defence of Moscow, 1941–4.

There is little doubt that Stalin's air force, including a number of death-defying pilots, helped save Moscow from massive destruction. Here are some facts:

In the first month of war the Luftwaffe made nearly one hundred attempts to penetrate Moscow air space, clandestinely, one at a time, at a height of 8,000 metres (24,000 feet). Only a few got through. From July to December 1941 there were 122 raids on Moscow by a total of 7,146 aircraft. Only 229 succeeded in getting close to the capital. The rest were shot down or chose less forbidding targets.

Then, on July 2, something unexpected happened that unnerved Hitler's pilots on the Eastern Front. A Heinkel He–111, with high-altitude engines, flew towards Moscow on an intelligence-gathering mission. On board was a colonel from the General Staff who had with him highly important documents including operational maps and codes. His aircraft was met by a Yak–1 piloted by Lieutenant Sergei Goshko.

The wooden-winged Yak–1, with a top speed of more than 300mph, was at times able to outmanoeuvre even the Luftwaffe's famed Messerschmitt Bf 109.

Suddenly, after an indecisive aerial battle, the Russian pilot struck the tail of the Heinkel with the wing of his fighter, sending it spinning to earth. It was the first ramming incident carried out by Moscow's air defenders.

For his exploit, Lieutenant Goshko was decorated with the highest combat medal, the Order of Lenin. Goshko brought down six more German aircraft by conventional means, making his last flight over a defeated Berlin on 8 May 1945.

At first, Luftwaffe crews refused to believe reports that a Russian pilot had rammed one of their aircraft near Moscow. But soon there were more reports of rammings. According to the record books, Stalin's 'Kamikaze flyers' had rammed German aircraft elsewhere over Russia prior to Goshko's daring performance. On the first day of the war a ramming incident occurred that is described in a document preserved in the Central Archives of the Russian Defence Ministry:

'At 0515 hours on 22 June 1941, about two hundred miles inside Russian territory, Flight Leader Junior Lieutenant Leonid Butelin rammed a German Junkers Ju–88 bomber, severing the tail with the propeller of his fighter. This was the first ramming of the war. No Luftwaffe pilot, however daring, used such tactics, then or afterwards.

Hitler believed that he could raze Moscow by massive air raids. For this purpose his General Staff chose more than 300 bombers of the newest types, including the high-altitude Heinkel He–111, the Junkers Ju–88 and the Dornier Do–215. Pilots for these raids were picked from famous squadrons, including the 'Condor' Squadron which had bombed Spanish cities during the Civil War, and others that had menaced the skies over London, Liverpool and Birmingham – or seen duty in Poland, Yugoslavia and Greece.

Aware that Moscow had a highly effective air defence system, the German High Command carried out careful reconnaissance before ordering mass air strikes against that city. The system, sometimes called 'Stalin's Sky Shield', has been described by Lieutenant-General Nikolai Suitov, former commander of the air forces of the Moscow Military District:

'Before the German attack on 22 June 1941 six fighter corps were created, half of which consisted of new types of fighters: the Yakovlev Yak–1, Mikoyan–Gurevich MiG–3 and Lavochkin LaGG–3. They were armed not only with cannon and machine-guns but also with rockets. At that time five top secret radar stations called 'Redut' could pick up targets at a distance of 120 kilometres (about 75 miles). By 22 July, 29 air regiments with 585 aircraft were protecting Moscow on round-the-clock duty. In 6th Air Corps we mobilised our test pilots, air club and air school instructors, including world record holders.

'In addition, Moscow was defended by nearly 1,000 anti-aircraft guns, 200 large calibre anti-aircraft machine-guns, 1,000 searchlights and hundreds of barrage balloons.

'To safeguard Moscow, Stalin's pilots shot down or rammed hundreds of German bombers, sending most of the crews to a fiery death. Official reports say that Russian pilots destroyed German aircraft by ramming on 300 occasions during the war. Most of these incidents took place on the approaches to the city or over Moscow itself.

'On the night of 22 July 1941 Hitler launched his first massive air strike against Moscow. Taking part were 250 bombers. Marshal Zhukov records that fewer than 20 Luftwaffe planes reached the capital, most of the bombers being stopped by the Moscow Anti-Aircraft Defence System (MAADS). About two dozen of the bombers were shot down outside the capital. The rest dispersed, dropping their bomb loads outside the city. This was the first of a long series of aerial battles for command of Moscow's skies.

'That same night over Mozhaisk, about 120 kilometres (75 miles) west of Moscow, a single aircraft, a Yak–1, engaged an incoming squadron of German Junkers Ju–88 bombers. The Russian pilot used his propeller to sever the tail of the bomber closest to him. The pilot, Boris Vasiliev, from the Georgian republic, was the first to ram a plane at night.

'At the beginning of August 1941 Russians crowded round a German aircraft that had been shot down not far from the capital. Near the charred metal was a wooden signboard with the words: "Tail of a German bomber downed by Senior Lt. Yevgeni Yeremeyev."

'Yeremeyev, who worked at a research institute of the Air Force, was a pioneer in night-flying. On the night of the first German raid on Moscow (22 July) he shot down a German bomber with machine-gun fire.'

'When at the end of July 1941 I saw a report about night ramming I did not believe it,' says General Yevgeni Klimov, then Commander of the 6th Air Corps. 'I called up Yeremeyev and he told me how it happened, and I recommended this hero of night ramming to be decorated with the highest award, the Order of Lenin.' But the pilot had only two more months to live. His life ended over Moscow when he was shot down by a Messerschmitt.

'We held discussions in all units about Yeremeyev's exploits by night.'

Among the people attending these discussions was Victor Talalikhin, a 23-year-old pilot who was already an expert on night flights. Two years earlier he had been decorated for heroism in the 'Winter War' with Finland, receiving the Order of the Red Star. Talalikhin was destined to enter the record books.

Here is a report from 6th Air Corps: 'Lieutenant Talalikhin at 22 hours 55 minutes on 6 August 1941 at the approaches to Moscow at a height of 4,000 metres saw an enemy bomber and attacked it several times. The enemy, returning fire, changed course and started to flee. Talalikhin closed and rammed the enemy aircraft, destroying it. He himself parachuted to earth.'

During the first four months of the war Talalikhin accounted for 27 German aircraft and was awarded the highest combat decoration, the gold star hero medal. Talalikhin's aerial saga became widely known in Russia and also abroad after he had posed for famed *Life* magazine photographer, Margaret Bourke-

White. But his luck ended on 27 October 1941 when his aircraft was destroyed in a duel with three Messerschmitts.

In the Defence Ministry Archives there is a wartime document entitled 'Air Combat Directive For Fighter Pilots', signed by the Deputy Commander of Fighter Aviation for the country's air defence: 'A situation may arise when duty toward the Motherland will demand from a Soviet fighter immediate ramming even if the armament of the aircraft is fully operational. An example: if the enemy bomber makes a run to bomb an object of state importance.' But according to the Directive, the pilots were not being sent on suicide missions. To ram the enemy 'is an act of the greatest heroism and bravery but is not an act of self-sacrifice,' it said. 'You should know how to ram.' There followed four pages of technical instruction on the techniques of ramming. Pilots who had rammed German aircraft early in the war and survived, instructed others on how to inflict this terrifying aerial blow. According to official reports, ramming fatalities were usually caused by head-on collisions, but some pilots survived if they had been able to bale out, and many managed to land their badly damaged aircraft.

Commenting on this Directive, Russian air ace Alexander Pokrushkin, who shot down 59 German aircraft, said: 'Everything is correct, it was just like that. A strike by ramming is the weapon of fliers with iron nerves. In the defence of Moscow this method was rightly necessary.'

Pokrushkin, who was to become an air marshal, said that 'at short distances, behind the tail of an enemy bomber, our fighter was invulnerable. He got into the 'dead cone' of enemy fire, inched closer and cut off a section of tail or a wing. One German pilot who baled out after his bomber had been rammed by Junior Lieutenant Fyodor Grul said when interrogated: "Rumours were around about rammings on the Eastern Front. But at first we did not believe in them. What a terrible thing it is!"'

The first high-altitude ramming was recorded during the Battle of Moscow. On 21 August, Lieutenant (later General) Alexei Katrich was ordered to destroy a Dornier Do–215 reconnaissance aircraft: 'My MiG–3 gained height, climbed to 1,000 metres, 3,000, then 5,000. It was cold in the cabin and it became difficult to breathe. I put on my oxygen mask. I was still climbing: 7,000 then 8,000 metres. After my second attack I saw flames from the left engine of the German aircraft. I pressed the button to fire again but there were no bullets left. Could I let the enemy go? What about Moscow? So, I decided to ram. With the tip of the propeller I cut the German's stabiliser and fuselage. The reconnaissance aircraft went down.'

During the defence of Moscow Yak fighter pilot Mikhail Rodionov brought off a 'double ramming' at a very low level. He had fired on a Junkers Ju–88 and knocked out one of its engines, then attacked again unaware that the Junkers had strengthened armour. Suddenly it went into a dive from 3,000 metres, but Rodionov caught up with it, now only 50 metres above the ground. With his propeller he put a deep gash in its right wing and then came in from the other side and delivered the *coup de grâce*, striking the bomber's wing with his own. Rodionov was awarded the Gold Star.

The Soviet Air Force records one more 'double ramming' when two Russian fighters were in pursuit of an enemy reconnaissance aircraft. Here is a report from 124th Fighter Air Regiment:

'After several attacks the machine-guns of the flight commander Boris Pirozhkov jammed. He closed to ram, slicing off the right half of the German plane's stabiliser. The Junkers Ju-88 lost height but did not fall. Then Lieutenant Viktor Dovgii, who was alongside, made a decision to ram it from above. At a height of only 1,000 metres he struck off the tail of the Junkers.'

Some of these aerial clashes seem incredible. The 606th Regiment had brittle wood and canvas biplanes that were no match for metal aircraft, and one of these, a Polikarpov R–5 bomber flown by Lieutenant Ivan Denisov on 7 October 1941 collided head-on with a Heinkel bomber. The twisted wreckage of the metal Heinkel fell to earth, but miraculously Denisov managed to bale out .

The last ramming in defence of Moscow occurred on 2 June 1943 when Lieutenant Gennady Sirishikov took off in a MiG–3 to take on a Junkers Ju–88 which was flying at a height of 8,000 metres. The Russian fired two bursts without result. The archive report says that the pilot 'refused to leave the field of battle without winning'. He closed in and used his propeller to saw off the tail of the Junkers.

The order to destroy enemy aircraft by ramming remained on the books until September 1944, but by that time Stalin's pilots dominated the skies.

The order to destroy enemy aircraft by ramming remained on the books until September 1944, but by that time Stalin's pilots dominated the skies.

But ... it seems that long after the war was over a Russian Air Force commander could still order a pilot on a suicide mission by ramming. In May 1960 when a high-altitude American U2 reconnaissance plane owned by the US Central Intelligence Agency was detected over Siberia, a Russian Air Force major was ordered to take his plane up and ram the intruder. (The U2 incident caused a sensation and resulted in the collapse of a planned Russo-American summit conference.) The pilot took off but never made contact with the U2. Meanwhile missiles were fired which brought down the CIA plane. But the missile forces on the ground, seeing more blips on their radar, didn't realise they had destroyed the intruder, and another Soviet plane that had been sent up was hit, taking the pilot's life.

'Night Witches'

During the war the all-women 46th Guards Night Bomber Regiment flew 24,000 missions.

No matter how pitiless the weather, Russian women pilots flew their tiny Polikarpov U–2VS two-seater close-support bombers (nicknamed 'ducks') – but only at night. When dawn broke their slow speed made them sitting ducks indeed, but in darkness they were difficult to detect when bombing bridges, trains or aircraft on forward airfields. The Germans dubbed them 'night witches', and it was said that pilots who shot down one of these little bombers would receive the coveted Iron Cross. It is recorded that the all-woman 46th Guards Night Bomber Regiment flew 24,000 missions.

Yevgenia ('Zhenya') Zhigulenko was a pilot-commander in the 46th. Her log book records a total of 968 combat missions. She was shot down twice. At the age of 24 she earned the country's highest military distinction: Hero of the Soviet Union.

Women fighter pilots began patrolling the skies over Stalingrad in the summer of 1942. The 586th Women's Air Defence flew 4,419 missions and were engaged in 125 air battles. All flying personnel of the 586th were cited for bravery.

But the 'night witches' flew more missions than the 586th.

The road to front-line duty had not been smooth for these young women pilots. When war came they insisted on seeing action immediately, but no women pilots were being sent to the front. They wrote countless petitions and appealed to everyone, including Stalin. Finally they got their wish and a women's air force group was formed. Their ground staff, mechanics and radio operators were women, and they too wanted to fly.

In the air there were no easy missions and few tranquil nights. In freezing weather hazards multiplied. 'During some flights', recalls Zhenya, 'we'd have to tear free with our hands the bombs that had got stuck under the ice-covered wings. The problem was that sometimes we used bombs which had been captured from the Germans and their lugs didn't properly fit our bomb-carriers.'

Many of her friends were killed in action. Zhenya remembers that in the space of one night eight girls perished fighting in the skies over the Taman Peninsula in the Crimea. These pilots in the Crimea had an exceptionally hazardous task in that they had to maintain a lifeline with the Russian Black Sea naval crews who had stormed the beaches in amphibious landing-craft and were under constant enemy fire. The 'witches' dropped ammunition, food and medicines, often flying at ground level across enemy lines.

Zhenya says: 'Flying was very frightening. After completing a mission your teeth would chatter, your knees would shake and sometimes you didn't even have the energy to talk. We would take off ten or more times a night.' After the war she became a script writer and film director.

> 'When all is said and done one can, if not get used to, at least reconcile oneself to many things: to being blinded by searchlights and shot at by anti-aircraft guns, to seeing bullet holes in the wings of one's plane, to being unable to speak and to feeling one's knees quaking after a touch-down, and even to missing a friend after a mission and hoping against hope that she will return.'

Even now, in her dreams, she finds herself once again in action and under fire, and now it is even more frightening because, as is the way with dreams, she feels helpless.

They Called her a 'Bolshevik Valkyrie'
In Norse mythology the Valkyries were the twelve handmaidens of Odin who selected those destined to be slain in battle and conducted them to Valhalla.

German soldiers called Mila Pavlichenko a 'Bolshevik Valkyrie'. British and American journalists had other names for her: 'The Queen of Fire' and 'Sniper Number One'.

Born in the Ukraine, the slight, trim-figured Mila was studying history at Kiev University when the war began. She walked into a military registration office, said she had experience in shooting, and was assigned duty as a sniper in the 25th 'Chapayev' Rifle Division.

During the defence of Odessa, on the Black Sea coast, Mila's marksmanship was the talk of the entire Russian coastal command. In the Odessa region alone this girl, described as attractive and gentle, killed 180 German soldiers with her sniper's rifle. Her name resounded across the country, and she appeared in a documentary film made by the well-known cinematographer Roman Karmen.

Men couldn't believe that this legendary sharpshooter was a slightly-built woman. At Sevastopol a burly sailor met her and later told his shipmates: 'Now there's a woman for you! By the looks of her she's just a dragonfly; but by the way she shoots she's a tiger!'

Mila's combat score rose relentlessly as she kept a bead on her foe, many of them first-class snipers. Once after a fifty-hour duel that ended in her favour, she crawled to her victim's body and found a record book in his pocket. The first entry read 'Dunkirk' and his score: four hundred British and French soldiers had met death at his hands. At Sevastopol he had brought it up to 500, but his duel with Mila was his last.

In April 1942 General Ivan Petrov issued Mila, now a lieutenant, a certificate as sniper-instructor. She was summoned to Moscow, was received by Commander-in-Chief Stalin, and was included in a delegation of front-line soldiers invited to the USA by Mrs. Eleanor Roosevelt.

On a visit to Chicago, Mila was given one minute to make a speech to a large audience. The Allies had not yet opened a 'Second Front', and Mila, looking especially slight in her army officer's uniform, stood before the microphone.

'I am 25 years old and have already destroyed 309 Nazis on the front line,' she said softly. 'I hope you will not hide behind my back for too long.'

The crowd froze. Then the auditorium filled with laughter and applause.

Nine Snow-White Cranes

There were many 'hero-families' in Russia during the war. Some of them lost four, five, even seven sons on the battlefield. Taso and Asakhmet Gazdanov raised seven sons in Ossetia, near the heart of the Caucasian Mountains. All went to war and none returned. From a homestead outside the city of Leningrad seven brothers of the Shaklein family went to the front. Seven death notices came back.

A greater tragedy in terms of numbers struck Yepistimiya Stepanova who lost her nine sons on the field of battle, from the second day of war almost to the day of victory. Alexander Sr. had lived for 17 years, Alexander Jr. – 20, Pavel – 22, Nikolai – 24, Ilya – 26, Fyodor – 27, Ivan – 28, Vasily – 35, Filipp – 36.

The day after the German invasion began, Lieutenant Pavel Stepanov died fighting in the border city of Brest. On the same day his elder brother Ivan, a machine-gunner, was severely wounded; taken prisoner, he escaped, was recaptured and executed.

Two other brothers – Alexander Senior and Fyodor – had fallen in other wars. At 17, Alexander had been brutally killed by counter-revolutionaries during the Civil War. Fyodor, a junior lieutenant, died a hero's death against Japanese forces who invaded Russian-protected Mongolia in the summer of 1939.

Vasily Stepanov, in his last letter from the front in 1943, wrote that by accident he had met his brother Filipp. It was the only time in the war that any of the Stepanov brothers met. Shortly afterward, Vasily, fighting with a partisan detachment, was ambushed by Gestapo forces, and shot.

At that time, Filipp was a prisoner, dying in a concentration camp. He lived until three months before Victory Day.

The year 1943 was the worst for the Stepanov family.

A few weeks before the Gestapo shot Vasily, his brother Alexander (who was named after his elder brother) met his fate on the banks of the Dnieper. He was commanding a company which captured a bridgehead; they were counterattacked and all his men were killed. Having no bullets left and not wishing to be captured alive, he ended his life with a grenade.

Days earlier, Captain Ilya Stepanov, commander of a tank company, fell at the Kursk bulge, one of the war's bloodiest battlefields.

Nikolai, the sole remaining brother, was unharmed until a few days before victory when he was severely wounded and hospitalised. Allowed to come home, he died in his mother's arms.

The mother Stepanova outlived her sons. When she died a few years ago at the age of 92, nine girls in snow-white dresses covered her grave with packets of earth brought from all the places and countries where her sons had fallen. A poem by the 19th-century poet Nekrasov was read which includes the words: 'She could no more forget her children than a weeping willow can lift its branches.' At her funeral service a gathering of thousands sang the verses of the poet Rasul Gamzatov: 'Sometimes it seems to me that the soldiers who did not return from the blood-soaked fields were not buried in common graves but were turned into snow-white cranes.'

Hero of the Drawing-Board

'I was shaken by the news that by noon of the first day of war we had already lost 1,200 aircraft – 300 destroyed in aerial battles, 900 on the ground. All this indicated that we had been caught napping. My mind was unwilling to accept the thought.' – Aircraft designer Alexander Yakovlev

Alexander Yakovlev, hailed for his famous Yak fighter, was widely regarded as Stalin's favourite aircraft designer. There were other talented designers, including Andrei Tupolev, Artyom Mikoyan – brother of Politburo member Anastas Mikoyan – Mikhail Gurevich and Sergei Ilyushin. Tupolev had been a victim of the purges before the war and sent to a special prison, one of the *Sharashki* where arrested scientists and engineers of known skills were allowed to continue working. Shortly after the outbreak of war he was released and went on to win high honours and a generalship in the air force.

But Yakovlev and his aircraft were continuously applauded and the country showered him with awards. (His Yak–3 could climb and match speed with the best German fighters.) Yakovlev was also authorised to publish his memoirs in which he described Stalin as being 'exceptionally modest'.

Stalin put great reliance on air power. Anything which disrupted the smooth running of his air force could make him lose his temper. He knew the 'vital statistics' including strengths and weaknesses of all current major combat aircraft, Russian and foreign. Once, when the American politician Wendell Willkie was visiting Moscow, Stalin complained to him that the United States and Britain were sending Russia inferior aircraft and withholding the best models. He said that Russia needed more advanced aircraft than the P–40s and Hurricanes that were being sent as part of Lend-Lease aid. He complained that when the Americans were about to deliver 150 advance-model P–39 Airacobras, the British grabbed the lot for themselves.

In June 1943 a serious flaw developed that grounded the mainstay Yak fighter. Stalin was furious. Preparations were under way for one of the greatest battles of the war, then just a few weeks off. But all the Yaks had a wing defect. The senior Air Force officers were shaken. It seems that the paint used on the Yaks was sub-standard and cracked under certain atmospheric conditions, causing the fabric of the wing to peel from the frame.

Summoned to the Kremlin, Yakovlev had never seen Stalin so angry. 'The whole of our fighter force is out of commission,' he thundered. 'There have been a dozen cases of the skin separating from the wing. The pilots are afraid to fly. How has it come about?' He let on that an 'important operation' was being held up because it could not be carried out without the highly durable and fast Yak fighter. He meant the impending Battle of Kursk.

Again Stalin barked: 'How did it happen? How could you produce several hundred planes with such a defect? Do you know that you have put the entire fighter plane force out of commission? Do you know what a service for Hitler you have performed? You are Hitlerites!'

A long silence followed. Yakovlev recalls that at last, after walking back and forth by his map table, Stalin calmed down and asked in a business-like tone: 'What are we going to do?' An associate of Yakovlev's who was present answered that all the aircraft would be 'fixed' immediately.

'What do you mean? Within what time period?'

'Within two weeks,' said the associate designer.

'You're not fooling me?'

'No, Comrade Stalin, we'll do it.'

Yakovlev says that he couldn't believe his ears. He was sure that the repairs would take two months. But the deadline was accepted, and Stalin, still extremely upset, ordered a military commission to investigate and punish the offenders.

Before he left Stalin's office, Yakovlev was again rebuked, but this time in a subdued voice: 'Doesn't your self-esteem suffer? How do you feel? You're being made a fool of, your plane is being sabotaged and you just stand by.'

'Comrade Stalin, I feel terrible as I fully realise the damage this misfortune has caused. But I swear that in the shortest possible time the defect will be corrected.'

Yakovlev and his design team worked without letup and managed to complete the repairs within two or three days of the start of the Orel–Kursk battle of July 1943 where the Germans deployed 150 bombers escorted by hundreds of fighters to blast the Russian front lines. Aerial battles raged, and both sides were using aircraft of advanced design. Yakovlev's design bureau supplied the Yak–7B; Semyon Lavochkin the LA–5 fighter-bomber and the LA–7 interceptor. The Russians also had the Ilyushin I1–2 ground attack fighter. The Luftwaffe was bolstered with the new Focke-Wulf Fw 190–A fighter and the Henschel Hs–129 ground attack/anti-tank aircraft.

In six days, according to Russian archives, the Luftwaffe lost 1,037 aircraft and Russians losses amounted to hundreds.

Yakovlev recalled that on the third day several hundred Russian fighters and bombers 'wiped out' the German main line of defence, destroying lengthy tank columns before they had a chance to engage the Russian ground forces. On 12 July the Russians began a successful counter-offensive.

A meeting of Stalin and Yakovlev which took place under normal circumstances helps explain why Stalin earned the respect of his generals and others who came in close contact with their Supreme Commander-in-Chief. Alone with Yakovlev, Stalin asked his opinion of a new fighter aircraft produced by a rival design bureau headed by N. N. Polikarpov, who had written a long letter to Stalin extolling his own aircraft. Yakovlev praised the Polikarpov plane, its speed and other characteristics. Stalin interrupted. 'Forget your corporate loyalty. How do you view it impartially?' Yakovlev said that he knew that only a few tests of the new aircraft had been carried out. On hearing this, Stalin – holding the letter in his hand – said that he did not believe in mere words. Only after extensive tests of the new aircraft had been made, particularly as to its range, would a decision be reached.

A Hero of the Airwaves

'In his inimitable ceremonial voice Levitan began – and suddenly Stalin shouted: "Why did Levitan leave out Marshal Konev's name? Give me the text!" There was no mention of Konev's name in the text. And I was to blame. Stalin was terribly angry. "Stop the broadcast and read it all again!" he ordered. I rushed to the telephone.' – From General S. M. Shtemenko's memoirs.

Yuri Borisovich Levitan was Stalin's chief radio announcer and in this job was able to observe Stalin close up, even to have brief chats with him. ('They were mainly "shop talk".') Meeting as he did officers of the General Staff on a daily basis as well as the country's top military and political leaders, he was privy to inside information.

As chief radio announcer, Levitan broadcast thousands of communiqués, citations for distinguished service and other announcements. His voice was known in every household that had a radio, and throughout the armed forces. Several armies awarded him honorary titles.

I met Levitan at the Central Broadcasting Studio in Moscow. Grey-haired and portly, although past retirement age, he was still working. Since he had been 'on the air' during the first week of the invasion, I asked if he knew whether Stalin was, as some have claimed, in an 'hysterical panic' on the day the Germans attacked.

Levitan replied: 'You can't say Stalin was frightened. But of course maybe he was a little disoriented at the time because it was a real surprise, a shock. War comes as a shock to everybody. But a few days later there was a meeting of Party leaders and they adopted a special directive which affected all radio coverage of the war. Also, war aims were outlined for soldiers, workers and partisans. Stalin himself read the directive. And, later, on 3 July at 6.30 p.m., there was a live transmission from the Kremlin when Stalin spoke to the people about Hitler's attack.'

On occasions Stalin, before delivering a speech, was introduced by Levitan.

'Although I introduced him, when we spoke it was mainly about technical details. This was during the days of the Great Patriotic War. We showed the transcripts to Stalin, which included our introductory words, and how we would present him to the listening audience. We – that is our staff – advised him whether to speak louder, softer, standing or sitting. But of course we never gave him advice on how to read, about his style.'

Stalin, according to Levitan, was an effective speaker. 'He was a clever, emotional speaker with a gift for making people believe in him. He had a gift of persuasion. But there was nothing special about his voice.'

'Many people have said he spoke with a thick accent...'

'Stalin spoke with an accent, a Georgian one. But his speech was always intelligible and his stresses, the emotional stresses, were always correct and impressive. It was a pleasant accent. And this was because he lived in Russia most of his life. It was a very soft accent. And his speeches were written by himself in perfect Russian.

'I'll tell you this: On 3 July 1941 I was standing near him. He had eight pages in hand – half of them in his handwriting. The rest was typed. Later I had a chance to look at these pages because we had to repeat his announcement. I saw the handwriting and I assure you it was on the mark. There were no faults. He observed all the commas, all the right punctuation. It was an educated person's writing, fully grammatical.

'His Russian was splendid. It was so that you couldn't drop a single word. It was precise, laconic, very emotional, and highly understandable. Personally, I derived pleasure from his speeches. Listening to them was like listening to a master storyteller.'

A different, highly critical opinion of Stalin's use of language comes from historian and critic Leonid Batkin. Stalin, says Batkin, used 'verbose rhetoric' and 'boring repetitions'. ('What does correct selection of cadres mean? – Correct selection of cadres means ...') Also, Stalin used endless enumerations, as for example 'Our five pillars of foreign policy' or 'Six tasks for the Party', etc.

Batkin dismisses Stalin's speeches as 'worthless', 'limp', 'insignificant'. He says further that Stalin's language was syntactically and lexically poor, full of the 'rhetorical devices' of a 'semi-educated' person; that he employed lots of 'bureaucratic jargon', that his sentences showed 'meagreness of expression', that there was an 'aridity' about his grammatical constructions.

On the other hand, Western leaders who met Stalin in wartime commented favourably on his language and speaking ability. President Roosevelt's assistant Harry Hopkins held lengthy conversations with Stalin. He said that talking to Stalin was 'like talking to a perfectly co-ordinated machine, an intelligent machine'.

Another American, Wendell Willkie, who met Stalin in 1942 said: 'He talks quietly, readily, and at times with a simple, moving eloquence.' Yugoslav intellectual Milovan Djilas gave this description: 'His Russian vocabulary was rich, and his manner of expression very vivid and plastic, and replete with Russian proverbs and sayings. As I later became convinced, Stalin was well acquainted with Russian literature.'

Although Stalin's chief radio announcer extolls Stalin's speech-making and writing, Levitan was no servile flatterer. 'You should not', he said, 'over-estimate Stalin's wartime role.'

> 'We had other leaders in the industrial sphere and in the military, who were very talented people, devoted to the country. They carried out their tasks well. These people were seasoned in the course of the war. And without the lower staffs – the well-trained, well-prepared, efficient junior workers – no leader, no matter how great, or even greater than Stalin, could do anything. Such were the talented people under him.'

Levitan said that 'deadlines' were always being advanced during the war. 'People worked and tried to do their best. For instance, the evacuation of plants and factories to the East was done very efficiently. People worked days and nights without food, standing in the snow.'

He recalled an unpleasant incident that took place while he was announcing those who were being honoured. The name of a famous Marshal – Ivan Konev – had been left out.

> 'Stalin was listening in his Kremlin office and called in. He asked: "Is this the announcer's mistake?" I was just ending my broadcast. I was still reading. And I heard the door squeak and the chairman of the Broadcasting Committee entered. I squinted and saw the chairman take a piece of paper and write something. And from my experience

I knew that when the chairman or any top official arrived during the broadcasting, and if he wrote something, it usually meant that there had been a slip of the tongue or some other mistake which must be corrected. So in those three or four minutes left for me to finish the announcement, I was feeling on edge. In my mind I was speculating on what the mistake was. A wrong date? Wrong town, city? Some other mistake? And the chairman, standing nearby with a piece of paper, waited for me to finish.

'Only a bit later did I learn that Marshal Konev's name had been omitted. Lucky for me, it was not my fault or that of the radio staff. Of course the announcement had to be read over again – which I did.'

REFLECTIONS

★★★ THE STALIN PHENOMENON ★★★

Censoring Marshal Zhukov

In 1989 the Russian public learned new details about Zhukov's censored memoirs. Whole pages, paragraphs and sentences had been cut from the original edition of his popular memoirs published 20 years earlier. Because Zhukov had given his approval for publication of his memoirs with the cuts – this was during the regime of Nikita Khrushchev who'd first exposed Stalin's 'cult of personality' – some wits called it the 'first capitulation of the undefeated Marshal'.

The censored parts of Zhukov's memoirs deal with such matters as Stalin's fallibility, his purge of the army in 1937–9 and Zhukov's observations as to how Stalin viewed the Nazi regime on the eve of war. This passage, for example, was excised from the original edition:

'I will not conceal that it appeared to us then [before the war] that Stalin knew no less but even more than we did about matters of war and defence and had a deeper understanding and foresight. When we had to encounter difficulties in the war, however, we understood that our views about Stalin being extraordinarily well-informed and possessing the qualities of a military leader had been erroneous.'

Nor did the following paragraph in the original ever see the light:

'At the end of May 1941 Marshal Timoshenko and I were urgently summoned to the Politburo. We thought that at last we would probably be permitted to put the border military districts on high alert. So one can imagine our amazement when Stalin told us: "The German Ambassador, von Schulenburg, has passed on to us a request of the German government to allow them to search for the graves of soldiers and officers killed during the First World War in battles against the old Russian army. For this search the Germans have formed several groups which will arrive at the border points according to our map."'

Similarly omitted was a conversation in which Stalin was first told that German armies had crossed the border into the Soviet Union. 'Stalin's reaction: "Isn't this a provocation by German generals?" Marshal Timoshenko, who was present, replied: "The Germans are bombing our cities in the Ukraine, Belorussia and the Baltic area – and land forces have launched operations on the border. It certainly cannot be called a provocation." Stalin commented: "If a provocation needs to be staged, then the German generals would bomb even their own cities." Further, he said that "Hitler knows nothing about it for sure. What is needed is to urgently contact Berlin."'

When the invasion began Zhukov met Stalin and raised the question of counter-strikes against the German armies. The following dialogue appeared in the original but an additional sentence was cut:

162

Stalin (irritated) What counter-strikes? Don't give me that rubbish!

Zhukov: If you think that as Chief of the General Staff I am only giving you rubbish, there is nothing for me to do here. So I ask you to relieve me of my duties and send me to the front. There I will apparently be of greater use to our Motherland.

Stalin: Don't get excited! But then, if you put the matter that way, we will manage to do without you.

Then Stalin added the following words which were not published: 'We have managed to do without Lenin, so we will certainly manage to do without you.'

The new uncut edition of Zhukov's memoirs though containing additional criticisms of Stalin, retains Zhukov's homage to his Commander-in-Chief: 'With strictness and exactitude Stalin achieved the near-impossible.' Also: 'He had a tremendous capacity for work, a tenacious memory, he was a very gifted man.' And: 'Stalin's merit lies in the fact that he correctly appraised the advice offered by the military experts and then in summarised form – in instructions, directives and regulations – immediately circulated them among the troops for practical guidance.'

Zhukov on Heroism. When Zhukov met General Eisenhower in Berlin in 1945 they spoke for three hours. During their talk the subject of patriotism came up and, records Eisenhower, he was stunned by Zhukov's words: 'You [in America] tell a person he can do as he pleases, he can act as he pleases, he can do anything. But we Russians tell him that he must sacrifice for the state.' Eisenhower says that he had great difficulty in replying.

A First Meeting. In the spring of 1940 Stalin invited Georgi Konstantinovich Zhukov, then Chief of the General Staff, to the Kremlin where they met for the first time. As was his habit, Stalin broke up some cigarettes and put the tobacco in his pipe. After slowly lighting up, he asked Zhukov to assess the fighting quality of Japanese soldiers.

General Zhukov (later appointed Marshal) had distinguished himself the previous year leading a combined Russian–Mongolian army to victory over a Japanese invasion force. 'Barbarossa' was just a year away.

In combat, said Zhukov, the Japanese soldiers were obedient, diligent and dogged. As a rule junior officers were fanatical warriors and when beaten on the battlefield often refused to surrender, sometimes preferring *hara-kiri*. Japanese generals and other senior officers lacked initiative and seemed to behave like stereotypes.

Stalin at that time had dominated Russia for more than fifteen years and was generally admired by the nation. Books, films and poems eulogised him. Zhukov says he instantly liked Stalin's directness and simplicity. Stalin listened closely as Zhukov discussed Japanese armaments and the Japanese air force. He then asked how Zhukov's own soldiers had done.

The burly general spoke in detail, giving praise as well as criticism. He singled out some 'poorly trained officers and men' and, discussing the performance of Red Army generals in Mongolia, called one of them incompetent.

Stalin asked probing questions about the difficulties in fighting, and wanted Zhukov's opinion on the real aim of the Tokyo government in opening hostilities. Zhukov said that Japan had covetous eyes on Siberia and wanted eventually to cut off the vital east–west Trans-Siberian Railway.

The future Marshal says that at first he was a bit awkward in Stalin's presence but gradually felt at ease. Stalin's absence of formality appealed to him. Before leaving he put his own question to Stalin. Puzzled by Allied inactivity on the Western front – this was the time of the so-called 'phoney war' – Zhukov asked how the international situation should be interpreted.

Stalin chuckled, saying:

'The French Government headed by Daladier and the Chamberlain Government in Britain have no intention of getting seriously involved in the war with Hitler. They still hope to be able to persuade Hitler to start a war against the Soviet Union. They refused to form an anti-Hitler bloc with us in 1939, because they did not want to hamper Hitler in his aggression against us. But nothing will come of it. They will have to pay a high price for their short-sighted policy.'

As Zhukov was leaving Stalin said: 'Now that you have combat experience, take upon yourself the command of the Kiev Military District and use this experience for training the troops.'

Zhukov says that he was deeply impressed with Stalin's appearance and manner, and 'the depth and concreteness of his judgement, his knowledge of military matters, the attention with which he listened to my report.'

After the German invasion, Stalin became Supreme Commander-in-Chief, and later made Zhukov his deputy.

'Are You Sure We'll Hold Moscow?' In 1970 Zhukov told an interviewer about a conversation with Stalin during the most critical hours of the Battle of Moscow in 1941. Advance units of the German armies were so close to the capital city that the onion domes of the Kremlin cathedrals could be seen through their binoculars. Stalin rang him up and asked:

'Are you sure we'll hold Moscow? It pains me greatly to ask you such a question. Tell me honestly, like a Communist.' Zhukov's replied: 'Yes, Comrade Stalin, we'll hold Moscow.' But he added that he would need reinforcements, including tanks and aircraft. He received them and the Germans were halted.

Maisky's Censored Memoirs

A couple of years after Zhukov's memoirs were published, historian-diplomat Ivan Maisky had his own troubles with the censor. To get his own memoirs published, every critical reference to the war and Stalin's role in it had to be removed.

Maisky, who was envoy to London from 1932 to 1943, was also a member of the Academy of Sciences and a respected historian. But Party leaders in the early 'seventies were apparently allergic to any criticism of the Party and refused to allow in print suggestions that Russia had not always been under 'competent leadership'.

In the censored edition of his book (*Memoirs of a Soviet Diplomat*), Maisky recalls how he felt after hearing a speech on invasion day – 22 June 1941 – by Foreign Minister V. M. Molotov:

'The speech of the People's Commissar for Foreign Affairs made a good impression upon me. It answered fully to my feelings.' But in the original MS this was followed by two sentences that did not appear in the book:

'But at that moment – I frankly admit it – I did not imagine what a terrible price we should have to pay for victory. But this was due to the fact that in the summer of 1941, like very many others, I did not clearly understand either the cult of Stalin's personality, or all the tragic consequences of that cult.'

Censored too was Maisky's mention of information that the British government had given him about Nazi plans to invade Russia. 'It seemed to me that they should give Stalin serious food for thought, and lead him urgently to check them and in any case, give strict instructions to our Western frontier to be on guard,' Maisky wrote. Also deleted was his comment that Stalin adamantly refused to believe that Hitler would attack Russia.

Western Praise For Stalin

After British Field Marshal Lord Alanbrooke met Stalin he commented: 'Never once in any of his statements did Stalin make any strategic error, nor did he ever fail to appreciate all the implications of a situation with a quick and unerring eye.' During the war Britain's Lord Beaverbrook declared that under Stalin Russia had produced the 'best generals of the war'. (When I mentioned this to General Volkogonov, a military historian, he said: 'Before he created good generals, Stalin destroyed a lot of other good generals,' and said that history and circumstances had combined to create the 'best generals' mentioned by Beaverbrook.)

Russian Critics

Roy Medvedev (*Let History Judge*, 1971) calls Stalin a mediocre military commander. Victory over Hitler, he says, was won by the Red Army and the people in spite of Stalin. Volkogonov, a Stalin biographer (*Stalin: Triumph and Tragedy*, 1992) says that Stalin had 'no professional military skills' and that his resolutions as set forth in military documents reveal the 'extremely contradictory nature' of their author. Marshal A. I. Eremenko in his memoirs blames Stalin for being too late in alerting the troops when Hitler launched his attack. He says that Stalin thought Germany wouldn't dare attack Russia. As a result, says Eremenko, Stalin did not mount effective security measures, lest this provoke Hitler. Another top-ranking Russian, Marshal Pavel A. Rotmistrov, said that the main reason for the big losses in 1941 was Stalin's 'personality cult'. According to Rotmistrov, Stalin concentrated huge power in his own hands, and believed that he alone could decide all questions, military ones included.

A Dissident General

Pyotr Grigorenko, whom I met a number of times in Moscow during the mid-1970s, made no secret of his dislike of Stalin. But he admitted that Stalin was an able and confident wartime commander. In his memoirs he said that an army colleague and friend, Lieutenant-General Pyotr P. Vechny, who had frequent meetings with Stalin, denied allegations that Stalin lacked understanding of military affairs. Stalin, said Vechny, who held a senior position on the General Staff during the war, might have trouble commanding a company, but he 'understood everything' better than those who worked with him. Indeed, Stalin didn't hesitate to speak out if a particular matter was unclear to him. He would, added Vechny, often ask different people the same question so that he could choose the best solution to a problem. If he didn't find this satisfactory, he would stick to his original opinion.

Western Experts on Stalin

Here is how some Western experts look at the wartime Stalin:

Adam Ulam (*Stalin*, 1989) says that Stalin left Russia 'rudderless' during the opening days of Hitler's attack. Albert Seaton (*Stalin as Warlord*, 1976) cites Stalin's 'uneven' knowledge of military affairs and says that he had 'no military training, or scientific instruction'. Robert Payne (*The Rise and Fall of Stalin*, 1966) says that Stalin displayed a 'vast ignorance of military affairs'. Alan Bullock (*Hitler and Stalin, Parallel Lives*, 1993) says that as wartime C-in-C, Stalin often failed to consult the General Staff when summoning commanders from the front and that he constantly intervened in operations, not being content with the strategic direction of the war. Alex de Jonge (*Stalin and the Shaping of the Soviet Union*, 1986) writes that Stalin 'would have been delighted to have others do his fighting for him'. Robert Tucker (*Stalin as Revolutionary*, 1974) told an interviewer in Moscow in 1991 that the start of Hitler's invasion of Russia was 'the most horrible defeat in military history and it was all Stalin's fault'.

From *Everyman's Encylopaedia*, 1978: 'Stalin interfered personally with the work of the military commanders, and assumed the ranks of Marshal and, later, Generalissimo.'

Stalin's Daughter and the CIA

The memoirs of Stalin's daughter, Svetlana Alliluyeva, are an unimpeachable source in the eyes of many historians. For example, Oxford scholar Alan Bullock in his 1,100-page biography of Stalin and Hitler, says that she was perhaps 'closest to understanding her father's mind'. In her memoirs she says that he suffered from a 'deep depression' after the invasion; that he had said cynically after the war that, 'together with the Germans we would have been invincible'.

But how objective are the writings of Stalin's daughter? Is it possible that not every word in her 1970 memoirs is her own? She herself once raised doubts about her memoirs.

In 1984 Stalin's only daughter returned to Russia (after her earlier defection) and stayed two or three years before again leaving for the West. Speaking at a press conference shortly after her arrival in Moscow, she said with a display of emotion that she was *not alone* in writing her memoirs; that standing behind her was a member of the Central Intelligence Agency. I was one of a handful of foreign correspondents in the room when she made this eye-popping disclosure.

Of course, she may have said this as a token of appreciation to her Moscow hosts who had expeditiously returned her old Russian passport and restored her citizenship. But in those years of Cold War mischief the bigger surprise would have been if a book being written on US soil by the daughter of Joseph Stalin had been totally ignored.

Svetlana's memory of post-invasion Stalin talking of collaborating with the Nazi regime is almost certainly hazy. Also doubtful is her statement that Stalin had 'not guessed or foreseen that the Pact [with Hitler] of 1939, which he had considered the outcome of his own great cunning, would be broken by an enemy more cunning than himself'. In fact Stalin has admitted that he expected Hitler to break the Pact, but not for another year or so.

Svetlana says further that Stalin 'never admitted his mistakes'.

Here is what Stalin told a large military audience in May 1945: 'Our government made quite a number of mistakes.' (He said this when admitting that the country had had some desperate moments in 1941–2, when the Red Army was in retreat.)

Khrushchev's Fallibility

In his 'secret speech' to the XX Party Congress in 1956, Premier Nikita Khrushchev said: 'We should note that Stalin planned operations on a globe. Yes comrades, he used to take the globe and trace the front line on it!'

But two high-ranking military men with a reputation for veracity, who know more than Khrushchev about this matter (they met Stalin sometimes daily during the war), disagree. Marshal Zhukov says: 'The widespread tale that the Supreme Commander studied the situation and adopted decisions when toying with a globe is untrue.' And General S. M. Shtemenko, who daily took to the Kremlin an armful of detailed maps of the various Fronts for Stalin's perusal says that: 'The talk of the Fronts being directed by reference to a globe is completely unfounded.'

Stalin: a Scared Rabbit?

Nikita Khrushchev also said that Stalin on hearing of the invasion acted like a 'rabbit in front of a boa constrictor'. But a man who was arrested at least six times by Tsarist police between 1902 and 1913 and who escaped five times – as Stalin did, mostly from Siberian and Arctic prison camps – is not likely to act the coward in moments of danger.

Stalin's 'Appointments Book'

Many experts have written that Stalin disappeared for a few days after invasion day, and it is difficult to be accurate as to his whereabouts during the opening days of the invasion. A few years ago his appointments book was found, and several pages detailing visitors to Stalin's Kremlin study are reproduced in Pavel Sudoplatov's *Special Tasks, the Memoirs of an Unwanted Witness*

– *A Soviet Spymaster*, 1994. And the Stalin biographer Edvard Radzinsky, on a visit to London in April 1996, disclosed that he had gained access to the 'presidential archives' in the Kremlin and found the journal listing Stalin's visitors for June 1941. He said this showed that Stalin had not, as previously thought, disappeared for a week or more after the invasion, but rather had received a steady stream of visitors.

That the country was not leaderless at this time is shown by the fact that a number of vital decisions were taken during the first week of the invasion and these had to be approved at the highest level. These included:

23 June (the day after the invasion): Adoption of a crash programme for production of ammunition; also approval of an economic mobilisation plan for the third quarter of 1941.

24 June: Adoption of a plan to move aircraft plants to the rear and to speed up construction of such plants in Siberia.

25 June: A decision was taken to increase output of heavy and medium tanks. Overtime working was made obligatory and annual holidays cancelled.

Marshal Zhukov mentions a telephone call from Stalin on the 26th, the fourth day of the invasion, summoning him to Moscow. 'In the evening of 26 June I landed at Moscow and went to Stalin's office directly from the airport.' Zhukov makes no mention of an incapacitated Stalin.

A week later Stalin gave a major radio address to the country, delivering it in person at the Central Broadcasting Studio. (Stalin's biographer Robert Payne says that Stalin recorded this address in the Caucasus, more than 500 miles from Moscow, but chief radio announcer Yuri Levitan says that he watched Stalin delivering this address at Moscow's Central Broadcasting Studio.')

Stalin's Visits to the Front Line

Stalin has been criticised by some observers (not generals) for not visiting his troops on the battlefield. General Shtemenko comments: 'It seems to me that Stalin could not visit the front lines more often than he did. It would have been unpardonably negligent for the Supreme Commander to lay aside overall leadership even for a time so as to decide particular problems on one of the Fronts. (In the summer of 1943 Stalin made a visit to the front lines, first to the command post of General V. D. Sokolovsky and then to that of General A. I. Eremenko.)

As to Stalin's nerves, or lack of them, his generals make no criticisms. Rather, Marshal Zhukov told a war correspondent that Stalin had 'nerves of steel'. The correspondent, author Ilya Ehrenburg, wrote (*The War: 1941–1945*) that the Marshal repeated these words to him several times when they met at a command post near the front line early in the war.

Even General Andrei Vlasov who had a great grievance against Stalin and, therefore, cause for resentment, told the Germans upon his capture that Stalin had strong nerves. Speaking to Dr. Goebbels, the Nazi Minister of Propaganda, he said that in the autumn of 1941, when the city of Moscow was threatened by advancing German armies, every one in the Kremlin had lost his nerve but only Stalin insisted on continued resistance to the German invaders.

Stalin Hangs a Traitor

General Andrei Andryevich Vlasov, son of a peasant, was 17 when he took part in the October Revolution. He rose swiftly in the Red Army, joined the Communist Party, was a military adviser to Chinese armies under Chiang Kai-shek, and distinguished himself at the Battle of Moscow in 1941. Vlasov received the Order of the Red Flag for bravery, fought in other fierce battles but was surrounded with his '2nd Shock Army' and taken prisoner by the Germans in the spring of 1942.

Pointing an accusing finger at Stalin for not doing enough to extricate his army from encirclement, Vlasov became chummy with a number of Nazi bigwigs. After Hitler's defeat, Vlasov was captured, tried for treason, and hanged by the Russians in the summer of 1946.

While in captivity Vlasov had told the Germans that he had lost all sympathy for the Stalin regime and, to show his new loyalty, he prepared an 'open letter' to all Russian POWs, exhorting them to join in fighting 'against Stalin, for peace and a new Russia'. Vlasov believed that only Russians could liberate Russia from Stalin and Bolshevism. While on German soil he trained deserters and POWs in a volunteer all-Russian army of liberation.

Vlasov's German captors found him intelligent and well-educated although, it is recorded, they resented his being 'Russian to the core'. But they gladly used him for propaganda purposes. Apparently even SS leader Heinrich Himmler took an interest in him but found unacceptable his dogmatic view that only Russians could conquer Russia.

In the opinion of historian von Rauch, German officials played a 'double game' with Vlasov, using him while making him believe that they agreed with his future vision of Russia and its non-Communist future.

In *The Goebbels Diaries, the Last Days*, edited by Hugh Trevor-Roper, Joseph Goebbels mentions meeting Vlasov several times and having long conversations with him. Vlasov, he recalls, described Stalin as a man of extraordinary cunning, even 'Jesuitical' training, whose utterances should not be believed.

Vlasov is mentioned by Alexander Solzhenitsyn and Nikita Khrushchev. Solzhenitsyn faults Stalin for Vlasov's plight; Khrushchev does not.

Solzhenitsyn, a Nobel-laureate, says that Stalin abandoned the General in 1942. This is refuted by Marshal Vasilevsky who in 1942 was First Deputy Chief of the General Staff, and was meeting Stalin, 'sometimes several times a day'. In his book, *A Lifelong Cause*, 1981, Vasilevsky says: 'I can with some authority confirm the extremely serious concern which Stalin displayed daily for the 2nd Shock Army and for rendering every possible assistance to them. This is proved by a whole series of GHQ directives that I personally wrote primarily to Stalin's dictation.' Vasilevsky mentions that he received daily telephone calls from Stalin about the 2nd Shock Army and General Vlasov.

Reviewing the Vlasov affair, Kremlinologist Edward Crankshaw, like Solzhenitsyn, defends the General who went over to the enemy. Vlasov, he says, was an 'angry and frustrated' man and not the opportunist-careerist depicted by Khrushchev. He blames the General's defection on the 'corruption, brutality and incompetence' of Stalin and his associates.

'Lashes and Prods'

Louis Fischer, a staunch anti-Communist author, after making a list of Stalin's abominations, nevertheless compliments the dictator's role in industry and education and in the victory over Nazi Germany. In these matters, says Fischer, Stalin 'deserved much praise'.

Fischer adds that under Stalin's 'lashes and prods', Soviet Russia built new cities and expanded her industrial production. Also, 'Stalin's strong arm put over the collectivisation and mechanisation of farming which regimented the peasantry and made possible an increased yield from the land. He greatly reinforced the nation's armed might.'

The 'Rokossovsky Phenomenon'

Russian historian Lev Bezymensky made a study of prominent citizens who suffered arrest under Stalin's dictatorship but were later released, men and women who quietly accepted their fate and, with apparent absence of malice, later served their country loyally. He calls this the 'Rokossovsky phenomenon' after the popular hero Marshal Konstantin Rokossovsky.

In 1937 he was jailed for no apparent reason. He was freed in 1940 and, beginning in 1941 at the Battle of Moscow, earned the highest decorations for his military skill, and led the victory parade on Red Square in 1945.

Edward Crankshaw, in a footnote to the Khrushchev memoirs, mentions Marshal S. K. Meretskov as another high-ranking Red Army commander who was released from detention and went on to win fame in fighting the *Wehrmacht*. Another who was released was General A. V. Gorbatov. (Roy Medvedev says that the 'extreme shortage of officers' in Stalin's army became evident in 1939–40 with the German invasion of Poland and Stalin's war with Finland.)

The celebrated aircraft designer Andrei Tupolev also suffered temporary arrest. In October 1937 police took him into custody on the fatuous charge that he had delivered blueprints of Russian aircraft to the German Messerschmitt aircraft firm which – according to one story – used them to produce the Bf 110 fighter.

But as aviation designers of Tupolev's stature were rare, he and other detained scientists and engineers were asked to continue working, although in confinement.

A true patriot, Tupolev bent his efforts to lifting the morale of his colleagues, telling them: 'We all love our Motherland not less but more than those who got us all together here. War is in the offing and, because of that, we must clench our teeth and make a first-class plane.' His colleagues agreed, according to the reminiscences of fellow-designer Leonid Kerber.

Tupolev went on to win two Stalin Prizes for his work on aircraft and was made a lieutenant-general in the air force.

Survivors of the Spanish Civil War

Many Russian generals who distinguished themselves in World War II had volunteered for duty in the Spanish Civil War. These men included K. A. Meretskov, P. I. Batov, N. N. Voronov, R. Y. Malinovsky, V. Y. Kolpakchi, A. I.

Rodimstev, M. N. Yakushin and S. M. Krivoshein. Admirals included N. G. Kuznetsov and V. A. Alafuzov.

In a memoir of his duty in Spain, General Pavel Batov saluted 'some members of the propertied classes' who fought alongside the Russians against the rebel forces of General Francisco Franco. Batov gives honourable mention to Esmond Romilly, a nephew of Winston Churchill's, and David Mackenzie, the son of a British admiral, who joined the International Brigade. Says Batov: 'I must say that they fought with a courage that their illustrious forebears could envy.'

Tragically, many Russian officers who fought in Spain returned home to be accused of treason and shot. Those who fell in the purges included Y. K. Berzin, G. M. Stern and Y. V. Smushkevich. From 1954, the Military Collegium of the Supreme Court began to rehabilitate thousands of officers, most of them posthumously.

The Generalissimo's Uniform

At the close of the war, the Red Army Chief of Supply, Colonel-General P. I. Drachev, appeared one day in Stalin's waiting-room dressed, says a bystander, in a 'magnificent' new military uniform. It was cut in the manner of Napoleon's time, with high collar, epaulettes, and gold-striped trousers. Drachev told onlookers that it was the new uniform for the Generalissimo.

Being told that Stalin was in an 'excellent mood', Drachev asked permission to show off the new uniform. But when Drachev entered, Stalin's face darkened.

'Whom do you intend to dress in that?' he asked.

'This is the proposed uniform for the Generalissimo.'

'For whom?'

'For you, Comrade Stalin.'

Stalin ordered Drachev to leave and then burst into an angry tirade. General Shtemenko, who was present, says that he 'protested against the excessive extolling of his personality, saying that it was foolish and that he had never expected something like this.' So till the end of his days, says Shtemenko, Stalin wore his Marshal's uniform, 'just like all the other Marshals'. He goes on to say that while Stalin backed modesty among Party, and government leaders spoke of the 'impermissibility of conceit and megalomania', he raised no objection to inflated praise of his own qualities and achievements.

Victory Parade

When in mid-May 1945 the idea of holding a victory parade on Red Square first arose, some of the leading Marshals asked Stalin (who now held the exalted rank of Generalissimo) to lead the parade on horseback. Stalin, already 66, brushed aside the idea, saying it was for 'you younger men' to ride in the June parade. But war historian Vasily Morozov gave me another version. According to him, Stalin's other son, Vasily, an air force officer, informed colleagues that Stalin had two or three times participated in rehearsals for the parade, riding with the troops. Twice, so the story went, Stalin tumbled off his horse, whereupon he said: 'To hell with it! Let Zhukov handle the parade! He's younger.'

Stalin's Medals

Stalin was awarded the highest medals during the war

On 24 June 1944 the first Moscow Defence Medal was pinned on Marshal Stalin's uniform by the Moscow City Soviet for his 'services in directing the heroic defence of Moscow and organising the rout of the German forces outside the capital.'

On 29 July 1944 the Order of Victory was presented to him by the Presidium of the Supreme Soviet of the USSR for his 'outstanding services in organising and directing the offensive operations of the Red Army that resulted in the resounding defeat of the Germans and radically changed the situation in favour of the Red army.'

On 26 June 1945, 'For having led the Red Army in the trying days of the defence of the country, and of its capital, Moscow, and for his energetic and resolute direction of the fight against Nazi Germany', Stalin was awarded the title of Hero of the Soviet Union, together with the Order of Lenin and the Gold Star Medal that go with the title. Also, a second Order of Victory was bestowed on him for 'skilful leadership in the Great Patriotic War which ended with complete victory over Hitler's Germany.'

On 27 June 1945 Stalin assumed the supreme military rank of Generalissimo. Marshal Vasilevsky says that the Front commanders recommended this high rank for Stalin.

★★★ STALIN AND INVASION DAY ★★★

It was the opinion of the US Ambassador Averell Harriman, who probably had more meetings with Stalin than any other Western leader, that he was obsessed with the danger of premature mobilisation of his troops. Stalin, he said, was unable to forget the consequences of hasty mobilisation that caused Russia to stumble into World War I.

Mobilisation of a country's armed forces is an extreme measure and the act itself can provoke war. The story of Tsarist Russia's early mobilisation on the eve of World War I is a gem of tragi-comedy. Stalin, an avid student of history (George Bernard Shaw once said that Stalin had 'won a point' against H. G. Wells on an event in British history), had no doubt studied the incident in detail.

In brief, this is what happened. At the end of July 1914, following the assassination of the Austrian Archduke Franz Ferdinand by a Bosnian revolutionary, Austria declared war on Serbia. The Russian Tsar Nicholas II, hoping to prevent the subjugation of Serbia, yielded to pressure from his ministers and signed an order for general mobilisation of the army. Meanwhile, Kaiser Wilhelm II of Germany, taking advantage of his close relations with Nicholas (they were related and called each other 'Willy' and 'Nicky') had sent him a telegram saying in effect that he, Wilhelm, wanted to reconcile Austria and Russia. But Wilhelm also tried to intimidate his 'dear cousin' with the threat of a catastrophic war.

Quite possibly the Tsar realised the danger in which he had placed his country. In any case, having second thoughts, he suddenly changed the order for general mobilisation to one of 'partial mobilisation'. His change of mind occurred when the head of the Mobilisation Section of the Russian General Staff was already at the Central Telegraph Office in St. Petersburg, and it was just a few minutes before the telegraphed order was to be sent to all parts of the country. The Tsar's ministers were shocked. Fearing the consequences of delay, the Foreign Minister, War Minister and the Chief of the General Staff again tried to persuade him to declare general mobilisation. Meanwhile Germany issued dire warnings if he did so.

Confident of changing the Tsar's mind, the Russian ministers asked for an audience. Sergei Dmitrievich Sazonov, the Foreign Minister, urged the Tsar to issue a new mobilisation order immediately. The ministers knew that once the army received a telegraphed order it would be too late to be cancelled.

To make sure, the Chief of the General Staff, General Nikolai Yanushkevich, told Sazonov that the moment he received the mobilisation order, 'I'll break my telephone and then take steps so that nobody will be able to find me.' When, shortly thereafter, the Tsar signed the new order to be telegraphed to the Army, Sazonov phoned General Yanushkevich: 'Now you can break your telephone.'

In less than 48 hours Kaiser Wilhelm declared war on Russia, opening the way to a national calamity. It was this affair which, according to Ambassador Harriman, gave Stalin pause in the summer of 1941 before he approved full-scale mobilisation.

But would early mobilisation have made a difference? Was it possible to check the Nazi behemoth by timely activation of the Red Army?

In his memoirs, Marshal Ivan Bagramyan says that he heard from Zhukov that it was Stalin's opinion that the superiority of Hitler's armies in equipment and combat experience was such that in a *Blitzkrieg* attack, the Russian army would be unable to hold the border areas. Bagramyan admits that on hearing this, he was staggered.

Despite the increasing strength of his armed forces, Stalin recognised that his country was now facing alone, as William L. Shirer put it, 'the mightiest military machine the world had ever seen'.

When the invasion began the population of Germany and her satellites totalled 290 million, Russia's, approximately 193 million. These human resources made it possible by June 1941 to bring the German front-line forces up to 8.5 million men. Hitler also had the spoils of war from his successful campaigns in the west. German and Russian documents show that more than 60 *Wehrmacht* divisions were equipped with captured French motor vehicles.

Stalin, although confident his country would win a war with Germany, believed with his military chiefs, such as Marshal Boris Shaposhnikov, that only through a protracted struggle could victory be won. A long war, in their view, gave advantages to Russia and disadvantages to Germany. Nobody knew better than Stalin what it was that had caused Napoleon's ruin in Russia.

Despite Stalin's miscalculation in judging the time of Hitler's invasion, there were immediate consequences favourable to Russia. On 22 June 1941 the

173

world identified Russia as the clear victim of aggression. On 12 July an agreement was concluded between Russia and Britain which, says the Annual Register, rapidly developed into the closest possible alliance. A similar *rapprochement* with the USA took place, though not carried out to the point of an alliance. Maxim Litvinov, an advocate of co-operation with the democracies, who had fallen into disfavour on that account in 1939, was appointed Ambassador to Washington.

Also early in July, President Roosevelt sent a message to Prime Minister Fumimaro Konoye, cautioning against a Japanese attack on the Soviet Union.

★★★ THE HORRIBLE AND BITTER TRUTH ★★★

A well-known Russian historian, Alexander Borisov, says that the fast-moving offensives of the Red Army into Germany saved its citizens from the tragedy that soon befell the inhabitants of Hiroshima and Nagasaki. In his view, if the war in Europe had continued beyond the spring of 1945, Germany could have been the first victim of the atomic bomb. The razing of the city of Dresden by 'only' conventional bombs showed that this war knew no restraints. But of course the headlong rush of these offensives added to the Russian casualty lists.

Total Russian battle losses in World War II are estimated as being in excess of 13,000,000 including POWs. Civilian deaths amounted to at least 8,000,000 and were possibly as high as 12,000,000. (Germany lost about 3,300,000 men and 7,000,000 civilians.)

Were these losses necessary? How much blame attaches to Stalin and his generals? There are no easy answers to these questions. In any case, the enormity of the Eastern Front and the legions of troops involved made high casualties inevitable.

Some scholars like Alan Bullock attribute Russia's swollen casualty figures, especially those sustained at the beginning of the war, to Stalin's failure to prepare for the *Blitzkrieg*. Yet according to General Ivan Shavrov, losses by the Red Army could have been still higher if prior to the invasion, Stalin had concentrated more armies at the border.

Few argue against the contention that in June 1941 Hitler's armies were virtually unstoppable. Looking back on the war, a few Russian generals, such as Eremenko, flushed with victory, said that negligence and miscalculation prevented a Soviet victory at the outset. But of course the capabilities of Stalin's raw troops at the beginning of the war cannot be compared with the combat-hardened veterans who stormed Berlin in April 1945.

Edgar Snow, a well-known American author and journalist who visited Russia during the war, weighed Stalin's responsibility for the lavish use of manpower in achieving Soviet victories. Stalin, he wrote, 'at least must have sanctioned the sacrifice of thousands of half-trained civilian militiamen in the costly salvation of Moscow.'

But Snow added a caveat: no matter how painful, such sacrifices contributed to the victory. 'They went to certain death, but the few hours they held the panzers back enabled the Siberian troops to reach the city and win that critical battle.'

Some critics point an accusing finger at Marshal Zhukov for his 'extravagance' in sending masses of troops to certain death as a way of overpowering an enemy. Some of the combat generals I interviewed in Moscow, while not wishing to detract from Zhukov's ability, said that he shared responsibility for some of the mistakes at the beginning of the war, and Zhukov has frankly admitted this.

When the Allies planned major campaigns, such as the landings in North Africa in 1942, Sicily in 1943 and the 'second front' in France in 1944, American and British political and military leaders weighed the human cost involved. Stalin saw things differently. But the situations were not analogous. Camped on Russian territory was a ruthless enemy.

The willingness or unwillingness to confront the Germans was touched on in a difficult conversation between Stalin and Churchill in Moscow in August 1942. Stalin said that 'those who do not want to take risks will never win a war'. He added that in order to become battle worthy, troops must go through a baptism of fire; that before troops were tried in action nobody could tell their worth. He added: 'One should not be afraid of the Germans.'

But it wasn't only people at the top like Stalin who took a hard-boiled approach to war. The harsh Russian attitude to life and death in wartime is perhaps summed up in a war-time letter addressed to Americans by the novelist Mikhail Sholokhov. He began with the message, 'We call you to battle.' The future Nobel laureate said: 'One cannot come through this war without smearing one's hands in blood. War demands blood and sweat. If denied it will take double the toll.' He added, 'You have not yet seen the blood of your kin on the threshold of your home. I have, and so I have the right to talk to you bluntly.'

The author had lost his mother, killed by a German bomb during an air raid on their tiny village along the Don in southern Russia. German shells had destroyed his house and library.

Like Edgar Snow, a number of experts have pointed to the Russian habit of often throwing troops at practically unbreakable positions, of continuing frontal attacks when they were unavailing. Liddell Hart says of the Russians that the abundance of manpower prompted lavish expenditure. (But Russian casualties must, I think, also be seen in the light of the fact that the Russians were literally fighting for their lives. At a conference of SS officers at the beginning of the invasion, Hitler's lieutenant Heinrich Himmler had said that 30 million Russians must be exterminated. This statement was made public at the Nuremberg Trials by SS General Erich von dem Bach-Zelewski who had, in 1944, brutally crushed the 'Warsaw uprising'.)

Hitler's generals, too, were prodigal in the use of troops to attain objectives, but Germany was able to draw on reserves of manpower from Axis partners. In April 1942 the *Wehrmacht* had 8.7 million men – more than when it first attacked Russia. Hitler demanded that his satellites send more and more soldiers to fight on the Eastern Front. Making a tour of Axis capitals in Europe at the

Führer's request, Field Marshal Wilhelm Keitel in 1942 persuaded Italy and Hungary to send an extra army each to the Eastern Front; Roumania agreed to send two more armies.

Taking advantage of a one-front war, Hitler concentrated more than 75 per cent of his armed forces (more than six million men) against Russia. These armies included 3,270 tanks, 3,400 aircraft and 43,000 artillery pieces.

The Allied decision to postpone the 'second front' until 1944 prompted a telegram from Stalin to Roosevelt on 11 June 1943. It began: 'Your decision creates exceptional difficulties for the Soviet Union, which, straining all its resources, for the past two years has been engaged against the main forces of Germany and her satellites ...'

At the end of 1942 Stalin gave details of the number of Axis troops facing Russia: 'According to authentic information, of the 256 divisions which Germany now has, no fewer than 179 are on our front. If to this we add 22 Roumanian divisions, fourteen Finnish divisions, ten Italian divisions, thirteen Hungarian divisions, one Slovak division and one Spanish division, we get a total of 240 divisions now fighting on our front. The remaining divisions of Germany and her allies are performing garrison duty in the occupied countries (France, Belgium, Norway, the Netherlands, Yugoslavia, Poland, Czechoslovakia, etc.), while part of them are fighting in Libya for the possession of Egypt against Great Britain. In all, the Libyan front is diverting four German divisions and eleven Italian divisions. Hence, instead of 127 divisions as was the case in World War I, we, today, are facing on our front no less than 240 divisions, and instead of 85 German divisions we have 179 German divisions fighting the Red Army.'

He added: 'You can now imagine how great and extraordinary are the difficulties that confront the Red Army, and how great is the heroism displayed by the Red Army in its war of liberation against the German Fascist invaders.'

When I asked General S. M. Krivoshein about the enormity of Russian losses in World War II, his reply was unexpected: 'In order to defeat the Nazi invader Russia was prepared to lose twice as many lives [as Russia actually lost].' The general mentioned the awesome figure of forty million. (This is approximately double the number usually cited for Russian war losses, between 20 and 25 million.)

Lofty patriotic sentiment must be considered when discussing Russian casualty lists. This can be seen, for example, in the diary of Red Army rifleman Lyova Fedotov, who wrote after Hitler's armies laid siege to Leningrad in 1941: 'I am absolutely positive that the Germans will never set foot in Leningrad. But if the enemy does capture it as well, that will only happen after the last Leningrader has fallen in battle.' In the 900-day siege of that city, more than half a million civilians perished.

During the war certain cities and strategic points were ordered to be held at all costs. German troops fought relentlessly at Stalingrad but were never able to capture that city. Nevertheless some Western historians assert that as a consequence of erroneous decisions, Hitler 'lost' Stalingrad; that given other circumstances the *Wehrmacht* could have taken that city.

Marshal Vassily Chuikov, who took part in the battle, disagrees: 'I declare with full responsibility that Stalingrad could have been taken by the enemy only on one condition: If all the soldiers died to a man. Not one of the defenders of Stalingrad would pass from the right bank of the Volga to the left. We gave an oath. This was an appeal from the heart.'

(In 1992 an official of the Russian Institute of Military History said that the Russians had to sacrifice lives at Stalingrad to make up for what the troops lacked in equipment and organisation. But Hitler's losses in killed, wounded, or missing at Stalingrad – about 800,000 – were at least as damaging to the Germans as the approximately 1.1 million dead were to Stalin's defenders. (These figures are taken from British historian Alan Bullock's well-documented book, *Hitler and Stalin, Parallel Lives*, London, 1993.)

In 1994 it was officially confirmed in Moscow that at least one million Russian soldiers perished in the Battle of Stalingrad, where Stalin had given the order: 'Not one step back!' Marshal Chuikov had told his 62nd Army that it could 'no longer retreat across the Volga', and that 'the only road leads forward'. (But at Stalingrad, Hitler had given a similar order to his generals: 'Surrender out of the question. Troops will resist to the end.')

The Berlin Operation was another costly victory – more than 300,000 Russian dead and wounded. Some observers say that these losses incurred on the eve of Germany's surrender were perhaps needlessly extravagant. Here is Marshal Ivan Konev's comment:

'I happened to hear arguments that the fighting in Berlin could have been conducted with less fury, fierceness and haste, and therefore with fewer casualties. There is outer logic in this reasoning, but it ignores the main thing – the actual situation, the actual strain of the fighting and the actual state of the men's morale. These men burned with a passionate and an impatient desire to end the war as soon as possible. Those who want to judge how justified or unjustified the casualties were, must remember this.'

Professor John Erickson of Edinburgh University, an expert on Russian military affairs, said in 1994 (*Barbarossa, the Axis and the Allies*) that the German invasion accounted for not 20 to 25 million but nearly 49 million soldiers and civilians. Erickson reckons that the drastic decline in Russia's birth rate at the war's end, resulting in population loss, was a consequence of the German invasion and should be added to the casualty toll.

★★★ LETTERS PRO AND CON ★★★

Debate about the wartime Stalin still percolates in all the republics of the former Soviet Union. This is not surprising if one recalls that General Volkogonov said that Stalin was one of the most complex figures in history – a man who belongs not only to the past but also to the present and to the future. The following letters about Stalin were published in newspapers and journals in the mid-1990s. I chose them mainly for their original viewpoints and because many of them add something to our knowledge of Stalin at war.

Pavel Kochegin, writer, war veteran, of Kurtamysh, Russia:
'The motto "For the Motherland! For Stalin!" was painted on the side of my combat aircraft. This fact alone makes me fear that my opinion of Stalin's role in the war may be biased.

'Indeed, the very beginning of the war and the summer of 1942 were hard on us because of Comrade Stalin's (and other people's) errors. During the Battle of Moscow (in the autumn of 1941) I happened to be in the capital. The situation deteriorated for our troops on the approaches to Moscow and the Germans managed to break through the front line. Industrial enterprises began to be dismantled, and cases of marauding and panic were recorded. The fact that Stalin stayed in Moscow had a sobering effect on the population. The capital changed beyond recognition; it was like a hardened soldier facing a mortal danger.

'From times of old it has been considered a disgrace to be taken prisoner. That is why soldiers have always preferred to be killed than captured, for the dead know no disgrace. Death was preferable to the disgrace of captivity even during wars between states with similar political systems, let alone a war against inhumane Nazism. Thousands of Soviet POWs wished that they had died on the battlefield instead of being captured.

'The suspicious attitude towards the overwhelming majority of former Soviet POWs could be attributed to the over-zealous security officers who lived according to the Russian saying "make a fool pray to God, and he'll smash his head". I could quote any number of examples, but I'll give you only one: on 20 October 1944 my aircraft was shot down over enemy-occupied Norway. On the 25th I got back to my detachment. The rest of our boys and the command were delighted to have me back, and I was decorated with the Order of the Red Banner for valour. The citizens of Norway who had helped me were also decorated.

'But there were people who found me suspect and began to gather material against me. Only the intervention of the head of our Political Department stopped all that. I received a new aircraft and carried on fighting. The detachments led by intelligent, human people, not zealous careerists, treated former POWs well, but there weren't too many of them, I'm sorry to say.'

Vyscheslav Kondratyev, writer, Moscow:
'Did we really fight and die for one man, Stalin? I'm sorry, but I fought for my country, Soviet power and Russia! And I believe that the majority fought for the same cause! Incidentally, even those hurt by Stalin – the children of persecuted people and de-classed peasants – fought as gallantly as the rest.'

Nikolai Voronkin, war veteran, Odessa, Ukraine:

'I was lucky enough to survive five naval raids in the enemy's rear in which 75 per cent of the troops were usually killed. In the autumn of 1941 none of the seamen yelled "For the Motherland! For Stalin!" Tipsy, after drinking the state quota of vodka, they cursed God Almighty, the Virgin Mary and all the angels in heaven. Later some men did shout "For the Motherland! For Stalin!" The question is, who did it, and why?

'Before a raid an officer from the Political Department would come and pick out two men from each of our motor-boats and brief them about the situation and the landing-party's orders. He would say:

"You personally will jump overboard as soon as we approach the shore and dash forward, and yell "For the Motherland! For Stalin!" to inspire the others.'

'Here, too, Stalin stood next to God. Near Novorossisk [on the Black Sea coast] we stood in formation and signed an oath "To the Great Stalin" which was written by someone at the top.

'It seems to me that Stalin was a combination of greatness and evil. What else? History will answer this question!'

Mikhail Vasilyev, war veteran, Gorky region, Russia:

'Yes, the Marshals won the war at the expense of the 25 million dead. What kind of genius was it if there was one dead German soldier per seven or eight dead Russians, Poles, Czechs and others? And what about our POWs? Why did Stalin abandon them? All other countries maintained contacts with their POWs via the Red Cross, and only Stalin rejected its help. If the Nazis allowed the Red Cross to visit their death camps, why did Stalin, a Communist, reject even that tiny chance of keeping in touch with the prisoners of war? Double cruelty was his line. During his rule the country lost far more than it gained.'

B. B. Konoplyanko, ex-KGB officer, no home town given:

'I'm a former security officer, and a Party member since 1939. I worked for the KGB [State Security Committee] for more than 28 years. I was posted to a department of the Red Army Special Branch in August 1939. When I agreed to be transferred to the Transbaikal Military District in Siberia, I had no idea of what such departments were doing or what was going on there. As I found out later, it was something atrocious. Nearly all the old members of the Special Branch had either been put behind bars for violating socialist law in 1937–8, arresting Soviet Army commanders without grounds, and beating up detainees, or sacked from the state security system. The remaining few honest security officers told us beginners about their "activities". Some honest security officers, as I found out later, had written to Stalin about the abuse of power in their system, but all those letters had been ignored, and the authors arrested and eliminated. The local Party bodies were also intimidated. I would put the blame for Stalin's cult not so much on Stalin himself but mostly on his environment – the cult was launched from the top, not from the bottom.

His toadies and bootlickers competed in currying favour with him by praising him to the skies.'

Leonid Mostipan, war veteran, Chernigov, Ukraine:
'A man I used to work with, who was born ten years after the war and graduated from an officers' school, is convinced that Stalin was an incompetent man who seized power by sheer chance, and who had all the people he disliked put up against the wall. He also thinks that the Politburo was Stalin's gang, and that together they did as they pleased; that Stalin, who was not a military man, usurped the post of Commander-in-Chief during the war. He also says that Stalin was to blame for all our failures. But I personally believe that Stalin was a great military leader.

'Stalin was right in saying that a soldier could choose only between victory and death, and that captivity was out of the question. I wonder what would have become of this country if the troops had thought there was no disgrace in being taken prisoner. There were enough weaklings who put up their hands and surrendered instead of attacking. No wonder they were eyed with suspicion after being liberated. It was only natural to check on the circumstances under which they had been captured, wasn't it?'

Lena Semenova, student, Yakutia, Siberia:
'What do we know about Stalin? We know that he was a man of unbending will and a fearless revolutionary. He purged the Party, but he often took honest people for enemies. He led the nation to victory in the last war but mercilessly destroyed most of the Soviet military leaders. Was this one of the reasons why the Nazis nearly reached Moscow? But didn't we win because our gallant troops went to battle for their country, for Stalin? Could it be that the people, feeling lost after Lenin's death [Lenin died in 1924], instinctively followed a new leader, for fear of being orphans encircled by enemies? There are still many questions to be answered.'

★★★ STALIN AS GENERALISSIMO ★★★

At the conclusion of his memoirs, Marshal Vasilevsky asks: 'Was it right for Stalin to be in charge of the Supreme High Command? After all he was not a professional military man.' And Vasilevsky's answer: 'There can be no doubt that it was right.'

The stocky Marshal, who had frequent, almost daily contact with Stalin throughout the war, held some of the highest posts in the Armed Forces: Chief of Operations of the General Staff; Chief of the General Staff; Deputy Defence Minister. In the summer of 1945 he was appointed Commander-in-Chief of Soviet Forces in the Far East in the war against Japan.

Looking back on the war, Vasilevsky mentions 'Stalin's growth as a general' although he does not fail to mention miscalculations by the Supreme Commander in the early months of the invasion. He points out that after a year or two Stalin 'successfully supervised the Fronts and all the war efforts of the country'.

Vasilevsky also informs us about Stalin's rank of Generalissimo. Not a few biographies and reference books say that Stalin promoted himself to the rank during the war. 'The rank of Generalissimo was awarded to Stalin by written representation to the Party Central Committee Politburo from Front commanders.' This, said Vasilevsky, occurred in June 1945. An official biography gives the day – 27 June.

While Zhukov praises Stalin, Vasilevsky goes one better: 'Stalin was the strongest and most remarkable figure in the country's strategic command.' (A number of generals I met called Zhukov 'the best among the best'. Vasilevsky agrees with this description. Zhukov and Vasilevsky, be it noted, were entirely different as men and generals: Zhukov was brilliant but pugnacious; Vasilevsky, also brilliant, had the calm exterior of a college professor. Unlike Zhukov, Vasilevsky, not surprisingly, had few run-ins with Stalin.)

When Marshal Ivan Konev was asked his impression of Stalin by the Yugoslav writer and political activist, Milovan Djilas (the year was 1944), he replied: 'Stalin is universally gifted. He was brilliantly able to see the war as a whole, and this made possible his successful direction.' This was not the automatic line that one would expect from a flunkey. Moments earlier, according to Djilas, he had sharply criticised three high-ranking Marshals, including Klementi Voroshilov, who was part of Stalin's inner circle.

General Ivan Chernyakovsky, who like Konev achieved outstanding success against Hitler's armies, made this original comment about Stalin: 'Here you have a dialectical process, not in theory, but as a living example. It's impossible to understand him. All you can do is to have faith.'

A perusal of memoirs, speeches and articles leads one to conclude that there is virtual consensus among Russia's wartime generals and admirals that Stalin was a military leader of extraordinary insight, that he was an exceptional Commander-in-Chief. This is apparent in the recollections of many Marshals, including S. K. Meretskov (*Serving the People*), Konstantin Rokossovsky (*A Soldier's Duty*), V. M. Vasilevsky (*A Lifelong Cause*), and I. K. Bagramyan (*Our Road to Victory*). According to these men there was nothing synthetic about Stalin's fame as Marshal and Generalissimo.

Various Western experts say that the reason Stalin improved in his ability as C-in-C was that his generals improved. This of course works both ways. Marshal Meretskov writes in his memoirs that Stalin 'thoroughly and consistently' delved into all army matters, and that Stalin's frequent meetings with his frontline generals and other top officers added significantly to his stock of military knowledge: 'I am inclined to believe that the Supreme Commander-in-Chief learned much about modern warfare from GHQ and the General Staff officers and other military experts. And of course they too acquired a great deal of knowledge from the Supreme Commander-in-Chief, particularly in the field of statesmanship and in economic and political matters. I was not an exception. Each visit to GHQ taught me something.'

In his book, *Reminiscences and Reflections*, Zhukov sums up his views about Stalin:

'I am often asked whether Stalin was really an outstanding military thinker and a major contributor to the development of the armed forces, whether he was really an expert in tactical and strategic principles. I can say that Stalin was conversant with the basic principles of organising the operations of Fronts and groups of Fronts, and that he supervised them knowledgeably. Certainly he was familiar with major strategic principles. His ability as Supreme Commander was especially marked after the Battle of Stalingrad.' He adds that Stalin had 'rich intuition and ability to find the main point in a strategic situation', which is high praise indeed from a soldier of Zhukov's stature.

When in the autumn of 1941 Hitler's armies were in sight of Moscow, Stalin assumed the post of Commander-in-Chief of Russian forces. Throughout the war he was also Chairman of the State Defence Committee and Supreme Commander-in-Chief of the armed forces.

General S. M. Shtemenko's standard work on the Soviet General Staff in World War II shows Stalin's hand in nearly every significant operation against the German armies. On each page almost (the book has 1,000 pages) the reader finds orders, counsel, reprimands, exhortations, violent arguments and the occasional kindly word from Stalin to his ablest officers.

On the negative side, there is trenchant criticism of Stalin by some commanders for his errors at the beginning of the war. Many generals regarded the pre-war purges as an indelible stain on Stalin's character. Curiously, only two or three of the dozens of generals I met voluntarily raised the subject of the purges. When I put the question to them they spoke briefly about it, as if wishing to bury the past. It seemed that they regarded the purges as 'the great mystery'.

On the Disasters at Kiev and Kharkov

In September 1941 Heinz Guderian's panzers drove 150 miles past Russian armies defending Kiev while Ewald von Kleist's panzers struck north, the two pincers joining far to the east of the Ukrainian capital. An estimated 650,000 Russian soldiers were taken prisoner. Hitler exulted: 'I declare today – and I declare it without reservation – the enemy in the East has been struck down and will never rise again.'

Stalin, who was reluctant to order the evacuation of Kiev, flared up when some military men advised it, insisting that his armies defend the city even after it became dangerous to do so. The following year, an ill-considered counter-attack to recapture German-occupied Kharkov led to the loss of three Russian armies totalling about 250,000 men. As Commander-in-Chief, Stalin bears ultimate responsibility for these disasters.

After the war, von Kleist said the Germans had hoped to receive important political advantages from these disasters. He told British military historian Liddell Hart that the German High Command had false hopes that after such costly defeats Stalin would be overthrown by his own people.

Among the military, Marshal Andrei I. Eremenko, who fought valiantly at Stalingrad and in other major battles, is the most severe of Stalin's critics, but his circle is a limited one. Eremenko strongly reproaches Stalin for the reverses at the beginning of the war. In his memoir, *An Arduous Beginning*, he blames Stalin for failing to mobilise the troops on the eve of 22 June 1941 and for the army's poor performance against the *Wehrmacht* in the early months. A main reason for this, he says, was the purge of many talented officers in the 1930s.

Eremenko lays part of the blame for the invasion day disaster on other 'superior military authorities'. But he attributes the early Russian setbacks to Stalin's 'faulty treatment of the question of defence'. 'What we witnessed was not an objective military lag on the part of a peace-loving state, but the effect of subjective mistakes made by Stalin', he says. Eremenko vividly recounts how, in September 1941, Hitler's troops had surrounded Russian forces of the South-western Front who were unable to break out and were fighting to the last man. He himself was in the thick of the fighting and was seriously wounded: 'This was one of the disastrous effects of Stalin's crude disregard for the elementary rules of military strategy.'

Another critic of Stalin is Nikita Khrushchev, who was a high-ranking political officer with the armed forces during the war and became Party boss and premier after the war. Khrushchev describes at length Stalin's responsibility for the disaster at Kiev and in other early defeats.

Eremenko and Khrushchev served together in various Fronts. Interestingly, both became severe critics of Stalin and both sought to justify their own military actions. Commenting on the disaster in the south, Russian war historian Colonel Vasily Morozov says that in their memoirs both Eremenko and Khrushchev 'whitewash' their own share of the blame. Marshal Vasilevsky, while not absolving Stalin of blame, alludes to Eremenko's culpability. Stalin, says Vasilevsky, 'seriously believed the firm assurances' of Eremenko about 'certain victory' over the attacking German forces. But 'this did not happen.'

Marshal Zhukov has described how he and other generals discovered Stalin's fallibility. Zhukov says that when encountering difficulties in the war, 'we realised that our views as to Stalin being extraordinarily well-informed and possessing the qualities of a military leader had been erroneous'. This was Zhukov speaking about the chaotic weeks and months at the start of the war. Later, Zhukov would write more flattering comments about Stalin, such as his ability to achieve the 'near-impossible'.

British historian and Stalin biographer Alan Bullock mentions Stalin's drawbacks as a military leader: 'Stalin devised a way of dealing with operational planning which preserved his reputation as Commander-in-Chief without exposing it to too much risk.' He mentions Stalin's 'declaration' read at General Headquarters in January 1942: 'We must not allow the enemy to recover his breath, we must pursue him westwards.' Bullock says 'This expressed a wish but lacked any precise strategic concept.'

This so-called declaration is mentioned by General Shtemenko. Actually it is a letter of instructions to Stavka – the General Headquarters – which sets forth enemy intentions and Russian objectives. It was obviously meant to be a morale-booster. Stalin's troops had just won a brilliant victory in the Battle of Moscow, the first big German setback in World War II.

'Our task', declared Stalin, 'is not to allow the Germans this respite, to drive them westwards without a halt, to force them to expend their reserves before the spring, when we ourselves will have new massive reserves and the Germans will have none, and thus ensure the total defeat of Hitler's forces in 1942.'

Such hopes were overly optimistic. But, at that time (1942), Stalin was also hoping for an Allied cross-Channel invasion of France.

Bullock goes on to say that 'what shocked the professional soldiers most was Stalin's complete indifference to the cost of an operation in lives – another characteristic which he shared with Hitler.' The British scholar bases this criticism on testimony which he says was provided by the historian, General Dmitri Volkogonov, who he says 'had access to the military archives'.

Stalin and his Commanders

When a critical situation developed on the South-western Front in June 1942, Marshal Timoshenko, the Front commander, urgently and persistently asked for reinforcements, especially infantry divisions. Red Army units had suffered big losses and were in disarray. Stalin allowed the Front four tank corps but refused to provide infantry. 'We cannot give you infantry divisions', he told the Military Council of the Front, speaking by direct line on 13 June, 'because we haven't any trained divisions at the moment. You will have to manage with your own forces and improve troop control.'

Timoshenko repeatedly cited the superior strength of the enemy's armour. Stalin replied: 'You have more tanks than the enemy. The trouble is that yours either remain stationary or are sent into battle in separate, unco-ordinated brigades. GHQ proposes that you concentrate 22nd, 23rd and 13th Tank Corps somewhere in one place, in the Veliky–Burluk area, for instance, and strike at the enemy's panzer groups. If our tank corps acted together and *en masse*, the picture would be quite different from what it is now.'

Timoshenko obeyed Stalin's instructions but insisted on reinforcements in infantry and weapons. To these continued requests, Stalin replied in writing: 'GHQ has no new divisions trained and ready for battle. Our resources of armaments are limited. Remember that we have other Fronts besides yours. Battles are won by skill, not numbers.' A few days later Timoshenko once again mentioned reinforcements: 'It would be a good thing if we could get one infantry division out of you.' Stalin replied: 'If divisions could be bought at the market I would buy you five or six, but unfortunately they are not on sale.'

Towards the end of July 1942 the Stalingrad sector was clearly becoming dangerous in the extreme. Stalin telegraphed the Stalingrad Front Commander, V. N. Gordov, telling him that the enemy had diverted 'our attention' to the south and at the same time 'have quietly brought their main forces up to the right flank of the Front. This stratagem succeeded because you lack reliable reconnaissance. This must be taken into account and the right flank of the Front must be strengthened by all possible means.'

Stalin issued orders that 90 per cent of all available aircraft be concentrated on the right flank. 'Don't pay any attention to the enemy's diversions and tricks,' he said, pointing out the manpower and weapons that GHQ had placed at the Front's disposal. Finally, he warned Gordov: 'Bear in mind that if the enemy penetrate the right flank and reach the Don in the Gumrak area, or north of it, they will cut your rail communications with the north. I therefore regard the right flank of your Front now as decisive.'

Shtemenko says that Stalin gave the Front another important task 'which had a considerable effect on the subsequent course of the Battle of Stalingrad. It concerned a defence line west of the Don which 'must be kept in our hands without fail'. Stalin: 'The enemy force that has driven a wedge into this line in the zone of the Guards division [the 33rd Guards Infantry] must be destroyed at all costs. You have the strength for this and you must do it. I categorically forbid any withdrawal from the indicated line of defence.' In reply, Gordov said that 'everything' was clear.

Stalin showed his faith in Gordov when, shortly afterwards, he made a suggestion to his General Staff about General V. Y. Kolpakchi, the commander of 62nd Army, who was to take up a position at the Stalingrad Front. 'Bear in mind that Kolpakchi is a very nervous and impressionable person. It would be a good thing to send him somebody firmer to keep up his spirits, and if Gordov himself goes there it would be even better.' He asked the General Staff to show this message to Gordov.

So vital was the strategic position of Stalingrad that Stalin ordered a large group of generals and colonels representing GHQ to go to that Front, size up the situation and help the Front command. Meanwhile the German Army had reached the threshold of the North Caucasus, having superiority in armour and aircraft and consequently in mobility and manoeuvrability. Stalin demanded from the General Staff a report as to where and how the defences of the Caucasus should be built.

On the night of 25/26 July, Stalin ordered Vasilevsky, who was then Chief of the General Staff, to get in touch personally with the Stalingrad Front Command and issue a severe warning: 'GHQ categorically demands of the Military Council of the Front to do everything to eliminate at once the enemy forces that have broken through, and restore the situation.'

On the 26th Stalin ordered that the Front be given an even sterner directive: 'The actions of the Command of the Stalingrad Front are evoking indignation at the General Headquarters of the Supreme Command. GHQ demands that in the next few days the Stalingrad Line [a major defence line west of the city] be restored without fail and that the enemy be thrown back beyond the River Chir [west of Stalingrad]. If the Military Council of the Front is not capable of doing this, let it state the fact clearly and honestly. GHQ demands from the Command of the Stalingrad Front a clear answer on its readiness to execute the given directive.' The answer arrived a little later, telling GHQ that its instructions would be fulfilled.

Out of the Stalingrad battle came the most famous order of the war, issued on 28 July 1942. Order No. 227, from the People's Commissar for Defence

(Stalin), stated that every soldier should hold his position under all conditions. Shtemenko calls it 'one of the most important documents of the war'. Stalin dictated the basic paragraphs of the order and told the General Staff to supervise its execution with the utmost rigour. Shtemenko calls the order 'an example of profound strategic prevision' because it outlined the conditions of the enemy and the character of the forthcoming stage in the war.

Order No. 227 began: 'Our Motherland is experiencing days of grave adversity. A complete stop must be put to all talk about our having plenty of territory, our country being great and rich, our having a large population and always plenty of grain.'

Some Western and a few Russian historians maintain that the order ('It is time to stop retreating. Not one step back!') was too harsh. But Shtemenko says that it 'had an extremely good effect on the men's combat ability. Everyone realised the necessity of standing to the last ditch and did everything he could for victory.'

From his experiences in the Civil War, Stalin knew the southern sector intimately and was able to help point out primary defence lines to his General Staff. Shtemenko says that Stalin and the General Staff, through joint efforts, worked out a plan for encirclement of Hitler's armies at the Battle of Stalingrad, a battle he says that 'may be said to have eclipsed Cannae'.

Marshal Vasilevsky says that anyone who reads the text of the document which Stalin dictated on 4 January 1943 and sent to the commander of the Transcaucasian Front will see clearly Stalin's skill as Supreme Commander-in-Chief. (The generals referred to are I. I. Maslennikov, M. M. Popov, and A. I. Eremenko.)

> 'First. The enemy is withdrawing from the North Caucasus, burning depots and blowing up roads. Maslennikov's Northern Group is turning into a reserve group with the task of carrying out an easy pursuit. It is not to our advantage to push the enemy troops out of the North Caucasus. We should gain more from keeping them there, so as to bring about their encirclement by a blow from the Black Sea Group. In view of this, the operational centre of gravity of the Transcaucasian Front is shifting into the area of the Black Sea Group, which is something that neither Maslennikov nor Petrov realise.
>
> 'Second: Get the 3rd Infantry Corps from the Northern Group on wheels at once and move it at all speed into the area of the Black Sea Group. Maslennikov can use the 58th Army, which is hanging about in reserve but could in the circumstances of our successful advance do a great deal of good.
>
> 'The Black Sea Group's first task is to reach Tikhoretskaya [east of the Sea of Azov] and thus prevent the enemy from moving their *matériel* out to the west. You will be helped in this by the 51st Army and, possibly, the 28th Army.
>
> 'Your second and principal task is to detach a powerful column of troops from the Black Sea Group, occupy Bataisk and Azov, break

into Rostov from the east and thus bottle up the enemy North Caucasian group with the aim of either taking them prisoner or destroying them. You will be helped in this by the left flank of Yeremenko's
Southern Front, which has the task of breaking through north of Rostov. [At this point, says General Shtemenko, who wrote out the
telegram, Stalin paused for a moment's thought, then continued]:

'Third. Order Petrov to start his offensive on time, without an
hour's delay, and without waiting for the arrival of all the reserves.
Petrov has been on the defensive all the time and he has not much
experience of offensive action. Explain to him that he must get into
an offensive mood, that he must value every day and every hour.'

Stalin added a fourth point, demanding that the Front's command proceed
immediately to the Black Sea Group's zone of action.

Vasilevsky says that those who read the order knew what it demanded –
that the enemy's escape route from the Caucasus be blocked by sea and land and
his formations cut off – and that the military situation after the Stalingrad victory showed the correctness of Stalin's strategy as contained in his orders.

In August 1943 a new and dangerous situation was taking shape around
the Ukrainian city of Kharkov with up to eleven German divisions, mostly
panzer and motorised, beginning to counter-attack Russian forces. These forces
had suffered a defeat there six months earlier. Now they were again taking
losses, and having only limited success, especially the major Front commanded
by N. F. Vatutin. Opportunities for breaking out in the rear of the large German
grouping at Kharkov had faded.

Stalin ordered Shtemenko (he was then a colonel on the General Staff) to
'sit down and write a directive to Vatutin. You will also send a copy to Zhukov.'
The directive shows how Stalin dealt with his best generals in difficult situations
when he had to give harsh criticism or offer advice. Clutching a red pencil and
pacing back and forth, Stalin dictated a first sentence:

'The events of the last few days have shown that you have not taken
into account past experience and continue to repeat old mistakes
both in planning and in conducting operations.

'The urge to attack everywhere and capture as much territory as
possible without consolidating success and providing sound cover for
the flanks of the assault groups amounts to a haphazard attack. Such
an attack leads to the dissipation of forces and matériel and allows
the enemy to strike at the flank and rear of our groups which have
gone far ahead and not been provided with cover on their flanks.'

Here Stalin stopped and read over Shtemenko's shoulder. At the end of the last
sentence the Supreme Commander wrote in his own hand, 'and to slaughter
them piecemeal'.

Stalin's conclusion was that the *Wehrmacht* had succeeded in breaking out
in the rear of a Russian tank army and had struck at the exposed flank of another

defending army; that as a consequence of the Front Commander's 'carelessness', the enemy on 20 August had struck at the rear of yet another Russian army and two corps. 'As a result of these enemy actions, our troops have suffered considerable and quite unjustifiable losses, and the advantageous position for smashing the enemy's Kharkov grouping has also been lost.'

Here, Stalin stopped, read what Shtemenko had written, and crossed out the words, 'profiting by your carelessness'. He then spoke of 'inadmissible mistakes' and demanded the liquidation of an important enemy grouping in the next few days. Without this, he said, there would be no success for neighbouring Fronts. 'You can do this because you have sufficient means with which to do it.'

Stalin glanced at the directive, emphasised the meaning of what was written by inserting a few words, and requested that the front commander 'not dissipate your strength'. Then he ordered Shtemenko to repeat the final text aloud. A few minutes later it was telegraphed to the Front.

Disagreeing With Stalin

Zhukov and Stalin would argue heatedly at times, their arguments even reaching the shouting stage. Other ranking officers also argued with Stalin although less vehemently. These men included Vasilevsky and Rokossovsky.

Vasilevsky, recalls Shtemenko, knew how to defend his own point of view in front of the Supreme Commander and he did it 'tactfully but with sufficient firmness'.

Shtemenko says that General A. I. Antonov, a top officer of the General Staff, enjoyed undisputed authority with Stalin, was outspoken and utterly frank in his reports, always presenting the facts exactly as they were no matter how negative. This, says Shtemenko, appealed to Stalin. He adds that Antonov 'had the courage to gainsay Stalin if necessary and was certainly never afraid to state his opinion'.

Marshal Rokossovsky was another officer who stood his ground in front of 'the Boss'. The Marshal said that Stalin would agree with an important decision by a Front commander 'if he offered weighty reasons for his action and stuck to his guns in proving his point'. Stalin did not mince words with his commanders in the field. In August 1942, when a general at Stalingrad expressed what was seen as undue anxiety over measures taken for the defence, Stalin sent a stern reply:

'I am astounded at your short-sightedness and confusion. You have plenty of forces but you lack the guts to deal with the situation. I am expecting a message from you to say that the alarming situation on your Front has been eliminated.'

The situation worsened as the enemy stepped up the pressure, but in a few weeks the German assault in turn weakened when fresh divisions from Siberia and Central Asia began to arrive.

Shtemenko closes his memoirs by saying that a number of Red Army setbacks in the summer of 1942 were caused by Stalin's decision to allow individual offensive operations which pulled apart and tied up the forces of a number of Fronts. But, Shtemenko says, these were in the nature of mishaps. He concludes by saying that history shows that Stalin's decision on strategic defence was fundamentally correct and that this made it possible for Russia's armed struggle to reach a historic turning-point in the war.

Vasilevsky, who was senior to Shtemenko and much closer to Stalin, devotes seven pages to summing up Stalin's qualities. Mainly, they laud the Generalissimo. 'Joseph Stalin', he says, 'has certainly gone down in military history.'

After citing Stalin's 'inadequate operational and strategic training' that was apparent in the first few months of the war, and mentioning the 'turning-point' for the Supreme Commander in the second year of the war, Vasilevsky explains why he thinks Stalin has a secure place in history:

> 'His undoubted service is that it was under his direct guidance as Supreme High Commander that the Soviet Armed Forces withstood the defensive campaigns and carried out all the offensive operations so splendidly.'

Stalin Prepares For War

At least four Marshals – and many generals – deny Stalin's alleged failure to prepare for the German invasion in June 1941. Marshal Bagramyan says a 'titanic' effort had been made to prepare for the coming war. Marshal Vasilevsky points to a 'whole number of very important measures' taken to counter the menace of aggression. Marshal Zhukov goes farther, saying 'every effort' and 'every means' was used to bolster the country's defences between 1939 and 1941. Marshal Rokossovsky says that the non-aggression pact with Hitler 'gave us the time we needed so much to build up our defences'.

Stalin's generals are virtually unanimous in pointing to Russia's accelerated pre-war industrial and military growth as the *sine qua non* for victory over Nazi Germany. This build-up started between the two world wars when the West had in effect quarantined the Soviet state.

Hitler's Armies – and Stalin's

Some Western academics and military experts, looking back from the 1990s at the Nazi–Soviet war, contend that Hitler's army in 1941 was not the 'wonderful war machine' everyone thought, that it was not fully prepared to launch a Blitz attack and conquer Stalin's Russia. It is a curious position.

At the war's end, the Slavs and other peoples of Russia who had been depicted by Hitler and his followers as members of 'inferior races' had defeated the *Wehrmacht,* an army that had been regarded by most military experts as 'unbeatable'. Hitler's trampling over most of Europe prior to 'Barbarossa' had 'proved' the prowess of his soldiers to the 'experts'. Moreover, the German army had a long militaristic tradition, which Stalin's forces did not. In June 1941 practically all the experts 'bet' on a lightning victory over Stalin's Russia. Thus it would be natural for some to seek reasons for the defeat of Hitler's vaunted armies in its own shortcomings rather than in the superiority of Stalin's armies, generals, and C-in-C Stalin himself.

Whether or not an army is a 'perfect war machine' that is 'fully prepared' to fight and defeat a potent enemy is a moot point. But to say, as some experts do, that Hitler's armies were not as ready as they should have been for war against Russia fails to put into the equation, or give sufficient weight to, the following: 1, the string of Nazi victories before 1941; 2, the participation in the invasion of more than 30 divisions of Hitler's allies; 3, the Nazi capture beforehand of the armaments and equipment of nearly 200 Czech, French, British, Belgian, Dutch and Norwegian divisions; 4, the munitions factories of Austria, Belgium, France and Czechoslovakia that were supplying the Nazi regime; and, 5, the fact that by the spring of 1941 almost 5,000 industrial enterprises in Nazi-occupied territory worked for Hitler's armed forces. In 1941 the industrial potential of Germany was estimated to be 50 to 100 per cent greater than that of Stalin's Russia.

An ever-present danger in 1941 was the need to keep a separate, huge army in the Far East to face a potential attack from Hitler's ally, Japan.

Stalin admitted the superiority of Hitler's war machine. He concluded prior to the invasion that the Red Army needed ten years to equal what he and his generals saw as the clockwork efficiency of the German Army.

Milovan Djilas, a Yugoslav writer and activist who met Stalin several times during the war, says that, prior to the Nazi–Soviet War, Stalin spared nothing to achieve military preparedness; and the speed with which he carried out the transformation of the top army command in the midst of the war confirmed Stalin's adaptability and willingness to open careers to men of talent. Djilas, an uncompromising critic of Stalin, says that the sweeping military purges had less effect than is commonly believed.

EPILOGUE

★★★ IF STALIN HAD MADE PEACE WITH HITLER ★★★

Sitting in the safe at GHQ were Hitler's plans to bring war to America's shores. The operation was to be carried out shortly after Stalin's defeat, something which his generals and practically all Western military experts had predicted would follow the *Blitzkrieg*. So heavy were the blows rained on Russia at the beginning of the war that rumours floated in the West to the effect that Stalin would no doubt send peace feelers to Hitler.

The first inkling of Hitler's intentions towards the USA came in a speech to aircraft manufacturers by Hermann Göring in July 1938. He promised his listeners that Germany would become rich, and spoke of the country's 'need' of long-range aircraft for bombing overseas targets. 'What we need is a bomber that could fly to New York with a 10-ton load and return home. I would be very happy to get such a bomber so as finally to shut the mouths of those upstarts there.'

Hitler rubbed his hands in anticipation of the havoc his bombers would cause on the other side of the ocean. Albert Speer, who was Hitler's industrial kingpin and was close to the Führer, says in his book, *Inside the Walls of Spandau – the Prison Diaries of Albert Speer*, that Hitler was obsessed with the idea of destroying New York in a hail-storm of bombs. 'Hitler described the skyscrapers being turned into gigantic burning torches, collapsing on one another, the glow of the exploding city illuminating the dark sky.'

For his plans Hitler counted on a four-engined long-range bomber that could reach the United States with a two-ton bomb load.

In his book *Conversations With Hitler*, Hermann Rauschning, former president of the Danzig senate and a personal friend of Hitler's before the war (he later became an anti-Nazi), quotes the Führer: 'We will create a new Germany in Brazil.' Rauschning says that "Hitler thought that it would be possible to break Anglo-Saxon influence in North America after the disintegration of the British Empire, and in its place implant German culture and the German language. That would be a step toward the inclusion of the United States in the German World Empire.'

Meeting the Japanese Foreign Minister Matsuoka in Berlin on 4 April 1941, Hitler told him that Germany would conduct a very active fight against America with U-boats and the Luftwaffe; that because of Germany's greater battlefield experience, which yet had to be acquired by the United States, she would be greatly superior, and that this was quite apart from the 'fact' that the German soldier 'naturally' ranked high above the American.

A proposed raid on the USA was discussed at Hitler's GHQ on 22 May 1941. Hitler spoke to Admiral Erich Raeder about the possibility of seizing the Azores as a base for operations. 'A need for that may arise even before autumn,' said Hitler. Germany declared war on the USA in December 1941, after the Japanese Navy had attacked Pearl Harbor.

On 11 June 1941, Draft Directive 32, dealing with post-'Barbarossa' objectives was sent to the armed forces. It laid out the Führer's strategy for world domination, including the conquest of Britain and the opening of hostilities against America. In July a 'secret order' declared:

'According to the intentions stated in Directive No. 32 on the further conduct of the war, I set forth the following principles regarding personnel strengths and *matériel*:

'Military domination in Europe after the defeat of Russia will enable us to reduce the size of the army in the very near future. Naval armament should be adequate for waging a war against England and, as the need arises, against America, too.'

'After the defeat of Russia ...'

In the summer of 1941 Hitler's armies raced east. Every expert in the West, with only one or two exceptions, reckoned that Stalin's armies hadn't the slightest chance against the Germans. After the invasion, Foreign Minister Ribbentrop, glowing with hopes of victory, sent a coded message to Japan via the German Ambassador, Jurgen Ott. Ribbentrop wanted him to convey to Tokyo's leaders his assurance that he would 'shake Japan's hand on the Trans-Siberian Railway before winter sets in'. He suggested that Ott draw the Japanese a picture of 'America completely isolated from the rest of the world'.

Ribbentrop's message was read in Tokyo by Dr. Richard Sorge, a confidant of Ambassador Ott. Sorge, who was also Stalin's chief espionage agent in Japan, radioed the information to Moscow.

A few months later Count Galeazzo Ciano, the Italian Foreign Minister, made an entry in his diary: '8 December. A night telephone talk with Ribbentrop. He is very pleased with Japan's attack on the United States.' A week later, Ciano said that Hitler had presented Japanese Ambassador Oshima with the Cross of the German Eagle after holding a long conversation with him on prospects for military co-operation. The stenographer's record of the talk says: 'He [the Führer] is convinced that Roosevelt must be defeated.' But Hitler had his order of priorities in his dream of conquest. The stenographer added these words: 'His first and foremost task is to destroy Russia.'

There were detailed plans for this undertaking, including ridding that country of most of its Slav population. Hitler's desire to make a giant colony of Russia involved the migration of millions of Germans to Russia's vast expanses. This was deemed obligatory after the collapse of Russia. Armed confrontation with the USA would follow the success of this 'foremost task'.

After the Red Army's victory at Stalingrad, the British scholar Joseph McCabe wrote of Hitler's grand strategy: 'There is little doubt that if Germany had succeeded in driving the Russians beyond the Volga, as at one time seemed possible, and if the Russians had not shown an amazing power of creating new armament industries, the Germans would again have turned upon Britain with a mighty air fleet before Britain was fully prepared, and it might have completed the conquest of Europe. Sweden, Switzerland, Spain and Portugal would then have openly joined the Nazi federation and one wonders if America could have been persuaded to enter the lists against a solidly Nazified Europe.'

In the event, the danger to America was averted.

But another danger arose: the possibility of a Nazi Germany in possession of the atom bomb. It is feasible that if the Russians hadn't pinned down Hitler's armies on the Eastern Front for four years, Germany would have had the opportunity to use her resources to develop the bomb. With the start of war in 1939, German physicist Werner Heisenberg (Nobel Prize, 1932) became the scientific head of Hitler's secret atomic bomb project. According to the US atomic scientist and Nobel winner (1963), Eugene P. Wigner, Nazi Germany had the ingredients for the bomb: uranium, heavy water and competent scientists. Not least, the chain reaction – the basic process in making the bomb – was discovered in Germany. But, says, Wigner, Hitler apparently believed that he could win the war before nuclear explosives were developed. Albert Speer, Hitler's Minister of Munitions, says in his memoirs that Hitler sometimes spoke to him about the possibility of an atomic bomb. He adds: 'I'm sure that Hitler would not have hesitated for a moment to employ atom bombs against England.'

At the time that rockets or 'flying bombs' were being launched against London and southern England, German scientists began research on multi-stage missiles with an intercontinental range under the so-called 'America Project'. Testing was also begun on submarine-launched rockets, the forerunner of the Polaris and Trident missiles.

The significance of this hardly needs explanation.

Edward R. Stettinius, who had been Secretary of State in 1944, said after the war that the American people were 'on the brink of disaster in 1942' and that, 'If the Soviet Union had failed to hold on its front, the Germans would have been in a position to conquer Great Britain. They would have been able to overrun Africa, too, and in this event they could have established a foothold in Latin America. This impending danger was constantly in President Roosevelt's mind.'

The peril for America if Stalin were forced to make a separate peace with Hitler was uppermost in the mind of Captain Eddie Rickenbacker when he arrived in Moscow in June 1943. The US World War I air ace said: 'Our War Department could not be positive of any action the Russians might take. If they collapsed, as in 1917, or signed a separate peace, several German armies would be released to resist us in the west. Or did the Russians have the capability and the determination to carry the war on to Germany?'

During his mission to Moscow, Rickenbacker met Marshal Zhukov and asked him about the possibility of a renewed German offensive. The victory at Stalingrad had been celebrated. Zhukov said that German armies were now concentrated 200 miles south of Moscow; that the Russians had already stopped two frontal attacks on Moscow and that the attacking German armies were thinking of going around to the south and 'coming in the back door'.

If the Nazis attacked, said Zhukov, the Russians would defend; if they did not attack until winter, the Russians would – and 'we will tear them to shreds'.

'His eyes bored into mine,' says Rickenbacker. 'I believed him completely.'

Rickenbacker reported to Washington his confidence that Russia's armies would hold, that Stalin wouldn't make peace with Hitler.

Stalin didn't. But the question is relevant: Could Russia have won without Stalin? Was Stalin indispensable to the Soviet war effort? An expert on Russia, Dr. Seweryn Bialer, has written: 'It seems doubtful that the Soviet system could have survived an extraordinary internal shock such as the disappearance of Stalin, while at the same time facing the unprecedented external blow of the German invasion.'

Another expert, America's wartime Ambassador to Moscow, Averell Harriman, says: 'We became convinced that, regardless of Stalin's awful brutality and his reign of terror, he was a great war leader.' (Replying to a question I put to him on his visit to Moscow in May 1975, Harriman called Stalin 'one of the most effective war leaders in history'.) Harriman is categorical: 'Without Stalin, they never would have held.'

Of course many do not share this view. For example historian Roy A. Medvedev (*Let History Judge*) writes: 'The patriotism of the Soviet people and the increasing experience of its army were chief factors that ensured a Soviet victory, despite Stalin's poor leadership.'

Here are two vividly contrasting views. Medvedev, a chronicler of the 'period of Stalin's cult' and a major critic of the dictator, suffered personally during that era. He informs us in one of his books that his father was a victim of the repressions that preceded the apocalypse of war.

Ambassador Harriman, an eye-witness to history, participated in many important wartime conferences with Stalin. But he also had an insider's knowledge of Russia. In the mid-1920s he had been given a concession to a manganese mine in the Caucasus. During the war Stalin sometimes jokingly referred to Harriman as 'our man from the Caucasus'.

Giving full support to Harriman but going a step further is Joseph McCabe, who has been described by eminent historians as 'one of our deeper thinkers' and 'one of the most learned men' of the 20th century. McCabe has recorded that when Hitler's armies fell upon Russia in 1941 Stalin became the West's leader in the gravest crisis through which the world has passed since the fall of Rome.

APPENDICES

★★★ THE COMMISSARS ★★★

Various bodies of Hitler's huge government machine worked tirelessly to plan a regime of terror on Russian soil. Under the so-called Order on Commissars of 6 June 1941, all captured political workers of the Red Army were to be shot on the spot. The order held that they were 'dangerous' because they would make it difficult to implement Nazi plans for the enslavement of the population.

According to General Viktor Nechayev (in his booklet, *Following the Traditions of Military Commissars*, Moscow, 1989), more than 100,000 Russian political officers were killed in action during World War II, many thousands having been executed immediately on capture. From various accounts it would appear that many of them died at their own hands rather than suffer capture.

According to Nechayev, those Red Army regiments, divisions and armies which had the most political workers won more victories. Inasmuch as the role of the military commissar was to foster discipline and patriotism, this is probably true.

But the system of commissars, from its birth in the Revolution, had its critics as well as admirers in Russia. Friction would often break out between military commanders and commissars. In the 1920s the commissar was the political assistant of the military commander, but sometimes hostility resulted because the former could independently contact high Party officials outside the army. There was, at the same time, a more subtle form of control in the army in the presence of secret police agents whose job was to check up on the loyalty of both commander and commissar.

The US military writer Hanson Baldwin of the *New York Times* once wrote that the main reason the Russian *moujik* (peasant) fought hard as a soldier in World War II was his fear of the punitive squads. The Russians reject this idea on the grounds that fear alone can't make heroes. (The many feats of heroism in Stalin's army were commented on by General Eisenhower at the end of the war when he remembered Marshal Zhukov's description of 'battalions of heroes' in the Red Army.) Even the Nazis mentioned the courage of the Russian soldier. A German military expert writing in the 19 July 1941 issue of the Nazi Party newspaper *Völkischer Beobachter*, said: 'The tough and staying qualities of the Red Army soldiers are beyond belief. They fight for every inch of ground even when their position is completely hopeless.'

The 'code of conduct' for Stalin's commissars was spartan: 'In a battle the commissar's place is where the greatest danger threatens his unit, where enemy fire is the heaviest and enemy assaults are the fiercest. Defying death, he is to set an example by standing to face a hail of fire.'

The commissars first appeared on the scene in the opening years of the 1917 Revolution. (Some historians trace their birth back to the French Revolution.) In April 1918 an Institute of Military Commissars was set up in the new Soviet armed forces, its members rallying the soldiers, forging discipline and conducting political education. They also had the job of checking on the loyalty of commanding officers, many of whom had served under the Tsar.

Doubts about loyalty were omnipresent. This is what Mikhail Frunze, an early Bolshevik military commander and Party leader, wrote: 'We were obliged to create the institution of commissars at a time when we had no army officers who were reliable from the class point of view, when in the building up of the Red Army we were involving people who were often hostile to our Soviet power. We knew this very well, yet went ahead, at the same time appointing commissars to work with them, the commissars being our proletarian eye.'

If taken prisoner in the early Civil War years, commissars were immediately shot. With the Civil War and foreign intervention in full swing, large numbers of Communists and Soviet officials were being executed without trial. In the summer of 1918 twenty-six, including commissars, who were members of the Baku Commune recently set up in Azerbaijan, were captured in the Trans-Caspian region (then occupied by British forces), taken into the desert, and shot.

By October 1918 there were approximately 35,000 political workers among Red Army troops. Two years later their number had risen to more than 300,000. Shortly before World War II military commissars were abolished and replaced by deputy commanders for political affairs, but they were reintroduced after Hitler's invasion in 1941.

By 1940 there were two military–political higher educational establishments and 25 special schools for political officers in the army and navy. A 'Political Textbook' was published for soldiers and sailors.

One of the first handbooks for political workers said that they must 'win attention and respect not by your post but by your work', and that 'You must be the first to enter combat and the last to withdraw from it.'

Women served also as political commissars. In 1919, during the Civil War, Olga Mitkevich headed the political department of the 13th Division of the 8th Army. It is reported that when her divisional HQ was surrounded by White Guards, she escaped and later, dressed as a peasant, led surviving soldiers out of the encirclement.

Also in 1919, another woman commissar, Maria Kostelovskaya, was appointed head of the 2nd Army's political department. When she protested to Lenin about her elevation to such a high post, he is reported to have said: 'It's wartime, the decision has been taken, and you are being sent where the situation is very difficult.'

In his memoirs, the late Soviet leader Leonid Brezhnev, who was himself a military commissar in World War II, speaks glowingly of political workers: 'How is one to gauge or assess a political worker's efforts at the front? A sniper picks off ten Nazis – all praise to him; a company repulses an attack and stands its ground – all praise to the company commander and his men; a division breaks through the enemy lines and liberates a community – the divisional commander is named in orders of the Supreme Commander-in-Chief. But great services are also rendered by the political worker who gives the men ideological weapons, who fosters in them noble feelings of love for their country, builds up their self-confidence and inspires them to acts of heroism.'

According to US General Phillip Faymonville, who had served at the American embassy in Moscow, the commissar had the functions of a quartermaster and chaplain. But he also had to understand military science, and be able to explain to the troops not only the reasons for an impending action but the best way of carrying it out.

★★★ STALIN IS ANGRY: ON 'VITAL SOVIET INTERESTS' ★★★

'PERSONAL AND SECRET MESSAGE

FROM PREMIER J. V. STALIN

TO THE PRIME MINISTER MR. W. CHURCHILL

Your message of 19 June received. [Churchill had explained why he ruled out a Second Front for 1943.]

'I fully realise the difficulty of organising an Anglo–American invasion of western Europe, in particular, of transferring troops across the Channel. The difficulty could also be discerned in your communications.

'From your messages of last year and this I gained the conviction that you and the President were fully aware of the difficulties of organising such an operation and were preparing the invasion accordingly, with due regard to the difficulties and the necessary exertion of forces and means. Even last year you told me that a large-scale invasion of Europe by Anglo–American troops would be effected in 1943. In the *aide-mémoire* handed to V. M. Molotov on 10 June 1942, you wrote:

"Finally, and most important of all, we are concentrating our maximum effort on the organisation and preparation of a large-scale invasion of the Continent of Europe by British and American forces in 1943. We are setting no limit to the scope and objectives of this campaign, which will be carried out in the first instance by more than a million men, British and American, with air forces of appropriate strength."

'Early this year you twice informed me, on your own behalf and on behalf of the President, of decisions concerning an Anglo–American invasion of western Europe intended to "divert strong German land and air forces from the Russian front". You had set yourself the task of bringing Germany to her knees as early as 1943, and named September as the latest date for the invasion.

'In your message of January 26 you wrote:

"We have been in conference with our military advisers and have decided on the operations which are to be undertaken by the American and British forces in the first nine months of 1943. We wish to inform you of our intentions at once. We believe that these operations, together with your powerful offensive, may well bring Germany to her knees in 1943."

'In your next message, which I received on 12 February, you wrote, specifying the date of the invasion of western Europe decided on by you and the President:

"We are also pushing preparations to the limit of our resources for a cross-Channel operation in August, in which British and United States units would participate. Here again, shipping and assault–landing craft will be the limiting factors. If the operation is delayed by the weather or other reasons, it will be prepared with stronger forces for September."

'Last February, when you wrote to me about those plans and the date for invading western Europe, the difficulties of that operation were greater than they are now. Since then the Germans have suffered more than one defeat: they were pushed back by our troops in the South, where they suffered appreciable loss; they were beaten in North Africa and expelled by the Anglo–American troops; in submarine warfare, too, the Germans found themselves in a bigger predicament than ever, while Anglo–American superiority increased substantially; it is also known that the Americans and British have won air superiority in Europe and that their navies and mercantile marines have grown in power.

'It follows that the conditions for opening a second front in western Europe during 1943, far from deteriorating, have, indeed, greatly improved.

'That being so, the Soviet Government could not have imagined that the British and US Governments would revise the decision to invade western Europe, which they had adopted early this year. In fact, the Soviet Government was fully entitled to expect that the Anglo–American decision would be carried out, that appropriate preparations were under way and that the second front in western Europe would at last be opened in 1943.

'That is why, when you now write that "it would be no help to Russia if we threw away a hundred thousand men in a disastrous cross-Channel attack", all I can do is remind you of the following:

'First, your own *aide-mémoire* of June 1942 in which you declared that preparations were under way for an invasion, not by a hundred thousand, but by an Anglo–American force exceeding one million men at the very start of the operation.

'Second, your February message, which mentioned extensive measures preparatory to the invasion of western Europe in August or September 1943, which, apparently, envisaged an operation, not by a hundred thousand men, but by an adequate force.

'So when you now declare: "I cannot see how a great British defeat and slaughter would aid the Soviet armies", is it not clear that a statement of this kind in relation to the Soviet Union is utterly groundless and directly contradicts your previous and responsible decisions, listed above, about extensive and vigorous measures by the British and Americans to organise the invasion this year, measures on which the complete success of the operation should hinge?

'I shall not enlarge on the fact that this responsible decision, revoking your previous decisions on the invasion of western Europe was reached by you and the President without Soviet participation and without inviting its representatives to the Washington conference, although you cannot but be aware that the Soviet Union's role in the war against Germany and its interest in the problems of the second front are great enough.

'There is no need to say that the Soviet Government cannot become reconciled to this disregard of vital Soviet interests in the war against the common enemy.

'You say that you "quite understand" my disappointment. I must tell you that the point here is not just the disappointment of the Soviet Government, but the preservation of its confidence in its Allies, a confidence which is being subjected to severe stress. One should not forget that it is a question of saving millions of lives in the occupied areas of western Europe and Russia and of reducing the enormous sacrifices of the Soviet armies, compared with which the sacrifices of the Anglo–American armies are insignificant.'
(24 June 1943)

NOTES

Part I HITLER AND STALIN

CHAPTER 1 Napoleon's gamble – and Hitler's

Fredborg, *Behind the Steel Wall*, 1944. Tippelskirch on Napoleon quoted in B. H.
Liddell Hart, *The Other Side of the Hill*, London, 1951. Late in 1941 Field Marshal von Kluge and other commanders were reading Napoleon envoy
Caulaincourt's account of 1812, according to General Gunther Blumentritt's
essay in *The Fatal Decisions*, London, 1956. Also Raymond Garthoff, *How Russia Makes War*, 1954.

Harriman's meeting with Stalin in A. Harriman and E. Abel, *Special Envoy to
Churchill and Stalin, 1941–1946*.

Quotations from Napoleon, Count de las Cases, Memoirs of the Life, Exile and
Conversations of the Emperor Napoleon, London, 1836.

Professor Tarle is quoted in Gerhard Schacher's *He Wanted to Sleep in the Kremlin*, New York, 1942.

Article in the *Petersburg Gazette*, reproduced in the *Annual Register*, London,
1812.

Karl von Clausewitz, Prussian General and noted 19th-century military strategist, wrote in his *Vom Kriege* (*On War*, 1833):

'Russia is not such a country that one can really conquer, i.e., occupy; this, at
least, is something that the modern European states cannot do, and that the
500,000 men whom Buonaparte had brought there for the purpose, could not
do. Russia is a country which can be brought to submission only through its
weakness and through the effects of internal dissension. In order to strike at the
vulnerable spots of its political body Russia would have to be stirred up at the
very centre.'

And: 'The march of 1812 failed because the enemy [Russian] government
proved firm and the people stayed loyal and tenacious, i.e., it failed because it
could not succeed.'

A decade after the war, a British General and historian, Sir William Jackson,
in his book *Seven Roads to Moscow*, raised a warning against new emulators of
Napoleon and Hitler, saying that any future attempt to invade Russia ran the
risk of nuclear annihilation of the world.

CHAPTER 2 Stalin's War Credentials

On Hitler's Iron Cross award see historian Igor Ovsyany's *The Origins of World
War Two*, Moscow, 1984. Also Werner Maser's *Hitler, Legend, Myth and Reality*,
London, 1971.

Guderian's reference to Hitler is in Werner Maser's biography.

For the size of the Red Army see General Viktor Nechayev's *The Traditions of Military Commissars*, Moscow, 1989 (in English).

Lenin's telegrams are to be found in Volumes 35, 43, 44 of *Lenin's Complete Works*, 1966 edition (in English).

Marshal Vasilevsky's memoirs, *A Lifelong Cause*, Moscow, 1981.

CHAPTER 3 Building Two Russias

John Littlepage, in *Reader's Digest*, October 1938; 'The Economy That Won the War', in *Pravda*, 25 March 1985;

Nuremberg Trial Documents (in *The Trial of German Major War Criminals*, London, 1946–50). Also A. R. Williams, *The Russians*, New York, 1943.

The H. G Wells rebuke is from his *Outline of History*, London. Curiously, a popular American novelist and political activist, Upton Sinclair, commenting on the Five-Year Plan, said that he had advised Moscow to 'push collectivisation at all costs', because only through mechanised farming could they permanently avert famine. And they had accomplished this, so he said. See *Terrorism in Russia? Two Views*, by Upton Sinclair and Eugene Lyons, New York, 1938.

For General Volkogonov's comment see *New York Times*, 1 August 1995.

For excerpts from Sholokhov's letters, see *Moscow News*, No. 28, 1987 and No. 14, 1988. For literary information on Sholokhov, see *Handbook of Russian Literature*, London, 1985.

For those interested in Sholokhov, in a Foreword to the 1934 English edition of *And Quiet Flows the Don*, he said that he often heard himself rebuked in English press reviews for his 'cruel' portrayal of reality; and that some English critics had spoken of the cruelty of Russian mores in general. In reply, he said that he accepted the first rebuke. His novel, he said, was not for reading during an after-dinner siesta – or for the sole purpose of aiding digestion. But, as to Russian mores, he didn't think the Russians were more cruel than any other people. And he wondered if the cultured nations were more cruel and inhuman who in 1918–1920 hurled their armies against 'my tortured Motherland' and tried to impose their will on Russia.

CHAPTER 4 An Army For Winning

Pierre Cot, *The Triumph of Treason*, New York, 1944.

The Album of the Red Army, Moscow, 1934.

S. M. Shtemenko, *The Soviet General Staff at War, 1941–1945*.

The letter to German Ambassador von Dirksen is quoted by L. Bezymensky, 'The Secret of Rapallo', in *New Times*, No. 16, 1982.

CHAPTER 5 Espionage in Stalin's Russia

On purge trials, see *The Times*, London, 28 January 1937.

On the arrest of 35,000 officers, see statement by General Igor Sergeyev in *Moscow News*, Nos. 8–9, 1990.

On the confessions: When Sir Bruce Lockhart, a British diplomat and intelligence agent who had served in pre-war Russia, wrote about the bizarre confessions, he offered the reader several explanations. Under certain conditions, he said, the injection of salts of barbituric acid can produce a dulling of the conscience which may produce confession. He mentioned other drugs that are supposed to act as a truth serum. But the ex-diplomat went on to say that the Moscow confessions were likely to have been obtained by a reaction to fear, exhaustion and, finally, indifference. Probably, he said, it was a combination of brutality and cajolery.

Sir Bruce, who had once been placed under house arrest in Moscow after the British arrested a Soviet diplomat in London, put forward this compelling idea: that when life-long Communists were put on trial, their confessions were sometimes evoked by a desire on the part of the victim to 'put himself right with history' and so devote his last words on earth to the cause for which he had given his life.

On the question of whether torture was used to gain confessions, remarkably, Western diplomats and journalists attending the open trials said of the prisoners that they saw no haggard faces, no twitching hands, no dazed expressions, and no bandaged heads.

Sidney and Beatrice Webb, who made an exhaustive study of life in Communist Russia, came up with this analysis of the confessions in *The Treason Trials in Russia, a New Civilization?*, London, 1940):

'The confessions of the defendants; the manner in which the several stories corroborated one another; their frank explanations of the way they had yielded to the temptation of giving their general adherence to a treasonable company of which they did not at first understand the scope; and how they had then found themselves unable to escape from the toils in which they had become entangled; – be it added, a certain amount of further corroboration deduced from incautiously public utterances by both German and by Japanese statesmen, convinced the British and American journalists present at the trial in January 1937 that the defendants were really guilty of the treasonable conspiracies with which they were charged.'

Some other foreign observers shared this view. For instance, the American engineer John Littlepage, who had spent ten years in Russia and had written about Stalin's Russia for various US publications, was asked by friends whether the accused were guilty. He said without equivocation that most of them were. What surprised Littlepage was that the men in the Kremlin had waited so long to realise that 'other Communists are the most dangerous enemies they have' (in *The Saturday Evening Post*, 1 January 1938).

For comments by General Behrens and Hoettl see Wilhelm Hoettl's *The Secret Front*, London, 1953.

Gerhard Schacher, *He Wanted to Sleep in the Kremlin*, New York, 1942.

On the GPU General's defection see *Oh, Japan* by Kimpei Shiba. Shiba (whom I met and befriended after the war) was an editor in Japan and personally knew Richard Sorge, Stalin's spy in Tokyo.

See also *The Times*, London.

Officer training statistics are taken from *The Armed Forces of the USSR*, Moscow, 1987, ed. by General Pavel Zhilin, a member of the Academy of Sciences.

On President Beneš, see 'The New Version of the Tukhachevsky Affair', in *New Times*, No. 13, 1989.

CHAPTER 6 **What Hitler Edited out of** *Mein Kampf*

Ivan Maisky's memoirs.

Joseph McCabe, *Winston Churchill: The Man and His Creed*, Girard, Kansas, 1944.

The London papers were the *News Chronicle* and the *Labour Herald*.

For Stalin's remark to President Roosevelt, see interview with historian Dr. Pavel Sevostyanov by APN (news agency) Moscow, 20 August 1986; also Sevostyanov's *Before the Nazi Invasion*, Moscow, 1984.

Mikhail Chernousov, *The Soviet Ambassador Reports Back*, Moscow, 1983.

For Stanley Baldwin's remark, see D. Irving, *Churchill in War. The Struggle for Power*, 1987.

CHAPTER 7 **The Hitler–Stalin Letters**

Nazi–Soviet Relations, 1939–1941, US Department of State, Washington, 1948.

See *Nazi Guide to Nazism*, ed. Rolf Tell, Washington, 1942 for Hitler's anti-Communist and anti-Semitic outpourings.

CHAPTER 8 **Master Stroke Or Blunder?**

On the Munich Conference 29–30 September 1938:

Russia never quite recovered from the trauma of the 1938 Munich Conference when the Western Allies quickly accepted Hitler's demands and in effect betrayed the sovereign state of Czechoslovakia. Until Britain and France declared war on Nazi Germany, the Kremlin had little reason to believe that there were substantial differences between the policy of the Hitler regime and that of the democratic states. Moscow was unsure that the Allies might not cook up a 'second Munich', this time involving Poland.

Moscow historian and diplomat Dr. Valentin Falin says that the Munich Conference opened the door wide to large-scale German military preparations and that even prior to Munich, the Western democracies missed a 'realistic opportunity' to halt Hitler's aggression and prevent a full-scale war.

According to British archives, another missed opportunity arose *after* Munich. These archives were made public after a statutory period of thirty years. On 1 January 1970 the English newspaper, *The Guardian*, wrote: 'The Cabinet papers for 1939, published this morning, show that the Second World War would not have started in that year if the Chamberlain Government had accepted or understood Russian advice that an alliance between Britain, France and the Soviet Union would prevent war because Hitler could not then risk a conflict against major powers on two fronts.' (Dr. Valentin Falin, *Izvestia*, 21 August 1989).

Alexander Yakovlev, 'The Events of 1939', in *Pravda*, 18 August 1989.

Moscow's comments on British, French and Soviet peace efforts on the eve of World War II. Documents and Records, Nos. 54 and 287, Moscow, 1976, Conversations with Maisky and Stalin in *History of Soviet Foreign Policy, 1917–1945*, Moscow, 1969; also Mikhail Chernousov, *The Soviet Ambassador Reports Back*, Moscow, 1983.

On instructions to British and French military delegations, see Fyodor Volkov, *Secrets From Whitehall and Downing Street*, Moscow, 1980.

On General Petrov's mission to Berlin, see *Moscow News*, Nos. 19 and 33, 1986.

On Western commerce with Hitler, see chapter 'Have English and American Finance Co-operated with Hitler to Destroy Democracy?' in *America is Worth Saving*, New York, 1941, by Theodore Dreiser. Information on Rolls-Royce engines appears in *Images of War, 1939–1945*, a Marshall Cavendish Collection in association with the Imperial War Museum, London.

Dr. Ingebord Fleischhauer, interview in *Lituraturnaya Gazeta*, Moscow, 16 August 1989.

Sir Bernard Pares, *Russia: Its Past and Present*, New York, 1949.

Stalin's speech, see J. Stalin's *On the Great Patriotic War of the Soviet Union*, Moscow, 1946.

Valentin Falin's observations in *Izvestia*, 21 August 1989.

CHAPTER 9 **A Russian Colonel In Paris**
Author's interview. See also Paul Carell's *Hitler Moves East, 1941–1943*, Boston, 1964

Kalinin's remark is quoted in Arthur Just's *The Red Army*, 1936.

CHAPTER 10 **The Russo–Finnish War**
Stalin's talk with Paasikivi is given in Robert Payne's *Rise and Fall of Stalin*, 1966.

Stalin's talk with Latvian Foreign Minister Munters is in Vilnis Sipols' *Diplomatic Battles Before World War II*, Moscow, 1982.

See Mikhail Semiryaga's *The Winter War*, Moscow, 1990.

Interview with Dr. Fleischhauer in *Literary Gazette*, 16 August 1989.

Max Jakobson, *Finland Survived*, Helsinki, 1984.

CHAPTER 11 **The Secret Speech**
Marshal Zhukov gives a good summary of the speech in his memoirs. A verbatim transcription exists in the Defence Ministry Archives. The part dealing with international relations is reproduced by Lev Bezymensky in *New Times*, No. 19, 1991.

CHAPTER 12 **The Hess Manoeuvre**
Lev Bezymensky's articles in *New Times*, 1980–1990, especially Number 46, 1990. The meeting during the Olympics between the Duke of Hamilton and Rudolf Hess is mentioned by Alan Bullock (Hitler, *A Study in Tyranny*, New York, 1964) and by *New York Times* diplomatic correspondent C. L. Sulzberger (World War II, 1970).

Several KGB documents on the Hess flight were made public in Moscow on 7 June 1991.

CHAPTER 13 **Plan 'Barbarossa'**
The Russian historian Lev Bezymensky has made wide use of German documents in reconstructing Hitler's designs in the war on Russia. For instance, his five-page article, 'The Code-word Was "Dortmund",' has much interesting

material on the Barbarossa Plan. It also has a 'timetable' of the war given by various German leaders. Some German generals gave their own timetable in their diaries or memoirs.

Statement by von Kleist to Nuremberg War Crimes Tribunal, quoted in *Moscow News*, No. 17, 1980.

For this and other statements by the Historical–Diplomatic Directorate of the Russian Foreign Ministry, see magazine *Vestnik*, (English) 1990–2.

For Stalin's pre-invasion moves, see Adam Ulam's *Stalin: The Man and his Era*, New York, 1974.

Stalin's remark to Timoshenko is given in *Izvestia*, 22 November 1989.

Joseph Davies, *Mission to Moscow*, New York, 1941.

For Stalin's statement to Churchill on the warnings of Hitler's invasion, in Alexander Werth's *Russia at War, 1941–1945*, London, 1964.

CHAPTER 14 Stalin Is Outraged

For information on Convoy PQ–17 see Admiral Kharlamov's memoirs, *Difficult Mission*; also General Shtemenko's memoirs.

Documents exchanged between Stalin and Churchill are to be found in their official wartime correspondence.

Stalin's quotation from the Bible is found in Daniel Yergin, *Shattered Peace*, NY 1977.

CHAPTER 15 The End Of *Blitzkrieg*

Interview with General Kurochkin, in *Moscow News Weekly*, No. 30, 1989.

CHAPTER 16 The Battle for Moscow

Much of the information on these battles was supplied by the Russian Defence Ministry's Institute of Military History. Especially valuable was their publication, *The USSR in World War Two, 1941–1945*, Moscow, 1985.

CHAPTER 17 The Battle of Stalingrad

The remark by Mao Tse-tung is in Boris Sapozhnikov's *The China Theatre in World War II, 1939–1945*, Moscow, 1985 (in English). Japanese historians writing in the five-volume *History of the War in the Pacific* state: 'By holding Stalingrad the Soviet Army saved humanity from Nazism–Fascism.' (Quoted by Doctor of History, Leonid Yeremeyev, in The *USSR in World War Two*, Moscow, 1985.)

Joseph McCarthy, *America's Retreat From Victory*, New York, 1952. The Cold War had, indeed, descended. Another senator, Robert Taft, in his book on foreign policy (*A Foreign Policy for Americans*, New York,1954), said that he had warned that Stalin's victories posed a greater danger to the United States than Hitler's victories. Walter Rostow, *The United States in the World Arena*, New York, 1960.

CHAPTER 18 The Battle of Kursk

From *The Battle of Kursk*, Moscow, 1974 (In English) with contributions by Russian Generals and several military historians.

CHAPTER **19 Operation 'Bagration'**
Operation 'Bagration', 1944, Institute of Military History, Moscow, 1980. Statement by Field Marshal Keitel, quoted by Lev Bezymensky, in *New Times*, No. 6, 1988.

CHAPTER **20 The Jassy–Kishinev Operation**
See *Soviet Armed Forces in the Second World War*, an official military history, ed. Marshal A. A. Grechko, Moscow, 1975.
On King Michael's contacts with OSS, see Alan Clark's *Barbarossa*, New York, 1965.
Information supplied by Colonel Malakhov in *Liberation Mission*, ed. Marshal A. A. Grechko, Moscow, 1975 (In English).

CHAPTER **21 Stalin's Jewish Generals**
For a list of Russian studies on anti-Semitism written during the Stalin era see S. M. Schwartz, *Jews in the Soviet Union*, Syracuse University, New York, 1951.

CHAPTER **22 The Death of Stalin's Son**
On executions of commissars and Jews, see Helmut Krausnick, *et al.*, Anatomy of the SS State, New York, 1968. Svetlana Alliluyeva, *Twenty Letters to a Friend*, London, 1967. Author's interview with military historian V. P. Morozov.

CHAPTER **23: Stalin: 'Who Will Take Berlin First?'**
The Conference at Cairo, 1943 in *Foreign Relations of the United States: Diplomatic Papers*, Washington, 1961. Also, Marshal Konev's memoirs.

CHAPTER **25 Mutual Cries for Help**
Correspondence Between Allied Leaders, 3 vols., Moscow, 1957.
German General Bodo Zimmerman, Chief of Operations on the Western Front, said: 'The war against the British and Americans in France was lost on the Eastern Front even before the landing of the Anglo–American armies on the Continent.' And: 'It would be no exaggeration to say that the Eastern Front steadily pumped all the efficient manpower and combat equipment out of the German armies in the west.' Quoted in historian Yeremeyev's *The USSR in World War Two*, Moscow, 1985.

CHAPTER **26 Tragedy in a Census**
For demographic details see Boris Urlanis' 'The History of One Generation' in *Sputnik* magazine, May, 1969; also 'A Heroic Generation' by Ella Maksimova, in a booklet entitled *Our Way to Victory – The Soviet People in the Great Patriotic War, 1941–1945*, 1990. On women at war: in early 1944 women accounted for 46 per cent of all military doctors in the Red Army and 23 per cent of medical orderlies. They made up 12 per cent of the signal troops. Hundreds of women were pilots and several thousand served in the air defence forces. (From Viktor Sokolov's *The Armed Forces of the USSR*, Moscow, 1985.)

CHAPTER **27 Stalin: a Perfectionist?**

See Shtemenko's memoirs; also Marshal Vasilevsky's *A Lifelong Cause* for Stalin's attention to detail.

CHAPTER **28 Toasting the Russian Character**

The toast is described in General Shtemenko's and other memoirs. See Stalin's 'The National Question and Social Democracy', in *Collected Works*, 1952 and 1967.

CHAPTER **29 'Kamikaze Pilots' and Other Heroes**

Details on ramming are to be found in official armed forces booklets, including *The Air Force* (1983), *Air Defence Troops* (1983), and *War Heroes, 1941–1945* (1984). See also *Izvestia*, 26 October 1986, and archives of Russian Defence Ministry.

For 'The Night Witches' see Zhenya Zhigulenko's account in *Moscow News*, No. 26, 1981; and *Soviet Women*, Moscow, April, 1985.

Mila Pavlichenko's story is condensed from *News From Ukraine*, undated, circa 1980. There are some details of her visit to the USA in the magazine *World At War*, New York, April 1943.

'Nine Snow-White Cranes', in *Moscow News*, No. 19, 1984. Also various issues of *Soviet Women*, 1980–4. Information on the Shaklein brothers is taken from *Izvestia*, 9 March 1981. (When writing this chapter I came across an article by an editor whose mother lost five brothers who were all killed instantly when they came together in a fateful rendezvous on the battlefield near Kiev early in the war. He wrote: 'Suddenly there were no more men left in the family, and the name disappeared. A family that had existed for centuries and had lived through numerous inroads of invaders was thus blotted into extinction.') Nikolai Nekrasov (1821–77) was a favourite poet of the radical intelligentsia. The lines are from his poem, 'Russian Women'.

Alexander Yakovlev's article 'A Hero of the Drawing-Board', in *Sputnik*, December, 1970.

For Stalin's complaint about delivery of US and British aircraft, see *Foreign Relations of the United States: Diplomatic Papers, 1942*, vol. 3, US Government Printing Office, Washington, 1961.

CHAPTER **30 The Stalin Phenomenon**

For additional details see Zhukov's memoirs.

Zhukov on heroism; see Eisenhower's speech in Washington, in John Gunther's *Inside Europe*, New York, 1966.

Remark by General Pyotr Grigorenko, in his memoirs, London 1983.

For Stalin's 1941 question to Zhukov on the ability to hold Moscow, see interview by Vasily Peshkov in *Soviet Life*, May, 1975.

Louis Fischer, in *Reader's Digest*, July, 1948.

On Stalin's visitors, see Pavel Sudoplatov's memoirs published in 1994.

On Edvard Radzinsky, see *The Times* (London), 21 April 1996.

Lev Bezymensky's 'The Rokossovsky Phenomenon' in *New Times*, No. 20, 1990. See also Zhukov's memoirs.

For 'Stalin rejects a Generalissimo's uniform', see Shtemenko's memoirs.

CHAPTER 31 **Stalin and Invasion Day**

Harriman made his remark on mobilisation at a Moscow press conference attended by the author on 7 May 1975. See also Harriman's memoir, *Special Envoy to Churchill and Stalin: 1941–1946*, New York, 1975

For Russia's 1914 mobilisation débâcle see *History of the USSR*, vol. I, Moscow, 1977

On the inability to hold the frontier areas, Bagramyan's recollection is quoted in Albert Seaton's *Stalin as Military Commander*, New York, 1976.

Roosevelt's message to Japan on a possible American response if Japan struck north at the Soviet Union, is given in *Memoirs of Cordell Hull*, New York, 1948. See also *Soviet–US Relations, 1933–1942*, Moscow, 1989.

CHAPTER 32 **The Horrible and Bitter Truth**

World War II took a toll of more than 50 million lives: 22–25 million were Russians; 7 million Germans; 6 million Poles; 6 million Jews; 5 million Chinese; 2.5 million Japanese; 2 million Indonesians; 1.7 million Yugoslavs; 1 million Filipinos; 800,000 French; 410,000 Italians; 375,000 Britons; 300,000 Americans.

Total material losses by all nations is estimated at four trillion dollars. The Soviet Union lost approximately one-third of its national wealth. Britain and France, by comparison, each lost less than 2 per cent of their national wealth. (These figures appear in *The Causes, Results and Lessons of World War Two*, Moscow, 1985, ed. by the General and Academician Pavel Zhilin.)

Mikhail Sholokhov, *At the Bidding of the Heart*, Moscow, 1973.

Lyova Fedotov's comment is given in *Moscow News*, No. 43, 1986.

For Marshal Chuikov's remark, see *Moscow News*, No. 46, 1982.

For Konev's remark, see interview with Russian historian Alexander Samsonov, in *Moscow News*, No. 15, 1985.

B. H. Liddell Hart, *History of the Second World War*, 1971.

John Erickson, *Barbarossa, the Axis and the Allies*, 1994.

CHAPTER 33 **Letters: Pro and Con**

From Russian newspapers and Moscow pamphlet *Stalin, For and Against*, 1990.

CHAPTER 34 **Stalin as Generalissimo**

Some Information for this chapter came from the memoirs of Marshals and generals including Zhukov, Vasilevsky, Eremenko and Shtemenko.

General Doerr's comment is quoted in *Life-and-Death Struggle Against Fascism*, Moscow, 1979; and in Hans Doerr's *Der Feldzug nach Stalingrad*, Darmstadt, 1955

EPILOGUE **If Stalin Had Made Peace With Hitler**

Count Ciano's memoirs.

Bezymensky's article in *Sputnik*, June, 1982.

For Hitler's remarks to Matsuoka, see *Trial of the German Major War Criminals. Proceedings of the International Military Tribunal, Nuremberg, 1945–6*, Parts 1–3.

On Hitler's atomic bomb research, see *International Herald Tribune*, 2 September 1992. Remarks by Nobel Physicist Eugene P. Wigner, in *Look* Magazine, 26 December 1967. See also David C. Cassidy's *Uncertainty: The Life and Science of Werner Heisenberg*, New York, 1992; Samuel Goudsmit's *Alsos*, New York, 1947; Albert Speer's *Infiltration*, New York, 1981.

For remarks by Stettinius see his *Roosevelt and the Russians*, New York, 1950. Rickenbacker, *Rickenbacker: His Own Story*, New York, 1967.

Harriman's comments are in Studs Terkel's *The Good War*, New York, 1984. Also my tape-recorded questions to Harriman in Moscow in May 1975.

APPENDICES

On the Commissars, see General Viktor Nechayev's *The Traditions of Military Commissars*, Moscow, 1989; also Professor Yuri Polyakov's tract, *The Civil War in Russia*, Moscow, 1981. For General Faymonville's remarks see A. R. Williams, *The Russians*, New York, 1943.

BIBLIOGRAPHY

Alliluyeva, Svetlana. *Only One Year*. New York, 1970.

— *Twenty Letters to a Friend*. London, 1967.

Armstrong, Hamilton Fish. *Chronology of Failure*. New York, 1940.

Bendiner, Robert. *The Riddle of the State Department*. New York, 1942.

Berezhkov, Valentin. *History in the Making*. Moscow, 1983.

Beria, Lavrenti. *On the History of Bolshevik Organizations in Transcaucasia*. 1939

Bezymensky, Lev. *The Death of Adolf Hitler*. London, 1968.

Bialer, Seweryn (ed.). *Stalin and His Generals*. New York, 1970.

Bidou, Henri (ed.). *Blitzkrieg: Eye-witness History of World War II*. New York, 1962.

Billington, James H. *The Icon and the Axe*. New York, 1970.

Blumentritt, Günther. *Von Rundstedt: The Soldier and the Man*. London, 1952.

Bohlen, Charles E. *Witness to History*. New York, 1973.

Bradley, Omar. *A Soldier's Story*. London, 1965.

Brzezinski, Zbigniew. *The Permanent Purge: Politics in Soviet Totalitarianism*. Cambridge, Mass., 1956.

Bullock, Alan. *Hitler and Stalin: Parallel Lives*. London, 1993.

Burns, James MacGregor. *Roosevelt, 1940–1945*. New York, 1970.

Byrnes, James F. *Speaking Frankly*. New York, 1947.

Caidin, Martin. *The Tigers are Burning*. New York, 1974.

Carell, Paul. *Scorched Earth, The Russo–German War 1943–1944*. Boston, 1970.

Carr, E. H. *The Russian Revolution: From Lenin to Stalin*. London, 1979.

Carr, E. H., and Davies, R. W. *A History of Soviet Russia: Foundations of a Planned Economy*. 3 vols., London, 1969–1978.

Cassidy, Henry. *Moscow Dateline, 1941–1943*. New York, 1943.

Chandos, Lord. *Memoirs*. London. 1962.

Chuikov, Marshal Vasili. *The End of the Third Reich*. Moscow, 1978.

Churchill, Winston. *Great Contemporaries*. London, 1947.

— *The Second World War*. London, 1954.

Clark, Alan. *Barbarossa, The Russian–German Conflict, 1941–1945*. New York, 1965.

Cohen, Stephen. *Bukharin and the Bolshevik Revolution, 1888–1938*. New York, 1974.

— *Commissars, Commanders and Civilian Authority: The Structure of Soviet Military Politics*. Cambridge, Mass., 1979.

Conquest, Robert. *The Great Terror: Stalin's Purges of the Thirties*. London, 1968.

— *The Great Terror: A Re-Assessment*. London, 1990.

— *The Harvest of Sorrow*. London, 1986.

Cot, Pierre. *Triumph of Treason*. Chicago, 1944.

Dalton, Hugh. *The Fateful Years: Memoirs, 1931–1945*. London, 1957.

Dangerfield, George. *The Strange Death of Liberal England*. London, 1936.

Davies, Joseph. *Mission to Moscow*. New York, 1941.

Deakin, F. W., and Storry, G. R. *The Case of Richard Sorge*. New York, 1966.

Deane, John R. *The Strange Alliance: the Story of Our Efforts at Wartime Cooperation with Russia*. New York, 1947.

De Jonge, Alex. *Stalin and the Shaping of the Soviet Union*. London, 1986.

Deutscher, Isaac. *Stalin*. Oxford, 1949.

Djilas, Milovan. *Conversations With Stalin*. London, 1962.

Dodd, William. *Ambassador Dodd's Diary, 1933–1939*. New York, 1941.

Dragunsky, David. *A Soldier's Life*. Moscow, 1977.

Dutt Palme, R. *Problems of Contemporary History*. London, 1963.

Eden, Anthony. *The Memoirs of Anthony Eden, Earl of Avon*. Boston, 1965.

Ehrenburg, Ilya. *The War: 1941–1945*. New York, 1964.

Eisenhower, Dwight. *Crusade in Europe*. New York, 1955.

Eremenko, Marshal A. *The Arduous Beginning*. Moscow, 1966.

Erickson, John. *The Road to Berlin: Stalin's War With Germany*. London, 1983.

— *The Road to Stalingrad: Stalin's War With Germany*. London, 1975.

— *The Soviet High Command: A Military–Political History, 1918–1941*. London, 1962.

— *Soviet Military Power*. London, 1979.

Feis, Herbert. *Churchill, Roosevelt, Stalin: The War they Waged and the Peace they Sought*. London, 1957.

Fischer, George. *Soviet Opposition to Stalin*. Cambridge, Mass., 1952.

Fischer, John. *Why They Behave Like Russians*. New York, 1947.

Fleming, D. *The Cold War and Its Origins, 1917–1960*. London, 1961.

Fuller, J. F. C. *The Second World War*. London, 1954.

Gardner, B. R. *The Year That Changed the World: 1945*. New York, 1964.

Gilbert, G. M. *Nuremberg Diary*. London, 1948.

Gilbert, Martin. *Winston S. Churchill, 1941–1945*. vol. vii, London, 1986

Gilbert, Martin, and Gott, Richard. *The Appeasers*. New York, 1963.

Goebbels, Joseph. *The Goebbels Diaries, 1942–1943* (ed. Louis P. Lochner). London, 1948.

Grechko, Andrei. *The Armed Forces of the USSR*. Moscow, 1972.

Grey, Ian. *Stalin, Man of History*. London, 1979.

Grigorenko, Pyotr. *Memoirs*. London, 1983.

Gromyko, Andrei. *Memories*. London, 1989.

Grossman, Vasily. *Red Army in Poland and Byelorussia*. London, 1945.

Guderian, General Heinz. *Panzer Leader*. London, 1952.

Gunther, John. *Inside Russia Today*. London, 1957.

Halder, General Franz. *The Halder Diaries*. Washington, 1950.

— *Hitler as Warlord*. New York, 1950.

Harriman, W. Averell, and Abel, Elie. *Special Envoy to Churchill and Stalin: 1941–1946*. New York, 1975.

Hilger, G., and Meyer, A. *The Incompatible Allies*. New York, 1959.

Hitler, Adolf. *Mein Kampf* (ed. John Chamberlain). New York, 1939.

Hingley, Ronald. *Stalin: Man and Legend*. New York, 1974.

Hoettl, Wilhelm (pseud. Walter Hagen). *The Secret Front*. London, 1953

Hoffmann, Heinrich. *Hitler Was My Friend*. London, 1955.

Hyde, H. Montgomery. *Stalin: The History of a Dictator*. New York, 1971.

Ickes, Harold L. *The Secret Diary of Harold L. Ickes*. New York, 1954.

Irving, David. *The Destruction of Convoy PQ–17*. London, 1968.

— *Hitler's War*. London, 1977.

Ishii, Kikujiro. *Diplomatic Commentaries*. Baltimore, 1936.

Ismay, Lord. *The Memoirs of General Ismay*. London, 1960.

Jackson, General Sir William G. F. *Seven Roads to Moscow*. London, 1956.

Jakobson, Max. *Finland: Myth and Reality*. Helsinki, 1987.

Jukes, Geofffrey. *Kursk: the Clash of Armour*. New York, 1969.

— *Stalingrad, The Turning Point*. New York, 1968.

Just, Arthur. *The Red Army*. London, 1936.

Kahn, David. *Hitler's Spies*. New York, 1978.

Kase, Toshikazu. *Journey to the Missouri*. New Haven, Conn., 1950.

Keitel, Wilhelm. *Memoirs*. London, 1965.

Kennan, George. *Memoirs, 1925–1950*. Boston, 1967.

— *Russia and the West Under Lenin and Stalin*. New York, 1960.

Kharlamov, Nikolai. *Difficult Mission*. Moscow, 1983.

Khrushchev, Nikita. *Khrushchev Remembers*. Boston, 1970.

Kovanov, V. S. *In the Name of Life*. Moscow, 1976.

Kovpak, General Sidor. *Our Partisan Course*. London, 1947.

Langsam, Walter C. *Historic Documents of World War II*. New York, 1958.

Laqueur, Walter. *Russia and Germany, A Century of Conflict*. London, 1965.

— *Stalin: The Glasnost Revelations*. London, 1990.

Lash, Joseph P. *Roosevelt and Churchill, 1939–1941*. New York, 1976.

Leach, Barry A. *German Strategy Against Russia, 1939–1941*. Oxford, 1973

Leahy, Fleet Admiral William. *I was There*. New York, 1950.

Leckie, Robert. *Delivered From Evil: The Saga of World War II*. New York, 1987.

Liddell Hart, B. H. *The German Generals Talk*. New York, 1948.

– *History of the Second World War*. New York, 1971.

Lockhart, Bruce. *My Europe*. London, 1952.

Louis, W. R. (ed.). *The Origins of the Second World War: A. J. P. Taylor and His Critics*. New York, 1972.

Maclean, Fitzroy. *Eastern Approaches*. London, 1949.

McCauley, Martin. *Stalin and Stalinism*. London, 1995.

McCauley, Martin. *The Soviet Union 1917–1991*. London, 1993.

Maisky, Ivan. *Memoirs of a Soviet Ambassador*. New York, 1968.

— *Who Helped Hitler?* London, 1964.

Manstein, Erich von. *Lost Victories*. London, 1955.

Maser, Werner. *Hitler: Legend, Myth and Reality*. London, 1971, 1988.

Medvedev, Roy. *On Stalin and Stalinism*. Oxford, 1979.

Molotov, V. M. *We Shall Not Forgive*. Moscow, 1942.

Montgomery, Bernard. *The Memoirs of Field Marshal Montgomery*. London, 1970.

Nekrich, Alexander. *June 22, 1941*. Columbia, S. Carolina, 1968.

Nicolson, Harold. *Diplomacy*. London, 1938.

Nove, Alec. *An Economic History of the USSR*. London, 1989.

— 'Was Stalin Really Necessary?', in *Encounter*, April, 1962.

Pares, Sir Bernard. *A History of Russia*. New York, 1965.
Password Victory, The Great Patriotic War. Moscow, 1985.
Pipes, Richard. *The Russian Revolution, 1899–1919*. London, 1990.
Polevoi, Boris. *The Final Reckoning*. Moscow, 1978.
Poliakov, Alexander. *Russians Don't Surrender*. New York, 1942.
Pritt, D. N. *The Autobiography: From Right to Left*. London, 1965.
Radzinsky, Edvard. *Stalin*. London, 1996.
Rauch, Georg von. *A History of Soviet Russia*. New York, 1964.
Ribbentrop, Joachim von. *The Ribbentrop Memoirs*. London, 1954.
Rickenbacker, Eddie. *Rickenbacker: His Own Story*. New York, 1967.
Rokossovsky, Marshal K. *A Soldier's Duty*. Moscow, 1985.
Roosevelt, Elliot. *As He Saw It*. New York, 1946.
Rothstein, Andrew. *The Munich Conspiracy*. London, 1958.
Salisbury, Harrison. *The Unknown War*. New York, 1978.
Schacher, Gerhard. *He Wanted to Sleep in the Kremlin*. New York, 1942.
Scott, John. *Behind the Urals: An American Worker in Russia's City of Steel*. Boston, 1942.
Seaton, Albert. *The Russo-German War, 1941–1945*. New York, 1971.
— *Stalin as Military Commander*. New York, 1975.
— *Stalin as Warlord*. London, 1976.
Service, Robert. *The History of Twentieth Century Russia*. London, 1997.
Sheinis, Zinovy. *Maxim Litvinov*. Moscow, 1988 (in English).
Shiba, Kimpei. *Oh, Japan*. Kent, 1979
Shirer, William. *The Rise and Fall of the Third Reich*. London, 1964.
Shtemenko, General S. *The Soviet General Staff at War*. Moscow, 1970
Shukman, Harold. *Stalin's Generals*. London. 1993.
Simone, André. *J'Accuse! The Man Who Betrayed France*. New York, 1940
Speer, Albert. *Infiltration*. New York, 1981.
— *Inside the Third Reich*. London, 1970.
Stalin, J. *On the Great Patriotic War*. Moscow, 1946.
— *The Essential Theoretical Writings*. ed. Bruce Franklin. London, 1973.
Steffens, Lincoln. *Autobiography*. New York, 1931.
Sudoplatov, Pavel. *Special Tasks: The Memoirs of an Unwanted Witness – A Soviet Spymaster*. Boston, 1994.
Taylor, A. J. P. *English History, 1941–1945*. Oxford, 1965.
— *The Origins of the Second World War*. London, 1969.
Taylor, Telford. *Sword and Swastika: Generals and Nazis in the Third Reich*. New York, 1952.
Tell, Rolf (ed.). *Nazi Guide to Nazism*. Washington, 1942.
Togo, Shigenori. *The Cause of Japan*. New York, 1956.
Trotsky, Leon. *Stalin* (ed. Charles Malamuth). New York, 1967.
Tucker, Robert. *Stalin as Revolutionary (1879–1929)*. New York, 1974.
Tucker, Robert, and Cohen, Stephen (eds.). *The Great Purge Trial*. New York, 1965.
Ulam, Adam B. Stalin: *The Man and His Era*. New York, 1974.
Vasilevsky, Marshal A. M. *A Lifelong Cause*. Moscow, 1981.

Volkogonov, Dmitri. *Stalin: Triumph and Tragedy*. New York, 1992.

Voznesensky, Nikolai. *The Economy of the USSR During World War II*. New York, 1948.

Warlimont, General Walter. *Inside Hitler's Headquarters, 1939–1945*. London, 1964.

Watson, Thomas J. Jr. *Father, Son & Co.: My Life at IBM and Beyond*. New York, 1990.

Weizsacker, Ernst von. *Memoirs*. London, 1951.

Werth, Alexander. *Russia at War, 1941–1945*. London, 1964.

Wheeler-Bennett, Sir John. *Munich: Prologue to Tragedy*. London,1964.

Wilmot, Chester. *The Struggle for Europe*. London, 1953.

Wuorinen, John (ed.). *Finland and World War II, 1939–1944*. New York, 1948.

Zhukov, Marshal G. *Reminiscences and Reflections*. Moscow, 1974.

Nazi–Soviet Relations, 1939–1941. US State Department, 1948.

Trial of Major German War Criminals: Proceedings of the International Military Tribunal Sitting at Nuremberg, Germany. London, 1948.

INDEX